The
Hunger
for More

ALSO BY LAURENCE SHAMES

The Big Time: The Harvard Business School's
Most Successful Class and How It Shaped America

THE HUNGER FOR MORE

Searching
for Values
in an
Age of
Greed

LAURENCE SHAMES

BOOKS

for Jade Albert

Library of Congress Cataloging-in-Publication Data

Shames, Laurence.

The hunger for more.

Includes index.

1. Success. 2. Wealth, Ethics of. I. Title.

BJ1611.2.S43 1989 178 88-29473

ISBN 0-8129-1656-5

Manufactured in the United States of America

9 8 7 6 5 4 3 2

First Edition

CONTENTS

//ACKNOWLEDGMENTS

THE MATTERS DISCUSSED in this book have preoccupied me for several years, during which time I have picked the brains of, and inflicted my opinions upon, a large number of colleagues, acquaintances, and occasionally strangers. In terror of the inevitable oversights, I will refrain from trying to thank by name all who have helped.

In particular, however, I would like to express my gratitude to the following friends, whose warmth, wit, and insight have been as manna to me during work on this project. Gerry Mallow and Françoise Davis-Mallow have taught me more than they realize about the art of living. Phil Landeck and Dr. Edith Langner have nourished me many times in many ways, most especially by their kindness. Jim and Janice Stanton have been convivial companions and playmates. Nancy Buirski has made me a beneficiary of her boundless enthusiasm. "Benno and Sally Collier" have my deep appreciation for their caring and their candor.

Better late than never, I would like to acknowledge an enormous debt to Rob Fleder, Marilyn Johnson, and Owen Edwards, who, a decade or so ago, had the generosity and/or the humor to treat me as a professional journalist and thereby allow me to become one. I would also like to thank Stuart Krichevsky, who does a far higher proportion of my worrying than he claims of my gross.

To Lawrence E. Joseph, who seemed to keep forgetting he wasn't actually working on this project, I give deep thanks. And to Ed Wetschler, he of the encyclopedic memory and unbamboozleable sensibility, I offer gratitude not only for much thought and trouble on behalf of this book but also for twenty years' influence in shaping my view of the world.

I would also like to thank the editors of *The New York Times,* in which a small portion of Chapter 13 first appeared, and of *Playboy,* which published an earlier version of certain material contained in Chapter 6.

Finally, I owe much more than the usual thank-you to my editor, Jonathan Segal, without whose steadfast conviction that this book should exist, it wouldn't.

PREFACE

THIS IS AN OPTIMISTIC BOOK whose first premise is that America has gotten about as rich as it's going to get.

Why, then, optimistic? Because it is my belief that, once we accept the realization that the days of automatically increasing wealth are past, a more serene and balanced future awaits us. Our hunger for more—one of our oldest and deepest national traits—will have to be nourished by things other than money. Our values will shift so that a sense of purpose, an ethic of service, and the desire to make a difference will be afforded a new respect. Perhaps we'll even learn to be more content with the tremendous wealth and privilege we already have.

This book, I should make clear, is not about economics, but rather about the thorough intertwining of economic expectations, social fashions, and personal values and outlooks. What I care about is the drama of real people making real choices bravely muddling along uncertain paths toward some version of fulfillment, some life that will, to them, appear "successful." What mix of history, economics, and sheer hype goes into the defining of success, of valid aims, of time well spent? What becomes of yearnings not included in the mix? What happens when, under the pressure of basically changing circumstance, a certain version of success no longer seems to work?

It is my conviction that the version of success that was dominant in America in the 1980s—a success defined almost exclusively in terms of money and virtually without reference to the substance of one's achievement—has served us badly. It has narrowed our options and cramped our imaginations. In the pages that follow, I do not intend to rail against success eighties-style on lofty moral grounds, but rather on practical ones: a vision of success based on money alone—*more* money each year—is a dangerous dead end at a historical moment when real wealth can no longer be counted on to increase. Over time, by the rigid rules of that game, there will inevitably be more losers, fewer winners, less joy, and more desperation in the contest. For reasons of simple self-interest, we need to cultivate a new definition of the well-lived life—a vision flexible and durable enough to float us through choppy economic currents. As this book goes along, I will be trying to suggest at least some of the components this new version of success might be made of.

My approach is observational, anecdotal—anything but technical. To establish certain premises and bolster certain arguments, however, I do make use (mainly in Chapters 2 and 3) of statistics, in whose selection I have employed two main criteria. First, I try to use numbers that have real meaning to most people—wages, housing costs, the price tag on a car or an education. Second, I limit myself to statistics whose ideological freight is either explicitly acknowledged or has been minimized by the methodology through which the numbers have been derived. Other statistics, it should be understood, could be used to tell a different tale; I tell the story that seems truest to me.

In telling that story, I also avail myself of the convenience of speaking in terms of decades, recognizing that such usage is, of course, approximate. Broadly speaking, I take the 1950s to have begun with Eisenhower's election in 1952, and to have ended, as a political and social episode, with the assassination of JFK in November 1963; economically, however, the fifties may be said to have lingered on until 1967, when inflation, fueled by the hidden costs of the Vietnam War, began creeping up. The sixties, economically speaking, ended with the oil shocks of 1973, but lingered on politically until the resignation of Richard Nixon in 1974. The eighties began with the election of Ronald Reagan, and as of this writing, it seems clear that they ended on Black Monday, October 19, 1987.

But why did the 1980s happen in the first place? Why did pocketbook issues become, apparently, the only issues, and how did money become so tyrannically central to our preoccupations? Why did business stories move onto page one and why was it suddenly sexy to have an MBA? Why did ethical lapses become so flagrant and so widespread, and why did a new and strangely elitist form of work ethic kick in?

These are some of the questions this book addresses; I believe they must be answered if we are to put the inglorious eighties behind us and move on to a riper stage of our development, both national and individual. We need to understand that there is nothing shameful about leveling off; the only shameful thing is to regard the leveling as an occasion for panic, selfishness, narrowness, and greed. We can do better than that; and in doing better there is much for us to gain.

Making a life consists of more than making a living; building a civilization means more than building an economy. Those are things that seem to have been forgotten in the 1980s. It is my hope for this book that it may play some small part in helping us remember them.

Shelter Island, New York
September 1988

The
Hunger
for More

Introduction:
The Day the
Eighties
Ended

/// **ONE**

    The smell of woodsmoke still clung to Benno Collier's pillow.

It had been carried down from Connecticut on his fingers, his sweater, and most of all in his hair, but he hadn't really noticed it until the alarm went off at six-thirty Monday morning. In the country the smell of smoke was as much a part of autumn weekends as brown leaves turning slowly in puddles with their stems turned up like masts; you savored the smell without the need of calling it by name. Here in the city, where you made your money and ate your food with sauce, the smell of burnt oak was exotic; right under your nose, it still smelled far away.

Benno propped himself on pillows and switched on the

TV. Looking past the peaks of his own feet and his wife's, he watched ten minutes of the early-morning business news. Sally Collier grunted once and dozed back off again. Since becoming pregnant she slept more soundly than she ever had and she smiled in her sleep.

In the shower, Benno softly sang a couple of Mozart arias. At the age of thirty-eight, he'd just started taking voice lessons. He'd wanted to for years, and now, somehow, the time seemed right. He felt settled in at Morgan Stanley, no longer awkward as the oldest guy in the equity salesman training program and in some ways the least likely to succeed. He didn't have an MBA and, though he kept the fact to himself, he was somewhat short on the carnivorous optimism of the kids who'd seen only bullish times. Still, he'd been selling stocks for three years, and doing well at it. He was, by Wall Street reckoning, almost an old pro. Taking voice lessons now struck him as one of those harmless eccentricities that old pros could afford to take the time for, that reconciled one to growing up, that saved one from being *just a stockbroker.*

Besides, it was one of the few things a Manhattan baby boomer could do without too much fear it would mark one as part of a trend. Six years before, Benno and Sally Collier had moved to West End Avenue because they liked the park, the architecture, the informality; then Amsterdam's opened, gourmet take-out appeared where *bodegas* used to be, and Yupper West Side became a phrase of scorn. Three years after that, Benno made the difficult and, as he saw it, damn courageous move of giving up his shot at a partnership with the law firm of Dewey, Ballantine in favor of the jazzier business of institutional trading, only to have no less an authority than *The New York Times* inform him that he was part of a wave of people "leaving the law for Wall Street." Well, thought Benno, drying his feet on the edge of the tub, just let them try to tell him he was part of a trend of urban males approaching forty, approaching fatherhood, approaching their first million in net worth, and studying operatic technique with old Hungarian ladies in fourth-floor walk-ups on Tuesday and Thursday evenings.

For that matter, let them tell him he was part of a trend toward the wearing of rebuilt shoes. *Rebuilt shoes.* The very phrase was archiac, and probably half the people Benno worked with wouldn't have the faintest idea what it meant. But Benno, who grew up not poor but prudent, could remember going to the shoemaker's with his father to have new soles and heels put onto uppers so uniquely creased and crinkled that they seemed to have the character of faces. The shoemaker's shop smelled like a sweaty saddle and had pots of glue with brushes standing straight up in them. Benno occasionally wondered if he was the only guy at Morgan Stanley who still went to the shoemaker. He had an old pair of Brooks Brothers cordovan loafers—Brooks Brothers itself, of course, having become terribly passé for almost everything except suspenders—and he was working on, oh, maybe his third set of soles and fifth of heels. The young guys shopped farther up on Madison, at places Benno hadn't bothered to learn the names of, and when it came to shoes, they always liked their next pair better than the ones they had on.

Benno liked the stuff he already had. He liked his old records, even though they hissed and popped. He liked the bruised attaché case he'd had since law school. And he liked his marriage. Almost to his surprise, he loved his wife more and more as time went on, and he was thrilled they were becoming parents. Tomorrow would be their eighth wedding anniversary. It would also be the day that Sally would have her sonogram and they would see the outline of their child for the first time. He'd marked the day in his book. Not that he was the sort of husband who would forget: October 20. This was Monday the nineteenth, and the year was 1987.

//// TWO

That day the Dow Jones Industrial Average sank 508 points, and the social and economic episode loosely defined as The Eighties ended.

With head-spinning suddenness, the habits, patterns, and expectations formed during that truncated decade came to seem outdated and, even worse, naïve. Advertisements, college curricula, career paths, lives—suddenly everything seemed due for a revision, and the revision was the more necessary in proportion to how quintessentially eighties the earlier version had been. If you were the Harvard Business School, what the hell did you say to your students that day? If you were the account exec on BMW or Rolex watches, what clever notions did you have as to how to move your product? For that matter, if you were a twenty-five-year-old trainee who'd sworn off sleep, sex, and the liberal arts in exchange for a slot in the go-go world of investment banking, how did you feel on Black Monday about what you'd gotten in exchange for your amputated youth?

The New York Times called October 19 "the end of business as usual," but it was much more than business that was changed. It was how people looked at their prospects, their choices, their priorities. Eighties values, dubious in the best of economic times, now seemed downright embarrassing. Not only were they narrow, selfish, fogeyish—it turned out they didn't even work. Delirious greed and runaway careerism had seemed amusing for a while, but October 19 killed that mood as fast as turning the lights up at a bar.

That, finally, was what made Meltdown Monday epochal:

THE HUNGER FOR MORE /// 7

not the mere evaporation of wealth but the shattering of a frame of mind and of a certain species of faith. How solid was the system, and who if anyone was in charge? October 19 didn't come out of nowhere. It was the culmination of five years of economic la-di-da followed by two months of market jitters in which the Dow had already given up almost five hundred points from its August high. The previous trading day had chalked up the first hundred-plus point drop ever. Saturday passed, Sunday passed, it couldn't have been clearer that the system was in trouble, and no one did a thing. Welcome to the free market, otherwise known as mayhem.

On Monday, the Dow lost 22.6 percent of its remaining value, or almost double the proportionate decline of Black Tuesday, 1929. More than 600 million shares were traded on the New York Stock Exchange, so overloading that institution's capacity that the ticker fell more than two hours behind. At brokerage offices around the country, over-revved computers flashed frenzied green question marks or simply went dead; for much of the afternoon, people who prided themselves on their coolness and their rationality were trading blind, selling, literally, at any price. IBM went down thirty-one dollars that day, GM dropped almost fourteen points.

In all, since August, one trillion dollars of value had been erased. One trillion dollars—this was a figure at once awe-inspiring, terrifying, and ridiculous. What *was* one trillion dollars, and where could it go? For that matter, where had it *been,* if it could just up and vanish so tracelessly and so blindingly fast? Then, too, the eighties had been a time when "success" was virtually synonymous with, and limited to, making money; had the country just become a trillion dollars less successful, a trillion bucks less worthy of esteem?

On October 19, 1987, no one had answers to any of those questions. No one, it seemed, could explain anything anymore. From the White House came the bland, questionable, and rather irrelevant assurance that "the underlying economy remains sound." But O.K., no one really expected anything pithy from the White House. It was the businessmen themselves, the eighties heroes, the smart pragmatic guys who were actually *doing* something, who should have a handle. But "leaders of major American companies [had been] caught . . . as much by surprise" as most stay-at-home investors. "I don't understand it," acknowledged the president of AT&T. "We don't know how to interpret it," conceded the chief financial officer of United Technologies Corporation.

Benno Collier, meanwhile, noticed a singular lack of sick jokes making the rounds that day. This was surprising, for Wall Street had a hard-earned reputation for yukking it up in the face of catastrophe; shit happened, as the saying went, and it was part of the Street's brave and unflinching realism to be able to laugh at it. From *Challenger* to the President's colon to the rough-sex defense, no subject was off limits. A plane went down in Colorado, a guy got rubbed out on Mulberry Street, and WATS lines would crackle with bleak hilarity before the bodies were cold. Not today. Today there weren't many attempts at wit, and what quips there were tended to call forth only forced, contorted smiles and a shuffling of feet. That was the thing about gallows humor. It depended a lot on who was getting hanged.

/// THREE

Sally Collier, to her immense chagrin, sat at home and followed the Crash on the tube.

She should have been covering the story herself. She was

a writer/producer for NBC News, and she'd been out on strike for sixteen weeks—the length of time was easy to reckon, since she'd gotten pregnant on either the third or fourth evening she'd been out of work. Her union, the National Association of Broadcast Employees and Technicians, had called a walkout over work rules and that now-quaint concept known as job security, and 2,800 people had been told to stay away.

It was, Sally believed, a stupid and perhaps a calamitous strike. The union leaders, old-timers mostly, didn't seem to understand how much the world had changed or to know who they were dealing with. This was no longer good old paternalistic NBC, and the money in broadcasting no longer flowed as freely as honey in summer. The network had been taken over; it was part of General Electric, and General Electric had the odd idea that showbiz should be efficient. The new management didn't mind using the ax, and the line going around the studios was that people had given their all for the peacock, and now GE was flipping them the bird. The union, Sally believed, was doing the hatchet men a great favor, providing a perfect laboratory for seeing just how few people the network needed to run well enough so that most people wouldn't notice it wasn't running very well.

Perhaps the biggest and certainly the culminating story of the decade was breaking, and NBC was covering it with bookkeepers and people from personnel, while professional journalists and cameramen stood on picket lines or sat in coffee shops and talked about how *they'd* have done it. This, thought Sally, was the kind of situation that drove you to distraction because it benefited no one. If you're losing and someone else is winning, O.K., that's life, but this just wasted everybody. Here she was, a thirty-five-year-old pregnant woman, who badly wanted to go to work now that the morning's dizziness and throwing up were over, being prevented from doing so by a union she no longer believed in, which was breaking its own back fighting a company not the one she'd been hired by and not the one she perceived herself to work for.

Around two o'clock she finally called Benno.

"What's going on there?"

"Damned if I know," he said, above the screaming and the slapped desks and scraping chairs of the bullpen. "I can't talk now."

"Are you all right?"

"No."

Sally sighed, hugged her belly, and went to the kitchen to get a glass of seltzer. Call it the Upper or the Yupper West Side, call it whatever you want, it was still a neighborhood where you could get seltzer delivered to your door in ancient wooden cases, forty-five cents per old-fashioned spigot-topped bottle. On days like this, a glass of seltzer was a comfort, especially when squirted over chocolate syrup and half-and-half.

//// FOUR

Wall Street, God knows, is not America, and in our grudgingly united states there were no doubt some tens of millions who took nothing but delight in watching the markets go down the tubes, in seeing lower Manhattan go into shell shock and observing the arrogant pin-striped Yalies at their most baffled, impotent, and tongue-tied.

But even before the end of trading on Black Monday '87, a new sort of "trickle down" theory was beginning to be grasped. Chicago journalist Studs Terkel acknowledged that even though Wall Street seemed to be "on some other planet," the debacle there could not but have an impact on "ghost towns [like] Youngstown, Ohio, [on] fourth-generation farmers being foreclosed, [and on] record-busting numbers of homeless." With investment banks in disarray, towns in Utah would have a much tougher time floating bonds to build municipal swimming pools. A basement tinkerer from Duluth would have a harder time finding someone to bankroll his brainchild. Anyone with a house to sell from Maine to Oregon had to calculate how much the value of his property had just been sliced, and anyone with a baby on the way had to wonder if the little one would be born into a recession, or worse.

The ramifications were national, even global, yet it was fitting that the epicenter of the anxiety should be Wall Street, because the eighties had essentially been a Wall Street contrivance all along. Wall Street had, so to speak, taken Ronald Reagan's message of unexamined euphoria and translated it into computer language.

Where had the eighties come from? As we will argue, the decade drew its energy from the collision of a long tradition of rising expectations and the widespread, if largely unspoken, fear that those expectations might no longer be met. By the late 1970s it was beginning to be suspected that America was no longer growing meaningfully wealthier. A traditional economic game was being played around the world—a game in which the score was kept by weighing steel, counting cars, measuring monumental bolts of cloth—and America was no longer winning it. Depending on your politics, you could blame this on labor costs or shortsighted management or wrongheaded government policies or the duplicity of foreigners; or you could simply give a philosophic shrug and pronounce that there were cycles to these things. The choice of villain was secondary. Paramount was the perception that America, the world's dominant nation for the entire lifetimes of most of the people currently breathing, was being aced out at the very game it had largely perfected.

So Wall Street invented a different game, if not quite from scratch, then by a radical reshuffling and redefining of the measurement and resonance of wealth. Make no mistake—the ingenuity coming out of the financial sector in the 1980s was epic. Junk bonds, index futures, leveraged buyouts, program trading—you didn't need an expert's understanding of the terms to grasp that these were enormously resourceful ploys in a contest being invented from day to day, a grand improvisation on the theme of finding money somewhere somehow.

Never before had business been conducted at such a high level of abstraction. Not only did no one touch products anymore, no one even touched money, but only moved the *record* of money. The beauty part of the new game was that it canceled out precisely those parts of the old game that America was no longer best at. Factories, widgets, customers—those concepts now seemed practically medieval. They had no place in the pure ethereal realm of electronic bucks. A six-and-a-quarter-cent price differential appeared on a computer screen, a couple of entries were tapped into a keyboard, and a number swelled in somebody's account. Next day's papers announced that the market had gone up again, and everyone felt reassured. America was winning again. America was coming back.

But coming back as what? Coming back as a nation in which, despite the longest stretch of economic expansion in our history, real earnings were virtually flat. Coming back as a nation in which, for the first time since World War II, economic inequality was not shrinking but widening. Coming back as the world's biggest debtor, with an embattled currency, an addiction to foreign funds, and a national case of *que sera, sera* about how things would shake out when the bills came due.

Ingenuity was one thing, vision was another, and it didn't

take the Crash to suggest that eighties-style prosperity was predicated on quick savvy rather than durable wisdom. Fortunes were made and fundamental problems went unaddressed. Today looked good, and if tomorrow looked bad you didn't have to answer phone calls. Abstraction, it seems fair to say, bred irresponsibility. It was just numbers, and not even numbers *written down,* but just made of cathode rays. That those eye-tiring squiggles might correspond to something out there in the world—a single mother losing a job, a town drying up around a shuttered factory—well, that leap into the concrete, the flesh and blood, was something you didn't really have time for. Real life was real life, but in the meantime the object of the exercise was juggling money.

But could the two—life and making a living—be so conveniently kept apart? Butchers, as a professional group, tend to have a meaty look. Go to a party and you can always spot an architect. The way people make their bucks rubs off on them; it rubs off on societies as well. When a certain way of making money is installed as the emblem of an era, when tales of financial wizardry lead the evening news and its practitioners stare out masterfully from covers of magazines and front pages of the papers, that style insinuates itself. That, finally, was what mattered about how the economic game was played in the eighties: not just that business was becoming unprecedentedly lean, hard-edged, focused all but exclusively on the numbers, but that American values and American life were becoming so as well. The long view was fading. The sense of shared purpose existed only in politicians' speeches. The future was being mortgaged, not only in terms of dollars but in terms of meaning. The more wealth-obsessed we became, the greater grew a kind of hunger that wealth could never satisfy.

Success lost its reference to accomplishment, to high intent, and was recognized only in terms of its reward. Ambition, which rightly has to do with finding balance and scope for all of one's abilities, was whittled down to mean getting on a career track. Taste and quality, much invoked in the eighties, were trivialized to mean largely what things cost and where they could be bought. Life itself had much of the juice and mystery sucked out of it on the way to becoming lifestyle; the marketplace told you what sort of goods, clothes, vacations went with your income level, and you dutifully bought those items, telling yourself all the while you were free and even privileged to be able to do so.

This was impoverishment, no matter how much money was floating around. People weren't truly choosing the work to which they would devote a large share of their waking hours, but only choosing the dollars that went with the job. They didn't even choose their leisure, really, but merely slipped into certain patterns that would define their standing. Still, as long as the national morale could ride upward on the numbers, it was easy not to notice that meaning and purpose were being drained, that the broader context in which some individuals were prospering was going sour. October 19 didn't start that process of souring, but only made it clear that a price was being paid all along. On that day, people began to realize what they'd been giving up in the name of being pragmatic, of being clever, of being what passed in the eighties for "realistic." They'd been giving up sleep. They'd been giving up friends. They'd been giving up a fair proportion of the freedom that, according to the conventional wisdom of the day, went with having bucks. They'd been giving up all the many grounds for self-affection and self-esteem that lie beyond the paycheck. If the paycheck, too, was taken away, then just what the hell was left?

//// FIVE

Benno Collier, if you figure in his year-end bonus, made around $400,000 in 1987. Sally Collier earned over $60,000, and followed the news to Moscow, Paris, and Beijing. Together, the Colliers bicycled through Tuscany and skied at Vail. They are not typical Americans or typical Manhattanites or typical yuppies or typical anything. By any measure, they are privileged. Yet by 5:00 P.M. on Meltdown Monday, neither Benno nor Sally could be mind-easy about the future. Neither was sure how much longer he or she would have a job. Neither was sure they'd be able to keep their country house, the place the woodsmoke came from. Both had cause to reflect upon, and perhaps fleetingly, secretly, to regret, picking this moment to bring a child into the world.

America, it seemed, was becoming a place where there were no more sure things. There was great wealth, there was ample opportunity, and there was also the chance that in a few hours it could all go smash. There were fewer and fewer safe spots on the game board. This was true whatever level of income or privilege you chose to look at. A workingman who felt lucky to have a union job that paid twelve bucks an hour and covered his kids' dental bills could lose it and end up going service sector for half the pay and no benefits at all. A manager at an acquired company, a guy who thought he'd done a pretty decent job these last twelve years, could find himself described as excess baggage. A stockbroker and a television journalist, veritable stars in modern America, could get zapped as innocent bystanders as Wall Street laid an egg and the network business went to hell.

The economic shocks could be fast and dire. But there were other, subtler consequences as well—consequences that existed at the intersection of economic circumstance and personal choice. In a time of such extreme volatility, when the painless rise of numbers could no longer be counted on, certain assumptions and values from the eighties had become bad bets, longer and longer shots with an insufficient payoff. If you equated success with a hot job and a glitzy pay stub, you could very well be defining yourself as a flop; as in Greek drama, you'd be barreling full speed toward the very destiny you most feared. If you measured progress solely in terms of a rising economic graph, chances are you wouldn't see much progress. You'd sell yourself short; you'd sell the country short.

But it didn't have to be that way. There were other, less fickle ways of defining success—success in service, success in originality, success, even, in contentment. There were other, more subtle ways of measuring progress—progress in equity, progress in social calm. And at the slag end of the 1980s it seemed only commonsensical that those other measures should be brought to bear. We'd learned that numbers could go down. It had got through to us that we were not sole masters of our fiscal fate. If we were to avoid utter bafflement and the numbing sense of personal defeat, we'd have to make an adjustment. The adjustment would not be easy; it would fly in the face of much of our history. Still, it seemed clear that the great moral and also imaginative challenge now facing us was to begin to cultivate a sense of purpose that had less to do with more, and more to do with better.

Part I

A
LEGACY
OF BOOMS,
A NOSTALGIA
FOR FRONTIERS

American democracy was born of no theorist's
dream. . . . It came out of the American
forest, and it gained new strength each
time it touched a new frontier.

—Frederick Jackson Turner

able but fine—the sorts of accomplishment that cannot be undone by circumstance or a shift in social fashion, the kind of serenity that cannot be shattered by tomorrow's headline —has gone largely unfulfilled, and even unacknowledged.

/// TWO

If the supply of more went on forever, perhaps that wouldn't matter very much. Expansion could remain a goal unto itself, and would continue to generate a value system based on bulk rather than on nuance, on quantities of money rather than on quality of life, on "progress" itself rather than on a sense of what the progress was for. But what if, over time, there was less more to be had?

That is the essential situation of America today.

Let's keep things in proportion: the country is not running out of wealth, drive, savvy, or opportunities. We are not facing imminent ruin, and neither panic nor gloom is called for. But there have been ample indications over the past two decades that we are running out of more.

Consider productivity growth—according to many economists, the single most telling and least distortable gauge of changes in real wealth. From 1947 to 1965, productivity in the private sector (adjusted, as are all the following figures, for inflation) was advancing, on average, by an annual 3.3 percent. This means, simply, that each hour of work performed by a specimen American worker contributed 3.3 cents worth of more to every American dollar every year; whether we saved it or spent it, that increment went into a national kitty of ever-enlarging aggregate wealth. Between 1965 and 1972, however, the "more-factor" decreased to 2.4 percent a year, and from 1972 to 1977 it slipped further, to 1.6 percent. By the early 1980s, productivity growth was at a virtual standstill, crawling along at 0.2 percent for the five years ending in 1982. Through the middle years of the

1980s, the numbers rebounded somewhat—but by then the gains were being neutralized by the gargantuan carrying costs on the national debt.

Inevitably, this decline in the national stockpile of more held consequences for the individual wallet. During the 1950s, Americans' average hourly earnings were humping ahead at a gratifying 2.5 percent each year. By the late seventies, that figure stood just where productivity growth had come to stand, at a dispiriting 0.2 cents on the dollar. By the first half of the eighties, the Reagan "recovery" notwithstanding, real hourly wages were actually moving backwards—declining at an average annual rate of 0.3 percent.

Compounding the shortage of more was an unfortunate but crucial demographic fact. Real wealth was nearly ceasing to expand just at the moment when the members of that unprecedented population bulge known as the baby boom were entering what should have been their peak years of income expansion. A working man or woman who was thirty years old in 1949 could expect to see his or her real earnings burgeon by 63 percent by age forty. In 1959, a thirty-year-old could still look forward to a gain of 49 percent by his or her fortieth birthday.

But what about the person who turned thirty in 1973? By the time that worker turned forty, his or her real earnings had shrunk by a percentage point. For all the blather about yuppies with their beach houses, BMWs, and radicchio salads, and even factoring in those isolated tens of thousands making ludicrous sums in consulting firms or on Wall Street, the fact is that between 1979 and 1983 real earnings of all Americans between the ages of twenty-five and thirty-four actually declined by 14 percent. *The New York Times,* well before the stock market crash put the kibosh on eighties confidence, summed up the implications of this downturn by observing that "for millions of breadwinners, the American dream is becoming the impossible dream."

Now, it is not our main purpose here to detail the ups and downs of the American economy. Our aim, rather, is to consider the effects of those ups and downs on people's goals, values, sense of their place in the world. What happens at that shadowy juncture where economic prospects meld with personal choice? What sorts of insights and adjustments are called for so that economic ups and downs can be dealt with gracefully?

Fact one in this connection is that, if America's supply of more is in fact diminishing, American values will have to shift and broaden to fill the gap where the expectation of almost automatic gains used to be. Something more durable will have to replace the fat but fragile bubble that had been getting frailer these past two decades and that finally popped—a tentative, partial pop—on October 19, 1987. A different sort of growth—ultimately, a growth in responsibility and happiness—will have to fulfill our need to believe that our possibilities are still expanding.

The transition to that new view of progress will take some fancy stepping, because, at least since the end of World War II, simple economic growth has stood, in the American psyche, as the best available substitute for the literal frontier. The economy has *been* the frontier. Instead of more space, we have had more money. Rather than measuring progress in terms of geographical expansion, we have measured it by expansion in our standard of living. Economics has become the metaphor on which we pin our hopes of open space and second chances.

The poignant part is that the literal frontier did not pass yesterday: it has not existed for a hundred years. But the frontier's promise has become so much a part of us that we have not been willing to let the concept die. We have kept the frontier mythology going by invocation, by allusion, by hype.

It is not a coincidence that John F. Kennedy dubbed his political program the New Frontier. It is not mere linguistic accident that makes us speak of Frontiers of Science or of psychedelic drugs as carrying one to Frontiers of Perception. We glorify fads and fashions by calling them Frontiers of Taste. Nuclear energy has been called the Last Frontier; solar energy has been called the Last Frontier. Outer space has been called the Last Frontier; the oceans have been called the Last Frontier. Even the suburbs, those blandest and least adventurous of places, have been wryly described as the crabgrass frontier.

What made all these usages plausible was their being linked to the image of the American economy as an endlessly fertile continent whose boundaries never need be reached, a domain that could expand in perpetuity, a gigantic playing field that would never run out of room, and on which the game would get forever bigger and more filled with action. This was the frontier that would not vanish.

It is worth noting that people in other countries (with the possible exception of that other America, Australia) do not talk about frontier this way. In Europe, and in most of Africa and Asia, "frontier" connotes, at worst, a place of barbed wire and men with rifles, and at best, a neutral junction where one changes currency while passing from one fixed system into another. Frontier, for most of the world's people, does not suggest growth, expanse, or opportunity.

For Americans, it does, and always has. This is one of the things that sets America apart from other places and makes American attitudes different from those of other people. It is why, from *Bonanza* to the Sierra Club, the notion or even the fantasy of empty horizons and untapped resources has always evoked in the American heart both passion and wistfulness. And it is why the fear that the economic frontier—our last, best version of the Wild West—may finally be passing creates in us not only money worries but also a crisis of morale and even of purpose.

///// THREE

It might seem strange to call the 1980s an era of nostalgia. The decade, after all, has been more usually described in terms of coolness, pragmatism, and a blithe innocence of history. But the eighties, unawares, were nostalgic for frontiers; and the disappointment of that nostalgia had much to do with the time's greed, narrowness, and strange want of joy. The fear that the world may not be a big enough playground for the full exercise of one's energies and yearnings, and worse, the fear that the playground is being fenced off and will no longer expand—these are real worries and they have had consequences. The eighties were an object lesson in how people play the game when there is an awful and unspoken suspicion that the game is winding down.

It was ironic that the yuppies came to be so reviled for their vaunting ambition and outsized expectations, as if they'd invented the habit of more, when in fact they'd only inherited it the way a fetus picks up an addiction in the womb. The craving was there in the national bloodstream, a remnant of the frontier, and the baby boomers, described in childhood as "the luckiest generation," found themselves, as young adults, in the melancholy position of wrestling with a two-hundred-year dependency on a drug that was now in short supply.

True, the 1980s raised the clamor for more to new heights of shrillness, insistence, and general obnoxiousness, but this, it can be argued, was in the nature of a final binge, the storm before the calm. America, though fighting the perception every inch of the way, was coming to realize that it was not a preordained part of the natural order that one should be richer every year. If it happened, that was nice. But who had started the flimsy and pernicious rumor that it was normal?

2

Normal Is
What You're
Used To

ONE

Measuring more is easy; measuring better is hard.

Measuring more requires nothing subtler than a scale, a calculator, a W-2 form. Measuring better requires values.

There are, broadly speaking, two sorts of values. The first might be called platonic, or religious, or spiritual, and has to do with eternal truths, with perfect mysteries, with things that do not change. The second sort of values—the kind we're mainly concerned with here—may be thought of as social, or worldly, or situational, and has to do with context. The first sort centers on what one feels to be right, necessary, absolute. The second revolves around what one deems to be fitting; and what is fitting, in turn, stands in some relation—conformity or rebellion, support, subversion, or disregard—to what one recognizes as normal.

But what happens to this second sort of values, and to our sense of what "better" means, if a culture adopts as "normal" a set of circumstances that really wasn't normal at all? This has been the case with American expectations of growth; it is why the shift away from *more* strikes us as so bedeviling.

Consider the 1950s in America. The fifties have become our reference point of normalcy, for a number of persuasive reasons. Insofar as there is such a thing as a typical American, she is a product of the fifties. The median age in the United States currently stands at roughly thirty-two years. Thus, the typical American of 1988 was born in 1956, a year of tailfins, of home permanents, of boomerang coffee tables, and with an inheritance of 8 percent economic growth. The midpoint of the postwar baby boom was 1955; the year of greatest fecundity was 1957. Using that cluster of dates as a reckoning point, it becomes clear that the fifties are absolutely central to the America we know, the America we took in with our breakfast cereal, our parents' faces, and our Saturday cartoons. This was "the decisive generation in our history."

Decisive, yes. The case can be made, in fact, that an understanding of the 1980s as well as a perspective on the balance of our century must be grounded in an understanding of the fifties. Earlier decades, while they have obviously left their legacies, were shaped by such "pre-contemporary" phenomena as the New Deal or the World Wars; later decades have been characterized by various symptoms of compensation for a solidity that seems to have been lost. But does that mean the fifties were normal? Not really. The habit of more, as we have argued, existed long before the postwar boom days came along; still, the 1950s raised that habit to heights unheard of until then. It was during the fifties that economic expansion was crowned as the successor to all our other versions of frontier, and the gospel of growth was spread to an unprecedentedly broad swath of the populace.

It was during the fifties that our common expectation of more coalesced into what might be called its wall-to-wall phase. If the fantasy was not yet described as "having it all," that was not for lack of material ambition or because of modesty of hopes; it was simply that, especially since most women still stayed at home, "all" was differently defined.

As for normalcy, was it normal that, after two centuries of worldwide decline in the birthrate of industrialized nations, Americans should go on a binge that made marriage and procreation all but universal, and that would increase the population by almost 50 percent between the years 1946 and 1964? (The baby boom, by the way, like the frontier, was a peculiarly American phenomenon; other Western nations had a postwar fertility spurt, but soon returned to prewar levels of reproduction.)

Was it normal that a nation which contained 7 percent of the world's people should produce two-thirds of its manufactured products, own three-quarters of its cars and appliances, and purchase 33 percent of all the goods and services available on earth, as the United States did in 1953?

Was it normal that millions of as yet shapeless American girls should have modeled themselves after a doll called Barbie, whose measurements, were she expanded to human size, would have been 39-23-33?

Was it normal that the operating budget of General Motors was larger than that of Poland, or that Americans spent more on entertainment than it cost to run Switzerland?

Was it normal that a higher proportion of dwellings in the city of Chicago should be equipped with television sets than with bathtubs, or that the average American should consume three and a half times as much food as the average foreigner, or that his income should be fifteen times as great, or that the number of swimming pools in the United States should have increased by 2,000 percent between 1950 and 1960?

No, none of these things was normal. In their various ways, they were all reflections of the giddily abnormal situation of the postwar years, when the United States, unscathed by bombs or political upheavals, leaped off to an enormous economic head start—as well as a head start in *image*— relative to the rest of the developed world. It was not, it should be understood, that the United States was competing more successfully in those years; rather, in the words of the economist Lester Thurow, it was that "there was no competition; a meaningfully competitive environment wouldn't come about till later." With its unravaged factories, undiluted dollar, and relatively undisrupted domestic market, America stood alone, and this was not normal.

Yet the fifties *seemed* normal, as did the contextual values that came out of the fifties, for a number of reasons. The first reason was the tendency, shared by every nation that has ever found itself preeminent, to regard its glory days as the typical days, its preeminence as earned yet inevitable. Nothing, one imagines, seemed more normal to the nineteenth-century Englishman than that Britain should have an Empire, and that locals from Nairobi to Bombay to the Falkland Islands should aspire to the dignity of Anglo-Saxon life, sipping Earl Grey tea, putting jelly on meat, and learning to beat their conquerors at squash. Analogously, it seemed normal enough to the 1950s American that every motorcade honoring every tinpot politician from Haiti to Cambodia should be led by a Cadillac or a Lincoln, that otherwise reasonable Frenchmen would go to absurd lengths to obtain a pair of Levi's, and that Italian moviegoers, in loving tribute to our frontier greatness, should flock to the spaghetti western. This view of normalcy was of course flattering, but it had its downside as well: when, in the course of events, some parity among nations reestablished itself, *that* would seem *ab*normal, and what was in fact a reasonable, necessary, and predictable leveling would feel like a defeat, even a humiliation, and would take us by surprise. Our national values did not prepare us to deal gracefully, or effectively, with the realization that other countries might do certain things as well as or better than we did.

A second reason the fifties passed for normal is that they were, or seemed, so much of a piece—though this is an aspect of the decade that has often been exaggerated. The fifties were not an unruffled sitcom-land, devoid of dissonant notes. The paranoia of McCarthyism belied the apparent assurance that our political system was so manifestly wonderful that *of course* everyone would be loyal to it. The early desegregation battles revealed the depths of American racism and exploded the comfortable myth that race's divisiveness was a problem limited to the South. The birth of rock 'n' roll suggested the existence of dark passions in the nation's young, passions not to be assuaged by the universally acceptable cooing of Johnny Mathis or the definitive phrasing of Sinatra. Finally, the emergence of the Beats, those pioneers of drug use, facial hair, and unhidden homosexuality, demonstrated that for some, at least, the promise of more could be taken or left, that the ethic of success seemed not worth its cost in conformity, constraint, hypocrisy, and squareness.

For all that, however, the fifties *were* a time of strong relative consensus, perhaps the last decade in which it made sense to speak of a national mood and a national idea—albeit a cockeyed one—of what better was all about. The mood was one of buoyant confidence, and the idea of better was inextricably tied up with the idea of "modern." *Better Living Through Chemistry.* Cars called *Jetstar* and *Futura.* Vacuum cleaners shaped like satellites. These were selling gimmicks, sure, but they were also summings-up of a national faith, a national awe, almost, at the chrome and urethane prospects of the frontier of modern consumerism. There was a boundless enthusiasm for all things new and preferably pastel, a positive pleasure in throwing last year's clock or blender in the garbage and seeing what would happen next.

Optimism colored everything. The Barbie doll, she of the improbable bosom, was shaped by the same unchastened exuberance that led gung-ho journalists to describe American prosperity in terms of "Himalayan peak[s]." The same trust in the future's benign manageability inspired both the flying-saucer desk lamp—this was normal, bringing UFOs into the home?—and the Diner's Club card, which launched the era of pocket plastic and painless debt in 1957.

The same headlong embrace of the new that sent tens of thousands of young couples to Levittowns in the certainty that this different life would be a better life, also induced in them the conviction that they "did not have to worry about what [they] would pass on to [their] children, because [the children] would have things unimaginably better." According to the fifties version of the habit of more, it was only normal that next year's car would have more horsepower, next year's dishwasher would have a built-in potscrubber, next year's sofa would have a chemical shield that would make a spilled highball bead up and roll right off. It was axiomatic that these exercises in more were also examples of better.

There is one further reason why the fifties have passed so long for normal, and that has to do with sheer force of numbers. The population bulge occasioned by the baby boom has been moving through the decades, to use the demographers' image, like a pig in a python; wherever the bulge existed at a given time, there seemed to exist the national style and even the national destiny. The "generational tyranny" of the vast baby-boom cohorts has had a crucial influence in "set[ting] the national temper." Thus, in the fifties, it seemed perfectly reasonable that the country was growing so fast because there were so many babies around and *they* were growing so fast. If not normal, things at least were in proportion.

The growth-spurt motif applied everywhere. Towns had growth spurts; schools had growth spurts. That wages might rise by 6 percent from one non-inflationary year to the next seemed in keeping with the general expansion.

As in the weedy years of childhood, growth and change through the fifties and into the sixties was so rapid and so relentless that the reaching of landmarks that would in retrospect appear momentous seemed perfectly normal, and slipped by almost without anyone noticing. Later on, when the frontiers of more were beginning to diminish and the horizons seemed no longer quite so infinite, those landmarks would take on the poignancy of a child's height measurements penciled onto a family-room wall.

In 1956, for example, in a development abnormal relative to the entire history of human labor, America's number of white- and pink-collar workers overtook the number of those engaged in the production of goods. This came about not because manufacturing jobs were yet becoming scarce—in fact 4 million new ones were added during the decade—but because clerical, secretarial, and retail sales employment was growing that much faster. Thus was born the reality if not yet the widely used term *service economy.*

In keeping with the confidence of the time, however, the service economy was not then thought of in terms of hundreds of thousands of people flipping burgers and shuffling files for minimum wage. On the contrary: the service economy was modern prosperity incarnate; according to the contextual values of the fifties, the move to services was a move toward both more and better. The service economy, it was believed, would make everyone middle class while holding forth the promise that soon no one would have to get his hands dirty or lift a heavy object ever again. Increasingly clever and well-educated people would go to work in lab coats—doing no one knew exactly what, and creating wealth no one knew exactly how. But whatever they did, it would be something modern, and if it was modern, it had to be good.

By 1964, American prosperity had become such a juggernaut as to arrive at what must be considered the watershed of the habit of more. That year, for the first time in any nation ever, urban Americans were able to pay for the necessities of food, clothing, and shelter with less than half their aggregate after-tax income. Fifty-two cents of every earned dollar was available for extras—for buying stereos, for putting down payments on summer houses, for sending the sons and daughters of working-class families to college. There was money to go to the very first discos, money to buy gold-plated bathroom fixtures, money for high school seniors to drive around in the just-introduced Ford Mustang. Moreover, there was, rather suddenly, enough money so that *and* rather than *or* became the operative notion in American spending; this was new. People could fix up the house *and* have a Florida vacation *and* move up from a Pontiac to an Oldsmobile. Freedom of choice was phasing over into freedom from having to choose; "having it all" was just beyond the frontier's next range of ups and downs.

In all, it was a swell time to be living in America, but normal it was not. America's preeminence was too lopsided to be normal. America's spending was too lavish and America's confidence too blithe to be normal. And the contextual values that inevitably went along with the seemingly effortless and presumably eternal prosperity and growth weren't normal, either. They were values that taught people to be happy and grateful at having more, but not to be content with what they had already. They didn't account for eventualities other than the eventuality of continuing frontiers. As for subtler ways of measuring better, those values didn't give us much to go on.

/// TWO

Barely had the 1980s begun, when people started pointing out that the new decade was a lot like the good old 1950s. And, if you didn't look too close, the resemblances were striking.

People were wearing their hair shorter again, and sometimes putting pomade in it, and a father-figure Republican was President. People were going bowling again, and serious urban restaurants were serving chicken pot pies. According to the fashion magazines, breasts were back in favor, and the Barbie doll, strange but true, had her greatest sales year ever in 1986. The tab-collar shirt enjoyed a brief revival. People were getting married again. A baby boomlet was heating up.

Yet none of these things had quite the same resonances they'd had in the fifties. They looked similar but felt different, and the image that irresistibly sprang to mind to explain the nature of the difference was that of two views from the same mountainside: the view one gets while climbing up, and the view one gets while coming down. The eyes see much the same vista, the legs and the spirit know otherwise. The eighties, in many respects, were a strained attempt at pretending the two views were identical. The new decade was informed by a yearning back to a version of normalcy that hadn't really been normal to begin with, and that, in any event, no longer fit the facts of the case.

Consider the 'burbs. As were the fifties, the eighties were (though less dramatically) a time of net outflow from the inner cities. People were moving both to the near suburbs—

the sorts of places they'd grown up in, and to which they'd sworn they'd never return—and, even more so, to the newer exurbs, farther outlying enclaves often centered around newly relocated company headquarters or clusters of small, high-tech firms.

But moving out of town didn't *mean* the same thing in the eighties as in the fifties. In the fifties, remember, suburbs were frontier, and moving to Park Forest or Fresh Meadows was thought of as an adventure in modernity, as participation in a great and *expanding* socioeconomic wave. Along with the values of a patch of lawn and new schools and safe streets for the kids went the values of belonging and, as it were, cooperating with the future. At their best, these values derived from a real sense of community; at their worst, they were simply a matter of "keeping up." Either way, they were grounded in the perception that more and more people would be buying houses, that the increasingly affluent suburban life was what the American future would look like, and that it was far better to be a part of it than not to be.

In the eighties, moving out of town tended to be more an adventure in individual financing, and being able to buy a single-family dwelling constituted personal progress *against* the general tide. Housing costs were outstripping almost every other economic measure, claiming an ever-larger fraction of an average family's resources. Buying an exurban acre and a home of one's own had become less a way of sharing in the national future than of outsmarting it.

The trend-line had been stood on its head—which is, of course, another way of saying we were walking back down the mountain. In the early fifties, with their postwar housing shortages, having a nest of one's own was still exotic; but it would be a great deal easier in, say, 1959 than it had been in 1951. Through the eighties, even before the Crash, owning a home was only getting harder. Instead of *wait till next year,* the operative notion was becoming *now or never.*

For another example of how the up-the-mountain/down-the-mountain dynamic affected the feel of the 1980s, consider the stage of life loosely defined as adolescence. For a quarter-century or so, beginning in the 1950s, adolescence itself was something of a frontier, adding years to its span, broadening its prerogatives, becoming ever more a hallmark of American life. In the 1980s, in ways that were unquantifiable yet palpable, adolescence began to shrink again. This contraction constituted one of the oddest yet most telling ways in which the anxious eighties mirror-imaged the eager fifties.

Regarded as a social fact rather than a glandular one, adolescence hadn't really existed until the fifties. That was when "teenagers" were invented, when kids started having their own music, their own ways of dressing, their own slang. Back then, adolescence began around age fifteen and was presumed to be over when you graduated high school and either went to work or became a housewife.

Over the next few decades, adolescence kept growing from either end. Bigger allowances and relaxing mores made children into adolescents sooner. "Preteens" now had their own dances, went out on dates, and had their own bubble-gum version of rock 'n' roll; older brothers and sisters felt honor-bound to hate the stuff, but no matter—the twelve-year-olds had their own money to buy the records, and very possibly their own hi-fis to play them on.

More dramatic by far, however, was the almost infinite elasticity of adolescence's yonder verge. College stretched it four years automatically—years spent juggling the priorities of getting educated, pursuing sex, and, in the Vietnam era, staying out of the army. Nor were those four years the limit of the undergraduate span; people changed majors, took incompletes, signed on for junior year abroad and somehow missed the plane returning. Those who swam most adroitly in the academic pond landed graduate fellowships that floated them for another few years. And no law stated that gritty gray adulthood had to start on the day one claimed one's final sheepskin. The hyphenated life was quite acceptable in the sixties and seventies; one could easily play out one's twenties as a cabdriver-novelist, a carpenter-painter, a waitress-playwright, or simply a guy with a master's who worked on oil rigs and pipelines while reading Wittgenstein and Svevo. There was a certain droll pride in doing—temporarily—menial work for which one was, by conventional measures, grotesquely overqualified. It was neither cool, civilized, nor generally considered necessary to decide too soon what you *really* wanted to do, or to make the decision primarily on grounds of money.

Whether these protracted years of schooling, dabbling, and making up one's mind were well or badly used was, of course, a highly individual matter. The point, however, is that an implicit set of values underlay the widespread tendency to zigzag toward adulthood, to meander toward long-term choices, rather than to race there. This set of values was one that the busy fifties had laid the groundwork for, but had not yet had leisure to practice, and that the nervous eighties—coming back down the mountain—seemed to have decided were luxuries that could no longer be afforded. Among these values was the conviction that examining one's life was a process worthwhile in itself. That a prime benefit of prosperity was the privilege of broad, general, and disinterested learning. That opportunity alone was insufficient reason for choosing one's lifework; one should have some feeling for what one did. That making money did not equal success and that just scraping by did not mean failure.

Make no mistake—these were values incubated in a confident time, values predicated in part on a passive trust that the economic side of life could wait, that prosperity would be there when one got around to claiming a share of it.

By the 1980s—well before the Meltdown, and despite the cheerful blather of the business rah-rahs—that trust seemed to have vanished. People talked confident, but lived scared. They grabbed at opportunities like diners at an over-crowded table; they comported themselves as though they knew damn well that economic life *wouldn't* wait, even for a minute. Especially among the young, it was critical to have . . . not so much a goal as a ticket: a law degree, a credential for computers, a track that would lead to Wall Street. It was crucial to find that ticket early, and to cling to it unflinchingly. Time, thought, effort, and yearning directed otherwise were time, thought, effort, and yearning wasted.

Those who remembered the fifties as "normal" looked on approvingly at this, and solemnly announced that the young were "getting serious" again.

Insofar as "seriousness" was equated with making a living, that was certainly true. What no one seemed to be saying, however, was that these "serious" grabs at personal prosperity were coming at the expense of precisely those civilized and civilizing privileges that prosperity was *for*. As adolescence contracted, there was less leisure and less disinterested learning. Lives zinged by too fast and too purposefully to be examined. People gave up the luxury of time in favor of the luxury of stuff.

Moreover, some of the hardest-driving young got *so* serious, so early, that they were ready for depressions very much like midlife crises at thirty-one or twenty-seven or twenty-two. The sense of being trapped, perhaps irrevocably, of running out of personal frontiers, came to third-year associates at law firms, or to second-year baby bankers in training programs, or to spunky young account execs who

realized one fine morning that marketing wasn't really the
be-all and end-all and they'd rather go outside. At some
point the sense of having missed something would assert
itself. The awful suspicion that maybe too much had been
traded for too little would begin to gnaw. But by then
there'd be a mortgage on the condo, a fat balance on
American Express, payments on the Saab. By then one
would have bought the scuba gear and would need warm-
water vacations to use it. Nothing was harder, or less
American, than stepping back.

So which was "normal"? Adolescence that lasted till the
temples turned gray, or adolescence that ended almost
before it began, adolescence in the form of a fourteen-
year-old boy already addicted to the stock tables, or a
sixteen-year-old girl already wearing horn-rimmed glasses
to look just right for law school?

Neither, of course, was normal. Normal was somewhere
in between—in a version of maturing not to be found in the
fifties, when the heady climb up the mountain of more
made grown-up prospects seem insupportably rosy, and not
to be found in the eighties, when fear about coming down
the mountain caused nearly all concerns other than pocketbook concerns to be jettisoned. Yet a normal—or at least
a civilized—vision of coming-of-age might contain elements
of each. It would recognize the bare facts of economic
responsibility while preserving the values of the examined
life, of work that is chosen for its content and not only for its
pay, of decisions made not out of secret fear but through
considered resolve.

/// THREE

If much of what was wonderful about the fifties wasn't
really normal, then much of what was normal about the

fifties wasn't that terrific. And it would seem that the resemblances between the fifties and the eighties are true resemblances to the same degree as they pertain to aspects of the two decades that were the least exalted, the most mundane.

Of politics, the less said the better.

But take, for instance, the prevailing views of higher education. In 1954, Nathan Pusey, then president of Harvard, pronounced that "the true business of liberal education is greatness." Well, that had a nice Athenian ring to it, and no doubt Pusey meant it, but outside of Cambridge it didn't really wash. For the overwhelming majority of American college students, the goal of education was a good job and a secure livelihood, period; this may not have been an exalted view, but it was practical, it was timely, and above all it was normal. Discounting the Ivy Leaguers and their cousins at the most prestigious Eastern schools, the typical fifties collegian was the first of his line to be heading for a diploma. It was an era when economic inequality was narrowing, and the object of the academic exercise was to move up a notch or two.

Through the fifties, then, the thrust in college education—*pace* Dr. Pusey—was unapologetically vocational. The decade's most heavily subscribed major was business administration—a field, by the way, whose students had the lowest median IQ of any but those who studied phys ed. At the very close of the decade, there was a jump in the number of engineering majors—not because people were suddenly following their souls' desire to nuts and bolts, but because, in the wake of Sputnik, money started flooding into math, physics, and engineering programs, and hard science, almost overnight, became a hot ticket.

It took the sixties and seventies to establish the broad belief that college should not just train but cultivate, that a degree should be not just a ticket to a better job but a passport to a more richly lived life. English literature and psychology were the hallmark majors in those decades, and while the well-rounded but undirected liberal-arts graduate has become a cultural cliché, the fact remains that you learn things from *Bleak House* that aren't to be found in Samuelson's *Economics*. Besides, was being "undirected" the worst thing in the world? Some of the people most widely studied and admired in the humanities curricula were undirected. Socrates just walked around. Freud kept changing his mind. Mark Twain didn't know whether to be a steamboat pilot, a bum, a writer, or a businessman. Moreover, a less ungenerous view of "undirectedness" might suggest the ability to move in *any* direction, and if one could move in any direction, one wouldn't run out of frontiers so fast.

In any case, academic vocationalism swept back in with a vengeance in the 1980s—and in this the decade truly did resemble the fifties. In 1984, more than twice as many undergraduate business degrees were awarded as in 1971; over the same time span, English majors decreased by almost 60 percent, with psychology, classics, and other "soft" disciplines suffering analogous declines. In case the attitudinal shifts that underlay these changes weren't apparent enough, an American Council on Education poll made them explicit. In 1987, in a survey of more than 200,000 college freshman, 76 percent acknowledged it to be "essential or very important" to them "to be very well off financially." Twenty years before, only 44 percent had made such a bald confession of fiscal preoccupations. On the other hand, in 1967, 83 percent of those interviewed thought it crucial "to develop a philosophy of life." By 1987, that percentage had shrunk to 39 percent.

Campus attitudes did not, of course, exist in a vacuum, but were one aspect of what was finally the most fundamental common ground between the fifties and the eighties: a frank, rather narrow, and almost salacious interest in the mechanics of doing business and making money.

In 1986, for example, it was observed that "shopgirls from Bloomingdale's read *The Forbes Four Hundred* as avidly as a corporate vice-president"; feminism and the two-paycheck household notwithstanding, what we're talking here is *How to Marry a Millionaire,* Marilyn Monroe, 1953. In the fifties, "captains of industry" routinely made the cover of *Time;* in the eighties, new monthlies such as *Manhattan, inc.,* took as their mandate the explication and glorification of the hot career, and *Money* magazine was the nation's fastest-growing periodical through much of the decade. Tom Wolfe, nonpareil coiner of phrases and *mots,* called the new media emphasis *plutography*—the graphic depiction of the acts of the rich. What was obvious about plutography was its trashy tabloid vicariousness, its unembarrassed ogling of luxuries beyond the reach of almost all; what was less obvious about it was its retro-ness. Eighties plutography hearkened back to those simpler times—the fifties being the last such—when wealth itself could be taken as evidence, if not necessarily of virtue, at least of *interestingness,* when a man, as in the America of John O'Hara, could be defined as worth listening to simply because he owned the town's only franchise to sell Cadillacs.

Similarly retro—though the fact was masked by ever-changing buzzwords and jargon—were eighties attitudes toward careers and business organizations. Conventional eighties wisdom had it that a new breed of cat was stalking America's corporate corridors. This new-style executive purportedly had a broad streak of entrepreneurship, valued action above security, hated hierarchy, was deficient in institutional loyalty but got away with it by sheer force of savvy, energy, gamesmanship, and guts.

This version of the eighties business turk made good copy, but it was basically malarkey. A handful of job-hopping MBAs and multimillionaire raiders aside, what the typical eighties businessperson craved was what the typical fifties businessperson craved: not high adventure, but a job that would still be there next week or next year, not a platform for the acting out of grand schemes, but a medical plan, a pension, a place to go in the morning.

Like the junior executives from the heyday of William H. Whyte's *Organization Man,* the typical eighties businessperson pursued his or her goals in big outfits held together by procedures and rules; for the great majority, the facts of working life hadn't changed all that much. William Whyte himself, in a 1986 coda to his seminal 1956 book, observed that the contemporary young executive "may talk differently than he once did, but he does not act so very differently; indeed, today's . . . young urban professionals exhibit a faith in the system every bit as staunch as that of the junior executives of former years. It is this faith, not disillusionment, that is unsettling."

Why had that faith become unsettling? Because it presumed a boundlessness of the economic frontier, an endless and eternal supply of more. It was a faith that had its roots in the seemingly automatic growth of the fifties—growth that was not normal because it resulted from world circumstances that were not normal. In the fifties, that faith had been reinforced by two things that seemed a perfect confirmation of the rightness of our methods and the adequacy of our values: Americans were getting richer relative to everyone else, and more equally rich relative to each other. By the 1980s, neither of those things was true. And, as Monet used to say about the quality of the light, a little detail like that made everything look different.

3

Why the
Middle Class
Isn't Funny
Anymore

ONE

One of the things that looked different was the American middle class, which, by the middle 1980s, had begun to look so different that it was increasingly difficult to find it at all. And the argument could be made that if we could no longer recognize the American middle class, then we could no longer recognize America.

As far back as 1782, when Ben Franklin was dispensing his advice to Europeans as to what they should and should not expect to find in the New World, America was already being described as a "Land of Labour," where "good Laws and Liberty" had given rise to an unprecedented equality, not just of opportunity, but of condition. "The Truth is," wrote Franklin, "that though there are in that Country few People

so miserable as the Poor of Europe, there are also very few
that in Europe would be called rich; it is rather a general
happy Mediocrity that prevails."

Along with economic parity went a proud and feisty sense
of social equality. "Birth," claimed Franklin, "[was] a Commodity that [could not] be carried to a worse market than
that of America, where people [did] not inquire concerning
a Stranger, *What is he?* but, *What can he do?*" The new
nation had no room for slackers and no need of gentlemen.
Contrary to tall tales of "houses til'd with pancakes"—an
early version of streets paved with gold—what America
offered was the opportunity to work hard in exchange for
the luxury of feeling inferior to no one. Among the various
freedoms America offered, not the least appealing or the
least historically radical was freedom from envy.

It should be understood that this vision of a virtually
all-inclusive (white) middle class was utterly unique in the
eighteenth-century world. Europe had its bourgeoisies, of
course, but they had evolved from previously existing social
structures. Europe's merchants and civil servants had clawed
their way to a degree of status as the money economy and
the national state displaced feudalism, and the new class
stood in clear contrast to the aristocracy above and the
peasantry, and later the proletariat, below. In America, the
middle class could not be said to have evolved, because
there was nothing for it to evolve *from*: no feudal or
monarchical traditions were in place before the middle
class arrived; there were no higher and lower orders for the
bourgeoisie to make a niche between.

The American middle class was coeval with America itself,
and was shaped by the same circumstances. Vast but diffuse
resources provided a living for everyone but—until after the
Civil War—discouraged the concentration of great fortunes.
Frontier hardships could not be bought out of; the relatively

richer man tromped through the same mud and horse ma-
nure as the relatively poorer one, and lived on the same
pumpkins when the hunting or the corn crop was bad. As
frontier shaped the American habits of optimism and the
expectation of better things, so it fostered a deep predilection
for an at least approximate equality. Other countries *had* a
middle class; America—with the notable but historically
overlooked exceptions of blacks and white sharecroppers—
was the middle class.

Shrewd observers from Crèvecoeur to Tocqueville realized immediately that that fact was absolutely central to the
formation of American values—and not always in a positive
way. In a milieu where, by custom and by law, no man could
presume himself superior to any other, how would distinction be recognized? How, if not by pedigree, would excellence be defined, and toward what, if not toward knighthood
or some other royal grant, should one aspire? One all-
too-obvious answer was money, since, going by the book,
political and even social equality was a separate issue from
the stacking up of personal wealth. If wealth has traditionally
been too much of a preoccupation in America, part of the
reason is that money has filled in for the other tokens of
preferment we have denied ourselves. Wealth has been
about the only medal civilians could wear.

And according to Tocqueville, for one, civilians will wear
medals. A species that seemed always to have had a
penchant for lords and serfs, chiefs and Indians, Brahmins
and Untouchables, would "never establish any equality with
which [it] can be contented." Men would contrive a hierarchy somehow—put houses on hills instead of on flatlands,
dress their women in fur rather than cloth, establish private
pews in church. All might be equal in the sight of God and
of the laws, but human eyes made discernments all their
own.

As it was in economic matters, so it was in matters intellectual: the ideal of equality was not an unmixed blessing. Tocqueville liked to think that the security and invigoration of democratic freedoms might lead "the mind of every man to untried thoughts." On the other hand, he was well aware of the potentially crushing social pressures inherent in a community of equals. Was a mere opinion—a thing of breath and vapor, and no more legally legitimate than any other—worth possibly offending one's neighbors over? What gave one the right to be smarter, bolder, more original? Against the explicit liberty to have and speak brave visions was the implicit suggestion that it would be more comfortable not to, and this was a circumstance that might "prohibit [the American] from thinking at all."

So, *did* the American bourgeois think at all? And if so, what was the quality of his thought?

A strange thing happened to the answers to these questions as time went on. As the middle class grew more and more prosperous, more and more self-esteeming, more and more secure in its prerogatives, the answers started getting funny.

In Tocqueville's day, the American middle class was a grand experiment, to be approached in the spirit of serious anthropological inquiry; you didn't make light of what then seemed the boldest foray into economic democracy since the early days of the Roman Republic. Half a century later, the experiment was seen to have succeeded, and middle-class mores, in the writing of Mark Twain and others, had become entrenched enough to become the stuff of relatively gentle comedy. By the turn of this century, with the bourgeoisie more wealthy and established still, Ambrose Bierce would up the comic voltage to a rollicking and edgy satire.

The focus of that satire, in various hands, was precisely

the bourgeois's implacable confidence, optimism, and seeming invulnerability; you were free to tweak him because you couldn't really hurt him. The historian Henry Steele Commager characterized the late-nineteenth-century burgher as a cheerful and unreflective fellow who "took comfort for granted," had "a quantitative cast to his thinking," and "was impatient of any but the normal yardstick[s]" for measuring the worth of individuals, institutions, or ideas. "Theories and speculations disturbed" him; "he had little sense of the past or concern for it"; "he felt instinctively that philosophy was the resort of the unhappy and the bewildered and knew that he was neither."

If this smug and boring little man made a tempting comic target when he was merely well-to-do, he became an irresistible mark when he grew rich. Wealth confirmed him in his dullness and he became a pompous ass. Success proved his wisdom and his virtue, and he was eager to share the secrets of his diet, his schedule, his credo. Sad to say, however, it was unlikely that our specimen parvenu had time to pick up much sophistication in the bustle of acquiring his fortune, and his lavish spending, rather than transcending middle-class sensibility, merely magnified it so that it might shine more brightly forth in all its bad taste, pretension, and naïveté.

When the *fin de siècle* American grew rich, he fancied himself, for want of more original fancies, a European lord. He wanted a palazzo, a Rhineland castle, a Versailles. A few American moguls—Carnegie, Frick—had the sense to hire well-versed advisers as to the deployment and display of their wealth. But more typical was William Randolph Hearst, who, at San Simeon, had a cavernous, baronial dining hall with walk-in fireplaces and individual ketchup dispensers at every chair. Mere satire was beggared by such evidence of middle-class frumpiness run amok, and simple observation

they could be counted on to chuckle at every emcee's imitation of Jack Benny or Ed Sullivan. Television was spawning a truly national culture, albeit an appalling one, based on favorite shows, brand awareness, and an ever-widening web of references to itself.

In tandem with the tube came a prosperity that dispersed itself almost as broadly as the airwaves. Over the half-century ending in 1953, real per capita disposable income more than doubled. Between 1947 and 1953 alone, it increased by 12 percent—and this during a time when the baby boom was adding close to 4 million new *capita* every year. As fast as the population was growing, personal income was expanding twice as fast.

Moreover, as wealth grew, the trend was unmistakably, even dramatically, toward more equal distribution. As of 1929, the richest 1 percent of Americans claimed 19 percent of the nation's total after-tax income; by 1946—largely because of the progressive income tax—that share had shrunk to 8 percent. At the opposite end of the economic spectrum, as of 1929—even after a decade of prosperity and even before the Depression settled in—only 20 percent of all American families were taking in more than $2,500 a year (roughly $4,000 in 1953 money and $16,000 today); by 1953, fully half of America's families had crossed the $4,000 threshold, which at that time was the generally accepted entry point into middle-class buying power.

As of 1953, 58 percent of American households were clustered in the great economic middle, taking in between $3,000 and $10,000 of after-tax earnings. "The U.S.," *Fortune* confidently concluded, "is becoming a one-class market of prosperous middle-income people," an "all-American" spending bloc who "essentially . . . buy the same things—the same staples, the same appliances, the same cars, the same furniture, and much the same recreation."

Together, then, television and broadening prosperity were giving rise to a new kind of culture in which the key word was *mass*. Mass communication. Mass media. Mass trends. Mass marketing.

It was telling that, while the term *mass market* had been in use at least since the beginning of the century, its meaning had to be totally revised to fit the fifties. Traditionally, the mass market had been defined in disparaging contrast to the "class market." This latter group was small, highly concentrated in the Northeastern cities, and rich enough to buy virtually anything it wanted; it was targeted—though no one used that parlance then—by importers of ivory and importers of governesses, by dealers in emeralds and roadsters and Havana cigars.

The old-style mass market, on the other hand, wasn't targeted at all. What was to be gained by courting a market that could and would buy only what it needed? The typical 1920s family had one or two hundred dollars left over after paying for basic clothing, shelter, and food. This puny amount of discretionary income simply wasn't worth the trouble of pursuing.

By the 1950s all of that had radically changed. The number of people with incomes of a million-dollars-plus after taxes had actually *shrunk* dramatically, as had the number of households with over 100,000 disposable dollars a year—again, because of changes in the tax structure. The squeeze at the top, however, was much more than made up for by the gains of the middle class. If virtually no one was buying one-hundred-foot steam yachts anymore, hundreds of thousands of people were buying twelve-foot dinghies with six-horsepower Evinrudes on them. If "the servant problem" was becoming critical in those households where maids and valets had always been the rule, dishwashers and Dispos-alls were becoming common in homes where leaking bags of garbage and scraping egg yolk with a fingernail had always been the rule.

What was happening was that the line between luxuries and necessities was blurring—blurring so much that new and in some cases oxymoronic definitions were called for. Things that had previously been called, simply, "luxuries," were now defined as "rare luxuries"—and their sales were in eclipse. Sales of "commonplace luxuries," however, were burgeoning. The "mass market," having caught the hunger for more, was spending like a "class market"; regular folks were now thinking of luxuries merely as necessities that were less necessary than others. In 1953, Americans had $34.1 billion dollars of income earmarked for luxury goods and services. The lion's share of that money—which was equivalent to the United Kingdom's total personal income for the year—was in the pockets of America's junior executives, unionized blue-collar production workers, mailmen, traveling salesmen, public school teachers, guys who drove trucks.

The result was a whole new species of mass-market consumer, and a whole new approach to reaching that consumer. It began to be understood that people didn't only buy to have; they bought for the pleasure of buying, and they felt privileged to be able to buy often. They would gladly trash their old still-working toaster in favor of the nicely contoured four-slice job like the one they'd seen on *The Donna Reed Show*. Products were more than function alone; they were supposed to make you feel good. Refrigerators had to come in modernistic colors like "Bermuda pink" and "lagoon blue." Tabletop radios had to be not just designed, but "styled." Cigarette lighters were supposed to look *atomic*. Cars had to be both exciting and easily surpassable. Nor was there anything the slightest bit clandestine about this; George Walker, the chief designer at

Ford, boasted to an interviewer that "we design a car to make a man unhappy with his '57 Ford 'long about the end of 1958." Curiously, the concept of obsolescence could be applied even to historical epochs long dead; in 1957, for example, *Look* magazine published a piece about "the new Early American look," pointing out how much more sophisticated and desirable this style was, relative to the Early American look of the first half of the decade.

The tastes of the new, suburban, television-influenced mass market were summed up by the design critic Thomas Hine in the felicitous coinage "populuxe"—a frankly contradictory attempt to combine populism with luxury, and with "a thoroughly unnecessary 'e,' to give it class." Populuxe was the Chrysler Imperial, Miami Beach, Con-Tact paper, the Barcalounger. Populuxe was the chartreuse vinyl dinette set and the festive dip made from a box of soup mix. Populuxe was mass-market Heaven, "an expression of outright, thoroughly vulgar joy in being able to live so well." Most of all, Populuxe was funny. Even today, you see one of those atomic wall clocks, or butterfly chairs that can swallow you alive, and you smile.

Why? Partly because, by our lights, the stuff is horrendous; but partly, too, we smile because those gaudy artifacts, meant to be used a year or two and then replaced by something sleeker, are the legacy of a middle class that really got a kick out of all the things it had, a middle class that reveled unabashedly in *more;* a middle class that had never had life so good, and was having it better every year.

/// THREE

Every year, that is, until 1968, when the rise in consumer prices first blipped past 4 percent, or 1973, when real wages started to fall, or 1974, when inflation hit double digits, gas lines stretched around the block, and 41 percent of American auto workers were laid off for at least part of the year.

Or 1975, when unemployment flashed at nearly 10 percent, and when the solace of blaming it all on OPEC was wearing thin in light of facts such as that America had been losing manufacturing jobs, as a percentage of all employment, at least since 1960, and in absolute terms, at least since 1970.

But it was 1978 when the middle class had its nose rubbed in a particularly unappetizing truth—a classic case of having insult heaped on top of injury, and a development that perhaps more than any other has changed the feel of things in America. By 1978 it had become clear that the more than thirty-year trend toward more equal distribution of wealth had reversed itself. The rich were getting not just richer, but relatively richer again. The poor were getting more numerous and less mobile again. And the middle class was getting screwed, squeezed, and whittled away from both ends.

As of 1985, families conventionally described as middle class—those with incomes between 15,000 and 35,000 1985 dollars—constituted 39.4 percent of American households; as recently as 1973, such households had been a 51 percent majority.

Of the roughly 6 million families that had vanished from the great middle, an undeterminable percentage had scratched their way upward, usually by combining his-and-hers paychecks. But while the two-earner household became almost an economic necessity through the late seventies and the eighties, the development had at least one substantial drawback, so far as relative equality was concerned. As more marriageable women maintained well-paying careers, men seemed to rediscover the maxim that it's as easy to love someone rich as poor. Male doctors now married not their nurses, but female doctors; male executives flirted with secretaries but wed vice-presidents. Matrimony was again taking on more of the character it had back in the days of dowries; it was a way of consolidating fiscal positions and concentrating wealth. In this, one ironic consequence of the women's movement was becoming ever clearer: females who had not been educationally privileged or simply were not workplace-ambitious were losing out on their traditional ticket to middle-class status and comfort; there were ever fewer prosperous men willing or able to "hire" them to make babies and keep house. For a woman to become middle class *without* a man was nearly as difficult as it had ever been, as women's median earnings still languished, as of 1985, at a mere 65 percent of men's.

Not that wage-earning males were having a terrific time of it, either. Between 1970 and 1985, real weekly earnings declined in construction, in retail trade, in wholesale trade, and in that whole enormous category known as services. In relatively high-paying industries like steel and autos, a combination of plant closings, long layoffs, and union givebacks pushed ever more workers back across the shadow-line between doing pretty well and just getting by. Even those who had not been economically "demoted" out of the middle class faced a new precariousness in their fiscal, and therefore their social, standing. This precariousness flew in the teeth of higher expectations as well as of the comic tradition of *Life of Riley*—with the Chrysler plant boarded up and the textile business gone to Singapore, you didn't do comedy about blue-collar guys moving to the suburbs and taking on the trappings of gentlemen.

Nor were there a lot of laughs in the situation of *white*-collar guys, who in many instances were doing even worse. During the 1970s, average earnings among such "smart" middle-class people as accountants, chemists, and engineering technicians all failed to hold even with inflation. Brewery workers, coal miners, and oil-field hands, meanwhile, all beat the consumer price index by comfortable margins—and they were out-earning the cited white-collar groups, except for the chemists, in absolute terms as well. No wonder that one in every five college graduates through the 1970s ended up in a job that didn't require college.

This, in turn, shed light on one of the biggest fibs this country had ever told itself: the fib, so essentially humane and so believable in the fifties, that as more and more people went to college and got good, practical, vocational degrees, the marketplace would grow smarter along with them, giving everyone a dignified and remunerative job that would really use his or her abilities and learning. Between 1955 and 1980, the number of Americans earning college degrees had nearly quadrupled. Education itself had been a leading growth industry, employing more people than autos or steel. It had turned out, however, that the supply of clean-hands jobs did not keep pace with the number of clean hands available to do them, and furthermore, that a discouraging number of those lab-coat sort of positions were not all they were cracked up to be. America had traded an idealistic view of education for a practical one, which had turned out not even to be practical.

Belatedly, people started acknowledging where much of the broad-based growth of the fifties and sixties, and most of the impetus toward economic equality, had *really* come from: from unglamorous, unmodern, generally unionized jobs in various aspects of manufacturing. Fancy it up however you like, wealth still came from finding a material that could be made into something someone wanted, hitting it with a hammer until it was the right shape, sticking it in a box, putting it on a truck, and delivering it to the guy who would pay you for it. If the equation worked out so that the people who performed those functions could also afford to buy the product, then general prosperity prevailed, then you truly had a working middle class, then things were in balance.

Between 1979 and 1984, more than 11 million people lost those sorts of production jobs, half of the people who lost them went back to work for lower pay, and it was becoming increasingly clear that the American economy was *not* in balance. There was still "growth," but the growth was cockeyed, paradoxical. In 1976, more Americans were employed than at any other time in history, and more people were unemployed than at any time since the Great Depression. Through the first half of the 1980s, nearly 2 million new jobs were created each year but those jobs were overwhelmingly concentrated in the service sector— and the service sector, which had sounded so modern and so full of promise in the fifties, was turning out to be perhaps the greatest engine of inequality this country had ever seen. In production jobs, the ratio between an average manager's pay and an average worker's pay was 1.5/1; in service jobs, the ratio was 3/1.

The trend toward broadening disparities could hardly have been clearer, or its implications for the middle class more dramatic. Home ownership, for example, that hallmark of mainstream status, was again becoming the prerogative of the few. Through the 1950s, carrying costs on a typical house averaged 14 percent of an average breadwinner's pay; by 1984, that figure had ballooned to 44 percent of what a thirty-year worker could expect to earn, and houses were moving beyond the reach of those erstwhile staple figures in suburban neighborhoods: "the nice young people just starting out." As recently as 1977, 36 percent of all homes purchased in America had been first homes; by

1980, only 18 percent were. Nor did the early-eighties drop in mortgage rates provide a great deal of help, since the median selling price of a new house increased by over 30 percent between 1980 and 1985, while real wages, as we have seen, were going almost nowhere.

The bottom line seemed to be that the American middle class was becoming too expensive a club to join at this late date. It was ever tougher to latch onto *more* unless you had a good bit to begin with, since the operative pattern had become trading up, not buying in. If you hadn't been around to stake a claim when things were good, when entry into the bourgeoisie seemed almost a perquisite of citizenship, there was a serious chance you'd missed out forever.

//// FOUR

Missing out carried with it emotional as well as economic ramifications—ramifications that exist at the intersection of financial security and self-esteem, and that are the crux of the reason the middle class isn't funny anymore. The middle class has lost the solid outlines that made it such a hittable target, as well as the confidence to laugh at itself.

By the early 1980s, the author Paul Fussell could persuasively argue that what had formerly been called "the lower-middle class"—that group made up chiefly of blue-collar guys doing unglamorous jobs, and old-style families in which the mother stayed at home—"doesn't exist as such any longer, [but has been] transformed into the high-proletarian class. What's the difference? A further lack of freedom and self-respect.... [Members of this class] are identifiable as people things are done to. They are in bondage—to monetary policy, ripoff advertising ... fast foods, consumer schlock."

At the same time as those with the most tenuous hold on

middle-class status were backsliding, those whose financial position was less threatened were engaged in a more or less mad scramble to disassociate themselves from the middle class. In 1965, being solidly bourgeois marked a person as a winner; by 1985, it did not. To be seen as "successful" in the 1980s, a time when both the carrot of ambition and the stick of fiscal worry had grown to preternatural size, you had to catapult straight on into the reaches of the wealthy. To stay in the middle was to lose, or, almost as bad, to be *seen* as losing. And what made the materialistic excesses of the eighties offensive, as we will argue, was not so much the excesses themselves as the fact that a desperate virtue was made of moving up at a time when the commonweal was moving down.

America, that historic bastion of the economic center, was becoming a society of extremes. Low-cost housing, as always, was in demand; waterfront property in the Hamptons of Long Island was routinely changing hands at a million bucks an acre; the soft spot in the market was in average houses for regular people. Porsche was selling one of every four cars it made in Southern California; Hyundai lowballed the market and became a major player almost overnight; meanwhile, there seemed to be ever fewer Buick types around. Bergdorf Goodman was doing terrific business, as was K mart; middle-market giants like Gimbel's and Ohrbach's had closed their doors.

So much for the one-class American market that *Fortune* had rhapsodized about in 1953, and whose brief existence had spawned the democratic pastels and boomerang motifs of Populuxe. By the 1980s, the only people who still seemed to want middle-class stuff were the people who couldn't afford it; the only people who still seemed to regard middle-class status as a goal worth shooting for were the people who probably wouldn't get there.

1

The
More
Factor

/// ONE

Americans have always been optimists, and optimists have always liked to speculate. In Texas in the 1880s, the speculative instrument of choice was towns, and there is no tale more American than this.

What people would do was buy up enormous tracts of parched and vacant land, lay out a Main Street, nail together some wooden sidewalks, and start slapping up buildings. One of these buildings would be called the Grand Hotel and would have a saloon complete with swinging doors. Another might be dubbed the New Academy or the Opera House. The developers would erect a flagpole and name a church, and once the workmen had packed up and moved on, the towns would be as empty as the sky.

But no matter. The speculators, next, would hire people to pass out handbills in the Eastern and Midwestern cities, tracts limning the advantages of relocation to "the Athens of the South" or "the new plains Jerusalem." When persuasion failed, the builders might resort to bribery, paying people's moving costs and giving them houses, in exchange for nothing but a pledge to stay until a certain census was taken or a certain inspection made. Once the nose-count was completed, people were free to move on, and there was in fact a contingent of folks who made their living by keeping a cabin on skids, and dragging it for pay from one town to another.

The speculators' idea, of course, was to lure the railroad. If one could create a convincing semblance of a town, the railroad might come through it, and a real town would develop, making the speculators staggeringly rich. By these devices a man named Sanborn once owned Amarillo.

But railroad tracks are narrow and the state of Texas is very, very wide. For every Wichita Falls or Lubbock there were a dozen College Mounds or Belchervilles, bleached, unpeopled burgs that receded quietly into the dust, taking with them large amounts of speculators' money.

Still, the speculators kept right on bucking the odds and depositing empty towns in the middle of nowhere. Why did they do it? Two reasons—reasons that might be said to summarize the central fact of American economic history and that go a fair way toward explaining what is perhaps the central strand of the national character.

The first reason was simply that the possible returns were so enormous as to partake of the surreal, to create a climate in which ordinary logic and prudence did not seem to apply. In a boom like that of real estate when the railroad barreled through, long shots that might pay 100,000 to one seemed worth a bet.

The second reason, more pertinent here, is that there was a presumption that America would *keep on* booming—if not forever, then at least longer than it made sense to worry about. There would always be another gold rush, another Homestead Act, another oil strike. The next generation would always ferret out opportunities that would be still more lavish than any that had gone before. America *was* those opportunities. This was an article not just of faith, but of strategy. You banked on the next windfall, you staked your hopes and even your self-esteem on it; and this led to a national turn of mind that might usefully be thought of as the habit of more.

A century, maybe two centuries, before anyone had heard the term *baby boomer,* much less *yuppie,* the habit of more had been installed as the operative truth among the economically ambitious. The habit of more seemed to suggest that there was no such thing as getting wiped out in America. A fortune lost in Texas might be recouped in Colorado. Funds frittered away on grazing land where nothing grew might flood back in as silver. There was always a second chance, or always seemed to be, in this land where growth was destiny and where expansion and purpose were the same.

The key was the frontier, not just as a matter of acreage, but as idea. Vast, varied, rough as rocks, America was the place where one never quite came to the end. Ben Franklin explained it to Europe even before the Revolutionary War had finished: America offered new chances to those "who, in their own Countries, where all the Lands [were] fully occupied . . . could never [emerge] from the poor Condition wherein they were born."

So central was this awareness of vacant space and its link to economic promise, that Frederick Jackson Turner, the historian who set the tone for much of the twentieth century's understanding of the American past, would write that it was "not the constitution, but free land . . . [that] made the democratic type of society in America." Good laws mattered; an accountable government mattered; ingenuity and hard work mattered. But those things were, so to speak, an overlay on the natural, geographic America that was simply *there,* and whose vast and beckoning possibilities seemed to generate the ambition and the sometimes reckless liberty that would fill it. First and foremost, it was open space that provided "the freedom of the individual to rise under conditions of social mobility."

Open space generated not just ambition, but metaphor. As early as 1835, Tocqueville was extrapolating from the fact of America's emptiness to the observation that "no natural boundary seems to be set to the efforts of man." Nor was any limit placed on what he might accomplish, since, in that heyday of the Protestant ethic, a person's rewards were taken to be quite strictly proportionate to his labors.

Frontier; opportunity; more. This has been the American trinity from the very start. The frontier was the backdrop and also the raw material for the streak of economic booms. The booms became the goad and also the justification for the myriad gambles and for Americans' famous optimism. The optimism, in turn, shaped the schemes and visions that were sometimes noble, sometimes appalling, always bold. The frontier, as reality and as symbol, is what has shaped the American way of doing things and the American sense of what's worth doing.

But there has been one further corollary to the legacy of the frontier, with its promise of ever-expanding opportunities: given that the goal—a realistic goal for most of our history— was *more,* Americans have been somewhat backward in adopting values, hopes, ambitions that have to do with things *other than* more. In America, a sense of quality has lagged far behind a sense of scale. An ideal of contentment has yet to take root in soil traditionally more hospitable to an ideal of restless striving. The ethic of decency has been upstaged by the ethic of success. The concept of growth has been applied almost exclusively to things that can be measured, counted, weighed. And the hunger for those things that are unmeasur-

generally sufficed to provide a good chortle at the expense of bourgeois taste writ large. "Must I show you this *French chateau* . . . on this street corner, here, in New York, and still you do not laugh?" wrote the turn-of-the-century architect and critic Louis Sullivan. "Must you wait till you see a *gentleman* in a silk hat come out of it before you laugh? Have you no sense of humor, no sense of pathos?"

In our own century, humor and pathos have played roughly equal parts in portrayals of the middle class, and the two elements have become ever more inextricably mixed. Perhaps the compleat bourgeois, Sinclair Lewis's George Babbitt, was at the same time loathsome, laughable, and sad, a man for whom "a sensational event was changing from the brown suit to the gray the contents of his pockets." The Babbitts of the nation, collectively considered, became the pitiable but also hilarious congregation that H. L. Mencken dubbed the "booboisie." And every Sunday, Dagwood Bumstead, the put-upon husband of the comic-strip "Blondie," could be seen mowing his patch of suburban lawn, or trying, always futilely, to enjoy a little peace in his recliner by the TV set, fretting meanwhile about the extravagant shopping habits of his wife and the unreasonable demands of his boss. Poor Dagwood—the quintessential provider of the sort of *more* that did not come easily yet absolutely could not be done without.

Not the least intriguing thing about the time-honored American tradition of tweaking the middle class has been the support given the genre by the middle class itself. Were the American throngs of pale, meek pencil pushers offended when James Thurber's Walter Mitty showed them the comic/pathetic discrepancies between their real lives and their fantasies? Not at all—they adopted Mitty as a mascot. Sinclair Lewis, his essential bleakness notwithstanding, was not just a Nobel Prize–winning author, but a best-selling one.

Millions of Americans guffawed at the early TV sitcom *Life of Riley*, which might be thought to have come uncomfortably close to showing them their own worst fears: Riley was the regular-guy working stiff who'd made it to the suburbs, and who was both baffled and bored by the newfound good life. He passed his weekends on a chaise longue (read: chaze lounge) in his miniscule backyard, terrified of insects, intimidated by his wife's appliances, and having not the faintest idea what use to make of his hard-earned leisure. By the 1970s, the black middle class was assured, perversely, that it had arrived, by being made the target of satires such as the *Saturday Night Live* skit "Stalking the Negro Republican." *Welcome to the club,* such vignettes seemed to say, *and congratulations on becoming conventional, pretentious, and utterly devoid of spontaneity.*

Why has middle-class-bashing been such a central part of American storytelling and American humor? And why has the middle class itself shown such an abiding willingness to chuckle at send-ups of its limitations and its prejudices? Part of the reason is that "middle-class America" has traditionally meant such a broad swath of the population that lampooning the bourgeoisie has been something of a communal rite. In a nation where 92 percent of the inhabitants call themselves middle class (even though, by usual economic reckonings, fewer than half that many really are), attacks on the bourgeoisie are no more to be taken personally than is criticism of humanity itself.

More subtly, however, America has been able to afford to spoof its middle class because, for much of our history and especially since World War II, the broad belief has been that ending up middle class was about the *least* one could aspire to. If grander visions fizzled, if more sweeping schemes failed, one could always take a job, maybe two jobs, and find a slot in the economic center; at the very least one could lay the groundwork so that one's children could join the bourgeoisie. And once you'd made it into the middle class, it was truly difficult to fall back out again. Raises came; savings interest outpaced inflation; pension money accumulated; property values rose as if by natural laws so that people effortlessly found themselves sitting on a nice piece of equity, substantial and respected citizens by definition.

The complacent bourgeois was laughable, then, because he was so awfully pleased with himself for something that in fact was so easy to achieve. Yes, it took work, often a great deal of work, to be bourgeois. It took sobriety, discipline, persistence, and the other middle-class virtues. But those virtues were common enough so that the lack and not the possession of them was surprising in a person. Given those widespread and communally reinforced traits, the American landscape would take care of the rest. First because of the literal frontier, later under the mechanics of more, becoming comfortably middle class seemed to happen almost automatically.

Well, beginning in the 1970s, it was no longer so easy to join the middle class, and people were actually falling out of its ranks every time a factory closed and every time the cost of living blipped ahead another notch. The middle class was no longer secure. And being insecure, it no longer seemed so funny, either.

//// TWO

If America, in theory, was a middle-class nation all along, it took the unique circumstances of the late forties and the fifties to create that particular version of the middle class immortalized by *Leave It to Beaver* and *Father Knows Best,* a vision of wholesome suburban normalcy in half-hour episodes with a moral.

This was a middle class characterized by kitchen counters full of space-age gizmos; by college-bound teenagers doing homework on the dining room table where no one ever ate; by stay-at-home mothers with perfect hair, shirtwaist dresses, and wooden-sided station wagons; and by fathers who carried briefcases and occasionally showed their love and their wisdom by skipping an important business meeting to get to little Jennifer's school play. Jennifer would portray a talking tea kettle, would get so excited at seeing her daddy, who before the second commercial had made her cry by saying he wouldn't be able to come, that she'd forget her lines but steal the show with an ad-lib straight from the heart; everyone would tell everybody else that they were wonderful, and they'd all go out for ice cream. This, in short, was the ideal if not the reality of the middle class that most Americans alive today grew up with.

Two factors made this middle class different from the versions that had gone before. The first was television, which blanketed the nation far more thoroughly and far more uniformly than any medium had ever done. Television blurred geography, downplayed or ignored ethnicity (except in the case of specifically ghetto-ized shows like *The Goldbergs* or *Amos 'n' Andy*), and made people more alike by *presenting* them as more alike. Sitcoms generally took place in Anywhere, U.S.A. Contestants on quiz shows might have Southern drawls or New Hampshire twangs, but their regional differences were assumed to go no further; once you got past the novelty of their accents, they were interchangeable in their hunger for the Samsonite luggage, the silver from Michael C. Fina, the Amana freezer, the travel provided by Trans World Airlines. Audience members, whether they were sixteen or sixty, could be expected to laugh at the same quips about the NBC peacock and the CBS "seeing eye";

The habit of more was not dying—hardly—but the prerogative of more was being concentrated in ever fewer hands. By 1983, more than a quarter of America's personal income was being taken in by the 15 percent of people who had household earnings over $50,000; projections indicated that by 1990, that quarter of the national income would grow to a third. This meant, among other things, that the terms *mass market* and *class market* were coming due for another redefinition. In the fifties, the mass market had become virtually synonymous with the middle class, and the mass market was where the action had been. That action was now greatly diminished, as the tens of millions who languished near the median income level found themselves with less discretionary money to spend. On the other hand, the sheer number of people who could be classified as wealthy was expanding enough that the class market—for European cars, exotic mushrooms, wineglasses that went *ping*—was itself becoming a mass market. It was, however, a "mass market" consisting of the fifteen richest people out of every hundred—not, as in the fifties, of one out of every two.

Those fifteen affluent people were by far the most sophisticated consumers America had ever had. They'd been to Europe. They knew which fork to use. They had taste. They weren't funny the way consumers in the fifties had been funny. You couldn't laugh at their hairdos, their man-made fibers, their pronunciation of words that once were French. The only problem with those fifteen people was that they no longer represented the main body of America, they no longer provided a model through which America could recognize itself, feel affection for itself, and even make fun of itself. Through the 1980s, the wealthy became ever more visible but ever less typical; the unwealthy were increasingly typical and ever less visible; there no longer seemed to be a middle ground.

The waning of the middle class raised a host of questions that didn't seem to get asked much in the 1980s. For those coming to be defined as "the high proletariat," the questions were immediate and clear: Where do I live? How do I educate my children? Why am I breaking my hump if there's no real progress to be made?

For the wealthy, the question was how long the trend toward lopsidedness could continue before conscience would protest—or, assuming conscience remained conveniently silent, before social unrest caused a serious reshuffling, or the economic system teetered from its own topheaviness.

There was a deeper question, too, a question of national definition. From Ben Franklin to Lee Iacocca, people who set themselves up as spokesmen for America had stressed that the nation was a haven of the economic mean, a place where advancement and equality were presumed not to be irreconcilably at odds. In America, comfort and self-esteem followed from playing by the rules, and if playing by the rules brought you to the middle of the middle class, but no farther, that was something you could be proud of. The middle-class virtues were rewarded not only materially, but by the satisfaction of feeling that one was in step with what the country stood for, that one was part of a tradition.

But if America *didn't* any longer stand for the supremacy and pride of the middle class, then what sort of country was it, anyway?

4 ///

Quiz Shows
and the
National
Purpose

/// **ONE**

So what kind of nation are we, anyway?

The question gets raised from time to time, generally at moments when it has become irrepressibly clear that some cherished but distant mythology is wearing thin. People notice that, except for arctic Alaska, there are no more empty places on the American map, and demand to know what kind of nation are we, anyway, if not one with a continent full of frontier. We find ourselves in a quasi-colonial war in Vietnam, and the question is asked, What kind of nation are we, anyway, if not one that has always been avowedly anti-colonial? The middle class comes under economic siege, and we ask ourselves, What sort of nation are we, anyway, if not one in which the regular joe has always held his head up high, and lived, if not magnificently, at least on an unenvying par with his neighbors?

National purpose is the ringing phrase usually intoned by politicians and pundits when such matters come under discussion; and debates about national purpose, once you get past the specific circumstances that prompt them, come down to questions about what we say we value, what we act like we value, and the sometimes extreme tension between the two. When the tension becomes too great, the discrepancies too bald, the hypocrisy too blatant, the public draws the line and the editorialists have a field day. Sometimes things even change as a result.

Crises of national purpose occur, as we say, from time to time. We had one after the assassination of JFK and the murder of Lee Harvey Oswald, when, rather suddenly, it began to be asked if we were a "sick society." We had one in the doldrums of the Carter years, when economic bafflement and political humiliation made people wonder if our morale had been irretrievably sapped.

But the argument can be made that the national purpose debate which continues to tell us the most about the America we know today is one that came out of the fifties. Just as the fifties were the pivotal moment in establishing the contemporary shape of the habit of more, so they were the moment when that habit first widely revealed its dark side. Already in the fifties it was beginning to come clear that more was not just an inadequate goal but potentially a dangerous one. Unless it was embedded in a context of solid values, more had a way of bringing out the worst in people. It could even make the whole system seem tawdry and a little bit absurd.

The crisis that brought these concerns into the spotlight centered on, of all things, a rigged television quiz show. Here, briefly, are the facts of the case:

In 1957, a man named Charles Van Doren, an assistant professor of English at Columbia University, won $129,000—roughly equivalent to half a million dollars in 1988—on NBC's *Twenty-One,* and became a national idol in the process. Van Doren was the right man at the right time, as far as public adulation was concerned. Through the fifties, the country had been shrugging off at least some portion of its traditional anti-intellectualism. It was the age of Sputnik, the "education gap" was looming, and the manliness and even the patriotism of being a professor was beginning to be accepted. Further, Van Doren was handsome, and when, in the sanctum of the "isolation booth," he furrowed his noble brow and shut his searing eyes in a monumental effort of recall, he looked more like a romantic lead than an egghead. *Time* called him "the finest product of American education, character, family background and native intelligence." So popular did Van Doren become as *Twenty-One*'s reigning genius, that when he was finally knocked off the show, NBC gave him a $50,000-a-year contract as a consultant and commentator on *Today.*

There was only one small problem with Charlie Van Doren: He was a fraud.

Not only had he been given the quiz show answers beforehand, he was even coached in his delivery, right down to the last pause and characteristic bite of the lower lip. He'd been able to dethrone Herbert Stempel, the 170-IQ champion who'd preceded him, because Stempel, a brilliant man but not box-office, had been persuaded by the producers to take a dive. And Van Doren, in turn, had intentionally succumbed to Vivienne Nearing, a well-briefed and carefully cast female who was both a lawyer and a telegenic blonde.

Not until 1959 did the truth about Van Doren come out, but this was not because the fix was hushed up that long. Herb Stempel, a high-strung man in the best of times, had blabbed to the newspapers as early as the fall of 1957, and was dismissed as "a raving lunatic," a case of sour grapes become delusional. No one would believe his detailed and consistent description of how the fixes were arranged. No one would believe that such a thing could happen in America. This was the airwaves, after all, public property, licensed by the government. Surely there was some invisible "they" who would prevent wrongdoing. Besides, Americans played fair, and everybody knew it. The American public would believe no evil of Charles Van Doren, or of the respected executives who managed the quiz show machinery, until it saw a smoking gun.

The smoking gun finally appeared in late 1959, in the form of a registered letter dated May 10, 1957, containing the answers for the show of May 13, 1957. Among the intellectual arcana revealed in that letter: the names of Snow White's seven dwarfs.

When the story hit, the public outcry was so widespread and so impassioned that getting to the bottom of the shocking business became national preoccupation number one. Now let's put this in context: In late 1959, the Berlin crisis was stewing, Castro had just come to power in Cuba, the United States was in the process of chalking up its first postwar trade deficit—and Congress virtually halted other business while a select committee ran several weeks of hearings on quiz-show fakery and other broadcast abuses.

At first glance, the elevation of the TV fiasco to top congressional priority seems wacky. In fact it made perfect sense. What was on trial was nothing short of America's image of itself. Central to that image, back in the most exuberant years of more, was the belief that American prosperity, American success, far from being at odds with American goodness, was the direct result of it. Winning was made of virtue and brains, savvy and nerve, blended up just right to produce the ability to rise to the occasion. Nothing summarized that process quite as neatly as the quiz shows: you played the game according to the rules, and money showered down on you from some apparently endless supply that came from God knows where. The spectacle of American plenty and the people who chased it may have looked like a rat race between nine and five, but by prime time it had become an orderly drama of fair and vivid competition.

The most compelling fantasies are the ones rooted most securely in fact; the quiz shows had captured the national imagination because they crystallized America's common promise, and wrote it large and fast. It was a vindication of our national pride that we were rich enough to throw fortunes at people who knew the name of Robert E. Lee's horse, that we could afford to give trips to Hawaii to people who could *Name That Tune.* It was a measure of our kindness and the depths of our resources that we could even show largesse to runners-up—no one ever called them losers. As fifties sitcoms showed a world where parents were always loving and children always adorable, so the quiz shows portrayed an America in which life was challenging yet fair, and there was at least a consolation prize for everybody.

It was the more distressing, then, that the congressional hearings went on to reveal that the fixes on *Twenty-One,* far from being an isolated instance of broadcast cheating, were part of a pattern, evidence of "a shocking state of rottenness . . . in the industry and in the individual." To mention just a few of the dozens of irregularities: A show called *For Love or Money* established winnings with a "dancing decimal machine" that was rigged. Bandleader Xavier Cugat was secretly briefed on his own career en route to winning sixteen grand in the "Tin Pan Alley" category of *The $64,000*

Challenge. Sponsors had muscled producers to keep popular champions afloat while at the same time keeping the lid
on payouts, and employees had been caught taking kick-
backs from contestants on *Treasure Hunt.*

This was white-collar crime, fifties-style, and if it seems
almost quaint today, it yet bears the germ of more virulent
varieties seen recently. The quiz-show malfeasances carried
the strong suggestion that there was beginning to be a break-
down, not so much in the rules, but in the values that underlay
the rules. Just as, in the Wall Street scandals of the 1980s, some
would try to lay the blame on insider-trading laws that were
unworkably vague, so some embroiled in the fifties scandals
claimed that they could not be held culpable because there
were no explicit guidelines on television quiz-show practices. That it was simply and self-evidently wrong to mislead
the public, to portray a rigged game as a fair one, seemed to
elude the go-go types who ran the programs. The idea of the
shows was *more*—more viewers, more sponsorship, more
money, more publicity. And if this magical *more* was a legitimate end in itself, then what did it matter if quiz shows were
scripted just as *Burns and Allen* was scripted? A rigged game
show was the perfect victimless crime. It didn't *take* money
from anyone—or did it?—and it harmed nothing except
maybe a couple of abstract values called truth and trust.

The only problem was that 1950s America took public
truth and public trust rather seriously; they were, supposedly, a big part of what the country was about. Americans
weren't used to being lied to, or at least weren't used to
finding out about it. They were used to thinking of themselves as beneficiaries, not dupes, of a system that, while
certainly not tamper-proof, was fundamentally just. Suddenly, very suddenly, they weren't so sure who was kidding
whom. People were outraged, yet at the same time embarrassed at their own naïveté in being shocked, and deter-

mined to remedy that naïveté. Like jealous lovers, the public now insisted on hearing the worst in graphic detail; and the 1950s, that supposedly most innocent of decades, ended in a mood of inquisition.

It was an inquisition that unearthed not bold crimes but sneaky offenses whose hallmark tended to be their slithery smallness. For instance, there was the widespread practice called *schlockmeistering*—plugging products in exchange for cash or merchandise. It was not mere wit that led Bob Hope to describe the NBC peacock as "a plucked pigeon with a Clairol rinse." Not for nothing did Jerry Lewis do gags whose punch line was "Look, Mom, no cavities," and not for nothing did Dean Martin once breathe deeply of Frank Sinatra's presence and ask if he was wearing My Sin. It was an open secret that payment would be made to any comedian who worked a mention of Playtex girdles into a routine, and Jack Benny, after dropping a reference to Schwinn bicycles, once turned his inimitable deadpan toward the camera and said, "Send three."

The schlockmeister scam, however, was a mere bagatelle compared to the systematic deceptions being put over by normal TV advertising. Windows did indeed look cleaner when the camera was aimed at an empty frame. Certain brands of dog food were in fact irresistible to dogs who'd been starved for a day or two. Shaving cream looked more like cake frosting than frosting did, and soap suds looked more like beer foam than beer foam. Still, it was hard to understand how four different cigarettes could all be lowest in nicotine, or why a certain medicine should be called "Little Liver Pills" when the product was nothing but a laxative. Under pressure, advertisers pledged to clean up their own ranks, but one agency head had the candor to state they were going about it "like cucumber growers during National Pickle Week."

Where would the parade of national venality end? And how drearily banal could the transgressions possibly get? Investigators found patterns of cheating in everything from newspaper crossword-puzzle contests to trading-stamp redemption capers.

Moreover, it was beginning to be suggested that dishonesty, far from being an occasional aberration, was an integral part of business-as-usual. Systemic corruption—this, at the time, was a radical and jarring idea. *Esquire* did a story on the young craft of public relations, observing that "however thin we slice it . . . [the practice of PR could] be called the art, science, skill, dodge or trade of lying." Payola—the giving of bribes, usually to disc jockeys, to get songs played on the radio—became a household word; so entrenched and formalized was the practice that one record company executive said it took exactly $22,000 to make a hit single in the Chicago market. A Cleveland DJ told *Life* magazine that payola was indeed rampant but should not be singled out for righteous criticism, because it was "typical of business morality—it stinks."

Of all the squalid revelations of 1959, one perhaps stands out as the most depressing and disillusioning of the lot: It came to light that, in a New York grand jury investigation into broadcast practices, at least one hundred out of 150 witnesses had lied under oath. Perjury on that scale had never before been discovered in America. And it was perjury by men in business suits and flat-top haircuts, by women in black pumps with tasteful clutch bags—not gangsters, not desperadoes, but conventional folks who were already in for their share of American plenty, already making it in a prestigious and remunerative business, and who had stumbled across the line of decency in a ravenous grab for more. The people who put their hand on the Bible, looked squarely at the duly appointed representative of government, and lied, were people very like one's neighbors—very like oneself.

So much like oneself, in fact, that many Americans, for the first time since the postwar boom had started to snowball, were "forced to think about the philosophy that lies behind the picture tube as well as the character of those who sit in front of it."

What was that philosophy—in real life, that is, not in high school textbooks? And the national character that America was so proud of—of what did it really consist?

In light of the television scandals, with their evidence of mass greed, opportunism, and an apparent majority of liars, the comfortable old verities didn't suffice to answer those questions. The standard belief was that the American was brave but prudent, independent but civic-spirited, ambitious but above all honorable; he had kept the frontier virtues, that is to say, while evolving into a savvy and responsible modern citizen.

In the mirror held up by the television follies, however, the unflinching observer could see neither frontier dignity nor modern smarts. The typical joe, rather, appeared to be a rather spineless fellow, a sneak, a follower who was more than ready to make an ass if not a felon of himself for a stove, a set of backyard furniture, a pair of airline tickets. The modern American, it seemed, was becoming less a proud member of a proud society, and coming to resemble more and more a contestant in a gigantic giveaway show, a guy who was in it for the money and the prizes, and who apparently didn't trouble much about what he had to do to get them.

/// TWO

President Dwight D. Eisenhower, a man not ordinarily given to flights of simile, likened the quiz show scandals to the infamous Black Sox affair of 1919, in which members of a major-league baseball team accepted bribes to throw a World Series, leaving a trusting public perhaps less angry than "bewildered."

The analogy was nearly perfect. In both cases the public felt betrayed by one of the institutions it loved the most, and with which it identified most strongly. In both cases, despite its indignation, the public re-embraced the institution almost immediately and perhaps more loyally than ever. And in both cases, while the immediate shock soon subsided, the disturbance rippled outward in the form of hundreds of editorials and political speeches condemning our fallen state, questioning our values, and fervently calling for a reexamination of the national purpose.

Asked California governor Edmund G. "Pat" Brown in late 1959: "Shall we allow a chromium-plated materialism to be the principal apparent goal of our national life?"

Warned Massachusetts senator John F. Kennedy, then stumping for the presidential nomination: "We have grown soft—physically, mentally, spiritually soft.... The slow corrosion of luxury is already beginning to show."

With the needs of Economic Man largely taken care of, observed New York governor and White House hopeful Nelson Rockefeller, "people are looking for a sense of direction."

And Chicago industrialist—later Illinois senator—Charles Percy correctly predicted that "national purpose will be a more important issue in the 1960 campaign than in any previous peacetime [election]."

But it was one thing to invoke the national purpose, another to define it. And when the politicians tried to shift from scolding to vision, they found they had little or nothing to say. They mumbled about greatness and destiny. They apostrophized the Founding Fathers and the Pilgrims. But they offered little that seemed germane to the contemporary conflicts between money and values, between a wealthier society and a better one, between the morality of earned rewards and the cheap excitement of the giveaway.

People noticed the omission, and a much-quoted editorial in the Gainesville, Georgia, *Times* nailed the opinion-makers on it. The politicians tell us, went the complaint, that "we have to sacrifice luxuries to carry out our job in the world. We're willing. But nobody tells us what to sacrifice and nobody tells us the purpose."

This was embarrassing. It was also confusing. It couldn't have been clearer that the typical American wanted more; yet everyone with access to a microphone or a printing press was warning against the dangers of wanting more. It was hard to explain *why* wanting more was dangerous, since it was as American as anything you could name and didn't *necessarily* make people into cheats and liars; but then again it was equally hard to justify what the more was *for*. By the close of the fifties, these questions in regard to the focus and purpose of American aspirations could no longer be dodged, but neither could they be answered. The result was a moral haziness, a want of certainty and authority that still pertains.

For at least the three previous decades, America had always had a clear and present crisis to give weight and dignity to its national strivings. Through the thirties, the urgent agenda was to do whatever was necessary to lift the country out of the Depression. Then came the even more specific goal of winning the war. Through the late forties and into the fifties, the perceived menace of international Communism became the goad that defined the national mission.

It is worth recalling that in the early days of the Cold War, the Soviet Union was regarded not simply as our habitual adversary and military nemesis, but as the leading exponent of a political and economic philosophy that had to be reckoned with. Karl Marx was taken dead seriously as an economic theorist, social critic, and would-be prophet; his arguments needed answering, both for America's own reassurance and as part of "the battle for men's minds" that was being waged in regard to the nonaligned and emerging nations. America had a global sell-job to do.

Marx had postulated that in late capitalist societies, the lot of the workingman must inevitably grow worse; well, we would prove to the world that in *our* late capitalist society, the workingman was having it constantly better. Marx had surmised that as capital was concentrated in ever fewer hands, class conflict would seethe and eventually explode; well, we would demonstrate that our ever vaster corporations were enlightened and benign, and that their cheerful, well-fed, and self-esteeming employees loved them.

There was thus an explicit political content and propaganda value to the early stages of America's postwar prosperity. Harvard Business School professor Norman S.B. Gras spelled it out very clearly in 1949: Communism's "implied threat to our way of life" would prod us forward to a humane "new business statesmanship," that in turn would "prove that Karl Marx ... had not formulated his theor[ies] ... with sufficient discrimination."

The desire to show up the Reds—the *mission* to do so—far from being a merely academic concern, was strongly present in mainstream thinking. *Time* titled its annual business wrap-up for 1953 "A Keystone of the Free World," and gleefully contrasted the U.S. businessmen "who had proved how well [free enterprise] works," with "the Soviet bosses [who] could not ... [provide] consumer goods for their empty-handed people." In those years, every American who put 10 percent down on a suburban house and ate more than his own weight in meat could feel that he was casting a vote for democracy. Spending more, relaxing more, even wasting more—these, in their way, were patriotic acts.

By the end of the 1950s, however, America found itself in the oddly dispiriting position of having nothing left to prove along those lines. Everyone already knew that the United States was the goingest outfit around. Everyone knew that Americans had the most shoes, the fullest pantries, the greatest number of kidney-shaped pools, the most elaborate battery-powered toys. Everyone knew that America was so rich that, on television, you could win more money than the average Communist would see in his lifetime, just by knowing the names of the Seven Dwarfs. Insofar as the postwar clash of ideologies was a race for the stockpiling, showing off, and disposing of material wealth, America had won, hands down, no contest.

So what was next? To what crusade would the country next turn its energies? How would it justify and ennoble its quest for more, if a suitable mission didn't come along? And what of the dim but gnawing hunger that persisted even in the face of our famous wealth?

Those, finally, were the questions that the whole national-purpose debate came down to; and as it turned out, the national-purpose debate was about to backfire in a major way. Some smart and modern people were beginning to suspect that maybe those questions didn't have satisfactory answers—and didn't really need to be answered.

The reasoning went something like this: Prosperity had been a goal for as long as anyone could remember, yet the simple fact of prosperity didn't seem to satisfy. Even though we called ourselves materialists—even though we blamed ourselves for being so—we seemed to crave some victory beyond wealth, whether that victory was called ending the

Depression, or winning the war, or acing out the Communists. But maybe we'd been kidding ourselves; if our notions of what the wealth was for could change so easily with every decade, every circumstance, every administration, maybe wealth didn't really have a meaning at all. Maybe the purpose and the meaning were tacked on afterwards, for effect. Maybe prosperity just meant having stuff, *more* stuff, and the rest was window-dressing, self-congratulation, evidence of just that sort of naïveté we were ready to shrug off.

As early as 1953, an investment banker, contemplating America's prosperity and the challenges confronting it, had boasted that "we have mastered production," but worried that "we have not yet mastered consumption." By the end of the fifties it was coming to seem that that bald and simple statement perhaps had more to say on the question of *What next?* than did all the high-flown speeches. Maybe what was next was frank and unadorned consuming—and maybe that was the best, most challenging, and most modern thing. We no longer had to knock our heads against adversity or measure ourselves against a foe. Now we could measure ourselves only against each other, and against some standard of living we would continually strive to surpass. More itself could be the streamlined modern agenda; we could define ourselves not in hyped-up terms of winning wars and championing democracy but in terms of what we could buy, what we could eat, what we could own. As in a television game show, the only real purpose was to try to have the most when the final buzzer sounded.

Consumption without excuses and without the need of justification—the beauty part was that it finessed the irksome question of values and of purpose. Except for unmodern and sentimental reasons, there didn't have to *be* a purpose. The mechanism didn't require it. Consumption kept the workers working, which kept the paychecks coming, which kept the people spending, which kept inventors inventing and investors investing, which meant there was more to consume. The system, properly understood, was independent of values and needed no philosophy to prop it up. It was a perfect circle, complete in itself—and empty in the middle.

/// THREE

It has by now become a truism that the so-called sixties generation did not reject the lessons of its parents and teachers but took them literally.

It was preached in social studies classes that in America all were equal before the law, and tens of thousands took to the streets to march for civil rights.

History instructors trumpeted that the swell thing about democracy was that it carried out the will of the people, and hordes of students demanded to know whose will it was to have a war in Southeast Asia.

Parents lectured that there were more important things than money and the crucial thing was to be yourself, and untold numbers of sons and daughters decided to major in psychology, climb the Rockies, go to Amsterdam or join the Peace Corps, and maybe get a real job somewhere down the road.

These were perhaps the most gullible people who ever drew breath.

They were even gullible enough to keep alive—for a while—the question of national purpose. Long after Charles Van Doren had been largely forgotten, long after the more hard-nosed and "modern" notion that there didn't need to be a purpose had moved into the ascendent, some people still kept asking *What next?* What is all that money *for*? Wasn't there some credible ideal of national goodness that would give to prosperity a more resonant and dignified meaning than simply having lots of stuff?

John Kennedy thought there was, and he labeled it the New Frontier. But Kennedy was dead before the program could become much more than a slogan.

Lyndon Johnson thought there was, and he tagged it the Great Society. But the Great Society was hamstrung by the lies and waste of Vietnam long before its promise was fulfilled.

Talk of national purpose, that is to say, didn't simply disappear, but, once the fifties were over, the discussion was repeatedly drowned out by the clamor of overwhelming events. The crucial questions were raised but never answered, and this constitutes a missed opportunity of epochal proportions. Through the sixties and into the seventies, the debate never seemed to get beyond what people *didn't* want. They didn't want their President playing cops-and-robbers with the opposition party. They didn't want holes poked in the ozone layer. They didn't want mercury in their swordfish.

But what *did* they want? Presumably they wanted a more economically just society, a less violent one, a less harried one, a less greedy one. What they got was the famously greedy eighties. Why?

In the middle 1970s, a new set of national and personal preoccupations socked in, radically narrowing the agenda, not just pushing the question of purpose onto the back burner but knocking it off the stove. Inflation. Oil shocks. A slide in real wages. Americans, both individually and collectively, were coming to the awful and somehow shaming realization that there were a great many things they couldn't predict and couldn't control. They couldn't predict the next recession. They couldn't control the supply of energy, of sugar, of coffee beans, or, for that matter, the supply of more. America was dizzied and enraged by a new sense of relative helplessness. And helplessness breeds obsession. People became obsessed with economic matters not because economic matters suddenly became fascinating, but because they carried a fascinating threat.

Thus the game-show atmosphere of the fifties devolved into the casino economy of the eighties. It was no longer true that there were only winners and runners-up, and that everyone went home with a prize and with his self-esteem intact. Now there were losers, lots of them. And the day's top priority was to avoid being swept into their ranks. Lots of things could be sacrificed in the 1980s, lots of concerns could be jettisoned. Lack of meaning? That could be handled. Absence of values? That could be got around. There was only one thing that could not be abided, and that was to be among those left behind.

So people hunkered down, got pragmatic. At the personal as at the national level, the fashionable stance was to chase the dollar while commenting gravely on the so-called luxuries we could no longer afford: introspection, compassion, too much asking *why*.

National purpose? In the 1980s, people seemed to have forgotten that such a vague and unproductive issue had ever been raised. Yet, for all the many reasons offered as to why the country wasn't running better than it was, a factor seldom mentioned was that it was tough to operate at peak effectiveness if you'd lost all sense of what it was you were trying to accomplish.

Part II

THE CELEBRATION OF WHAT DIDN'T WORK

The exclusive worship of the bitch-goddess
Success. That—with the squalid cash
interpretation put on the word
success—is our national disease.

—William James

5 /// "To Know No Boundaries"

/// ONE

Sally Collier shifted in the green vinyl waiting-room chair while Benno used the hallway telephone yet again.

It was ten-thirty, they'd been waiting at the hospital for an hour, and he'd checked in with the office four times so far. Each time he'd patted Sally's hand nervously, a little guiltily, and said he'd be right back. Each time he'd come back looking a little more harried than he'd looked before. This was Tuesday, October 20, 1987, the day the markets almost closed, the day of the apocalyptic whispers. It was a hell of a day to have your boss stroll by and see an empty chair in the place you were being overpaid to sit.

Sally, on the other hand, was quite serene. An amazing thing, this being pregnant. A new recipe of hormones kicked in and clarified the world. There pertained a sort of calm that derived not from optimism, but from a suspension of the categories of optimism or pessimism. That which truly mattered would be taken care of. For a professional woman, a woman operating in what was still essentially a male arena, there was a certain pressure to downplay what might be called the pregnant view of things; like menstruation, the shift in outlook was a fact of life but something you were supposed to *rise above* in the name of being treated as an equal. But what about the *non-pregnant* view of the world, with its scatter and anxieties, its petty worries, its byzantine hierarchy of concerns? That view, too, was shaped by some mix of gland juices and enzymes in the blood. Who could say which brain cocktail gave the truer picture?

Sally looked out the window. Columbia Presbyterian Hospital is roughly nine miles uptown from Wall Street, yet it fronts on a different universe. Manhattan gets skinny up there and is arranged in narrow north-south strips: Broadway, Riverside, the park, the Hudson, the palisades of New Jersey indistinctly orange in the autumn light. To get to the hospital you drive through Harlem, and Harlem in the morning, it seemed to Sally that day, was not only unthreatening but something like a vacation. *Don't ever romanticize the poor,* a mentor had once told Sally, *because you know damn well they'd rather be rich.* Well, O.K., banish the thought of any honky liberal sentiment.

Still, south of 110th Street there were two great tyrannies— tyrannies in which Sally and Benno were privileged to conspire, yet in whose thrall they were. One of those tyrannies was money and the other was the news. South of Harlem there was so much wealth that it was hard not to feel like a jerk if you didn't latch on to some, and there was so much "news" that people made a fetish of being "informed." There was a considerable leap, of course, in equating knowing the news with being informed, and an even greater leap in presuming that being informed put one in control of one's fate. No one knew better than Sally what an arbitrary construct the news finally was. It was like the unpregnant view of the world. It passed as absolute because so many people subscribed to it, but it wasn't absolute. Occurrences *A* through *Z* transpired, and items *D, M,* and *V* were selected out as news because they fit the conventions of the news. *This was a terrible tragedy, and here's the empty house where it happened.* That was one convention: the reporter just slightly off-center in front of the side-by-side duplex where the massacre took place, with quick cuts of the neighbors saying things like "We just can't believe it—he used to play catch with our kids."

News conventions went in and out of style—covering protests, for example, had really slipped—and Sally had noticed that, through the 1980s, one convention that gained a lot of ground was the startling but straight-faced money story. It was assumed that everyone out there was dying to hear about money, and that an item containing figures sufficiently large automatically crossed the threshold into being news. It was this development that closed the circle of the two downtown tyrannies, joined media to bucks with such a snug seal that lower Manhattan was quite perfectly airless, and a trip uptown, where people swung their arms when they walked rather than clutching *Times*es or *Journal*s or *Womens Wear Daily*s against them . . .

A nurse in a stiff white cap poked her head through the waiting-room doorway. "Ms. Collier?"

"Oh," said Sally. "Just a minute. My husband's on the phone."

///// **TWO**

What Benno was hearing from his colleagues in the bullpen that morning was that the system by which they all made their livings appeared to be straining beyond its limits. Certain barely conceivable things were going on.

Sweetheart stocks such as IBM and Merck had stopped trading—there was no one who wanted to buy them. The absence of buyers didn't just hammer prices but made them meaningless: no buyers, no transactions; no transactions, no going rates; no going rates, no market. One boutique brokerage had merged—on a handshake, at 3:00 A.M.—with Merrill Lynch to avoid being wiped out instantly. Banks were withholding credit from major securities firms. Rumor had it that Goldman, Sachs and Salomon Brothers were pressing for a temporary shutdown of the Big Board; exchange chairman John J. Phelan would later be quoted as having said, "If we close it, we [will] never open it." The whole financial system was on the brink, and perhaps the most bedeviling thing is that it had reached the edge of ruin "in the absence of any true calamity." On the basis of internal pressures, private panic, and systemic glitches alone, the money business had hit the wall.

This was the more befuddling in light of the eighties' rather shrill insistence that there didn't need to *be* a wall. Whether by the voodoo of supply-side or the abracadabra of leverage, ingenuity would find a way to keep the boundaries receding. Forget that America's productivity wasn't really growing and forget that the typical American wasn't really better off and forget that the next century was being mortgaged. Somehow the supply of more, or at least the semblance of it, could be maintained. This was the central tenet of eighties faith. It was also a central way in which the eighties turned out not to work.

The failure could not be laid to a lack of belief or of ritual. The gods of growth had been adequately propitiated. The mythology of the endless frontier had been sufficiently invoked.

For that matter, it had been relentlessly invoked. Through the eighties, the frontier myth had been dusted off in Washington, repackaged on Madison Avenue, and dangled over us like a fat and scrumptious worm being fed to famished baby birds. Consider, for example, one of the hallmark ad pitches of the decade, the Merrill Lynch "Your World Should Know No Boundaries" campaign.

A series of lavishly produced television spots showed the firm's trademark bull galloping along an endless crescent of surf-licked beach, cavorting across an unfenced plain, romping through fertile fields delimited only by the far horizon. The imagery was unabashed frontier-romantic, and the visuals were accompanied by the strains of what had originally been a theme song for a James Bond movie. Thus, a suggestion of boundless independence and freedom was wedded to a hint of sex and of high swashbuckling adventure—and all you had to do to be a part of it was to have a couple of dollars to invest.

This was pretty nice. The only problem was that the mythology had *bupkis* to do with what American life was really like in the 1980s. By most measures more substantive than the Dow Jones average, and for most people outside the "newsworthy" group of movers and shakers and yuppies, the 1980s were a time when the boundaries of personal opportunity had perhaps become more prominent features on the landscape than the opportunities themselves. Stampeding bull or no stampeding bull, contemporary America featured only limited spaces in which yearnings might roam free. James Bond theme song or no James Bond theme song, the decade was a sorry time for most sorts of adventure.

People no longer referred to the baby boomers as "the luckiest generation"; now they were dubbed "the generation doomed to wait in line." Even as they were going gray around the temples and ribbed around the middle, they were waiting in line for promotions that didn't come, for security that eluded them, for snug houses that remained just slightly out of reach. The boomers—and their younger cousins even more so—were waiting for all the promises of their youth to be delivered, and they desperately wanted the fruits of those promises in hand before the arrival of a vastly indebted future that threatened history's most monumental renege.

The real frontier had offered a comforting array of second chances. In the ersatz frontier of "knowing no boundaries," even first chances were getting harder to come by. The surest of sure things were no longer sure. Suddenly there were too many doctors and not enough patients, too many teachers and not enough students, too many lawyers and not enough clients. There even seemed to be too many farmers, notwithstanding that there were fewer farmers every year. For some time people had been saying there were too damn many MBAs; nobody really believed it until October 20, 1987, when it began to be whispered that maybe ten or fifteen thousand of them would get the ax in New York City alone. Again and again, the rush to perceived opportunity was closely followed by a pattern of gluts and cuts, obstacles and bottlenecks. This was not frontier; it was gridlock.

Life, meanwhile, was getting inexorably more expensive. That this should be happening during a time of quite low inflation only made the process more mysterious: what was there to blame it on? An average-priced new car cost the average person twenty-three weeks' pay in 1987, up from seventeen weeks' a decade before. Sending one kid to a private four-year college gobbled up fully 40 percent of median family income. Further, there was no longer a virtual guarantee that buying the kid a diploma would at least get him or her out of the house. As eighteen-to-thirty-four-year-olds found it ever tougher to get a toehold on self-sufficiency, increasing numbers of them swallowed their pride, packed up their albums and their contraceptive paraphernalia, and moved back home. By 1987, 19 million people in that age group—up from 13 million in 1970—were living with one or both parents.

Oddly, however, the broad perception that everything

from ice-cream bars to sweatshirts to medical insurance now seemed to cost too much didn't dissuade Americans from making purchases. Indeed, insofar as the Reagan "recovery" was anything more than a triumph of creative accounting, it was an uptick caused by a somewhat hysterical binge in consumer spending. As faceless, forbidding, and arcane as the Economy had become, the homey truth was that fully two-thirds of the GNP derived from real flesh-and-blood individuals buying stuff, and it was "the super-consumer whose mighty wallet [was] power[ing]" the moderate apparent growth that pertained at mid-decade. As of 1982, only 27 percent of American households had a microwave; by 1987, nearly two-thirds did. VCRs, barely heard of as recently as 1981, were owned by half of America's families in 1986; not one of those machines, as Jesse Jackson was fond of pointing out during his 1988 presidential campaign, had been manufactured in America. In 1986, although 99 percent of the country's homes already had television, fully 25 percent acquired a new set. Through the middle years of the 1980s, consumer spending was increasing at an average annual rate of more than 4 percent, while real wages were going nowhere.

This, of course, is another way of saying that each year people were living a little more above their means. Why? Why were Americans buying so much—so much that they couldn't really afford and didn't really need; so much that depleted their savings to all-time lows and put them ever deeper into high-priced debt; so much that exacerbated the country's trade situation, since so many of the new gizmos were imported?

Why? Well, partly it was because we'd all been taught that our world should know no boundaries. The key word was *should*; a habitual sense of *fittingness* was involved. That *should*, however, was in conflict with observable fact, and the resulting dissonance was driving us more than a little bit crazy. Secretly oppressed by a new awareness of limits, we bought into the fib that limits could be done away with. Privately mortified that we weren't getting richer, we defiantly spent as if we were. Rather than honestly addressing the question of life becoming more expensive—which is to say, the standard of living ceasing to rise or even beginning to fall —we put the blinders on the bull and let that sucker charge.

Then, too, America went shopping in the 1980s because there didn't seem to be a great deal else to do. In terms of social fashion and the sort of things that made it onto the news, what was there that seemed compelling beyond the making and spending of money? Worthy causes were few and far between. Sex was down the tubes. There didn't seem to be many thrills around, except the sort of thrills you could carry home in a shopping bag. And, even accompanied by the measures of a James Bond theme song, those sorts of thrills weren't really all that thrilling.

/// THREE

The crisp white paper that covered the examination table crackled as Sally Collier settled onto it. Benno, feeling oddly shy, retreated to a narrow chair squeezed between a wall and a steel cart full of disinfecting jars.

"Sally, you look wonderful," said the doctor, who was probably younger than the Colliers and always worked in black high-top sneakers. *You look wonderful*—this was the sort of thing an obstetrician said, and usually really believed. There were an almost infinite number of ways to measure wonderful, to decide if things were as they ought to be, if the universe was in order. The different ways went with different occupations, since different occupations put the center of the universe in different places. For an obstetrician, the rightness of things was measured by high color, swelling breasts, blue-veined skin pulled taut across big bellies. "Benno, you don't look so good. Nervous?"

"Yeah," said Benno, "I'm a little nervous."

The doctor lifted Sally's sweater, listened to her heart, asked about her weight. It was terrific having someone smile upon being told how much you'd gained. He introduced the sonogram technician, a green-eyed West Indian woman named Ms. Mariah. Then he left.

Ms. Mariah wheeled the computer alongside the examination table and smeared lubricant on Sally Collier's belly. Then she crooked a finger over toward Benno. "Daddy," she said, "you won't be able to see a thing from way over there."

Daddy. Benno had been called that, teasingly, raucously, by friends. This was the first time he'd been called it straightfaced, by a representative of the outside world. He went and stood behind Mommy and put his hands on her shoulders. They watched the screen—very like the one on which *he* was accustomed to measuring the rightness of things, to watching the state of the world flicker by.

Ms. Mariah slowly moved the scanner across Sally Collier's tummy. At sixteen weeks there's a fair amount of empty space in the amniotic sac, and the fetus floats and tumbles like a turtle in a tidal creek. It swims high, it dives low, it isn't always easy to find; and as the small search continued, Benno realized that his heart was racing. He leaned forward and pressed his face against his wife's hair.

Finally the child appeared, traced in line by line across the screen. It was big-headed, with a terrifyingly delicate strand of neck, and hindquarters narrow and squat like those of a chimp. It seemed to be growing out of its umbilical cord like a tune being blown through a trumpet. "Beautiful," said Ms. Mariah, freezing the image. "Ten fingers, ten toes. Do you want to know the gender?"

Benno and Sally had discussed this question many times,

and had decided that they would. If no one knew, that would be one thing. Given that the technician and the doctor would know, however, it seemed that they should, too. There was suspense enough remaining. "Please," said Sally.

"You see that tiny little thing over there?" said Ms. Mariah. "Really tiny?"

Benno and Sally didn't see it, but mumbled that they sort of did.

"You're going to have a boy."

//// FOUR

Adventure. Or, to put it another way, the suspense of believing that life has not yet peaked, that there will be more challenges, more gratifications, more wonders to see, more changes in the world that will be worth making changes in oneself in order to measure up to. The assurance that one's possibilities have not congealed.

It was the hunger for those things that the shapers of the "know no boundaries" rhetoric correctly identified as a widespread need in 1980s America, the hook on which they could hang their political or commercial sell-job. The only problem was that the hunger could not have been more real—it cried out for substantial nourishment, for honest food—and people were trying to satisfy it with empty calories.

The hunger was not to be satisfied by fantasizing boundaries out of existence—by showing a bull romping through Wyoming, or by positing a financial market that would presumably go up forever, or by having the President read a speech about America coming back. The need, rather, was to play a personal part in stretching the boundaries that existed, in moving them back even an inch by the serious and self-chosen application of will and passion. And that was precisely the sort of frontier-expanding that *wasn't* being done in the 1980s.

You didn't hear much in the 1980s about middle-class sons and daughters going to do good works in bad neighborhoods. You didn't hear about people trekking off to Nepal with eighty dollars in traveler's checks and fourteen packages of trail mix. It had become decidedly unfashionable to pursue any sort of art one wouldn't be likely to sell. Even romance seemed to have lost its tinge of emotional adventure; the sweet desperation of falling in love had paled into considerations of suitability and scheduling, geography and bucks. In 1987, the batch of people then in their twenties was dubbed "the unromantic generation." Wrote the journalist Bruce Weber after interviewing members of this stolid-hearted crew: "I'd ask about love; they'd give me a graph."

Analogously, the moral adventure of questioning authority, of speaking truth to power, had fallen into such thorough desuetude as to appear downright quaint. In 1986, addressing the "problem" of radical sentiment on college campuses, an administration official commented that the potentially subversive activities came less from the students than from "those faculty that were students in the late sixties." Thus the melancholy image of balding professors with hairy ears and receding gumlines striving mightily but without result to incite their depressingly well-behaved students to do something other than study.

No, the 1980s were a sorry moment for adventure. Of the two great raw materials for gallant commitment and consequential risk, the outside world and the self, people were working meaningfully on neither. Rather, they were just trying to reconcile the one to the other without tampering with either very much. They were trying—economically, intellectually, emotionally, morally—just to slide by, to make accommodation.

But accommodation is an inglorious concept, a strategy and not a philosophy. It makes hay but does not account for yearnings. And the more that accommodation became the dominant mode in America, the greater grew the need for a rhetoric that would make matters appear otherwise: compensation-by-hype. The eighties were essentially a meek, dull decade in which a great deal of money and brainpower were expended to make things seem brave and entertaining.

This compensation-by-hype, as we will argue, took many forms. The more people accommodated themselves to the gray realities of latching on to whatever sort of work by which they could make a living, the greater became the need to portray the routine processes of business as a scintillating *agon,* a contest as thrilling as war and as sexy as the movies.

The more obvious it was that inequality was widening and compassion was evaporating, the more strident and self-assured grew the speeches about tough-mindedness and pragmatism, as though selfishness and patriotism had conveniently merged.

The more painfully clear it became that economic security and a sense of doing something other than trivial were ever harder to come by, the more fervently people hankered for "success"—not knowing precisely what they meant by the word, except that it was something in excess of what they had so far.

Thus, under the aegis of eighties-style ambition, people tried to make themselves feel good by feeling bad about what remained beyond their grasp. By the dictates of the eighties business myth, they substituted for adventure a clenched and sober striving, and told themselves they were having a jazzy time. In accordance with eighties fashion in owning and consuming, they wallpapered a lifestyle over their lives, and called it having sophisticated taste. The 1980s were a time when millions of people fibbed to themselves every day about what they wanted and how it might best be gotten, and they called it being realistic.

6

Attack of the Business Rah-Rahs

ONE

Being realistic, eighties style, was largely taken to mean being businesslike, as if businesslike behavior and reasonable behavior were necessarily the same, as if business logic were logic, period, as if there were no other persuasive model for what a functioning adult should be. In the 1980s, acting responsibly meant acting "professionally," being intelligent meant being shrewd. As for creativity, the motto of one New York ad agency seemed to sum it up: "It isn't creative unless it sells." There seemed to be no other convincing norms, no other agreed-upon criteria for what was admirable, what made sense, what constituted rational behavior.

This equation of business with realism was curious,

because the case could be made that, historically speaking, America's attitudes toward business were not realistic but rhapsodic, not logical but mythic. Making money, as has often been observed, is America's civil religion; and religions, civil or otherwise, proceed not by syllogism but by revelation. Faith drives the machine, and "rational" explanations come afterward.

So it has been from the start of business in America. Tocqueville wrote of the Americans' "trading passions," which he saw not as a calm and orderly pursuit of wealth, but as an essentially nonrational gambling obsession in uneasy coexistence with the steady labors of the farmers-artisans who were the real grist of the democratic mill. When Washington Irving, in 1837, coined the disapproving phrase "the almighty dollar," he was speaking not out of an aversion to profits per se, but because of the perception that commerce, American style, made people frenzied, flighty, and "jumbl'd in their wits." Henry Steele Commager observed that the typical turn-of-the-century American was pragmatic in his religion, pragmatic in his philosophy, pragmatic in his marriage—and quixotic when it came to enterprise. Americans were so quixotic about enterprise that they applied to it the constitutionally forbidden terms of aristocracy and the archaic ones of classical antiquity. Calling business bigs the Robber Barons and referring to J. P. Morgan as "Jupiter"—this was logical?

When Calvin Coolidge made his notorious remark that "the business of America is business," he wasn't suggesting that the country was as plain as a warehouse or as bland as a store; he was suggesting, in fact, something rather more egregious: that the stores and warehouses were the emblems and repositories of the grandeur and virtue of the nation. "The *persona* of the American civilization has been the businessman," the historian Max Lerner has argued, and "where other civilization types have pursued wisdom, beauty, sanctity, military glory, predacity, asceticism, the businessman pursues the magnitudes of profit with a similar singleminded drive."

That drive is elemental, primal, previous to logic. It is the raw material of national as well as personal myths, the drawing board of iconographies both sacred and profane. So basic is that drive that it shapes norms in its image rather than being shaped by them, and so rambunctious that it cries out for the *apparent* logic of business—or, as the case may be, of Hinduism, saintliness, or the samurai ethic—as a way of giving focus to its energies. Business rationality is, as it were, an overlay, a distillation of the seething broth of ambitions, aggressions, yearnings, and terrors that define the American tribe.

The story of American business can be thought of, then, as at least one of our national epics—and epics, by definition, are not rational texts but magical ones. Stripped of its conventions and imagined without its familiarity, the story of business is as "realistic" as Wagner and about as grandiose. In the ritualized pages of the business section throb a million fantasies struggling to be given voice. The stock tables are a Delphic code, the want ads a blueprint of destiny. Alongside the endless series of mundane and routinized business functions there exists a masked and poignant ardor for the exalted, the heroic.

This fantasy side of business, as we say, has existed nearly as long as America itself. Yet it seemed to take the economic anxieties of the late 1970s and 1980s to make those fantasies explicit—and this was a prime example of compensation-by-hype. In the face of a woeful shortage of other good and gripping stories to tell, of other adventures to record and other ambitions to celebrate, the juiced-up business romance came forth with a vengeance. Business books topped the best-seller lists. Business magazines became the hot category. The world stopped when television's evening soap-opera moguls strutted their stuff. And the mythic elements that had previously been merely hinted at in the tales we tell about business began to be spelled out in gaudy headlines and in prose whose piquant cadences had probably never before been called into the service of describing the processes of buying and selling, of numbers going up or numbers going down.

///// TWO

Consider, as an early illustration of this burgeoning genre, a 1978 article from *Saturday Review* entitled "The New Entrepreneur: Romantic Hero of American Business."

In this piece it was observed that "our fabulously successful economy has always been powered by entrepreneurs—people of vision and daring." One specimen entrepreneur, a man who made a fortune in suburban shopping malls, thereby helping to kill off the American downtown, was apotheosized as "an urban philosopher of extraordinary eloquence." Another, whose wealth derived from holdings in coal and gas, was praised as "a convivial companion, a connoisseur of fine food, vintage wines, and four-star restaurants, an engaging conversationalist with serious interests in the fine arts." Also presented as exemplars were the starters-up of Silicon Valley, who, in a reprise of a very familiar tune, were glorified as "technological frontiersmen."

Now, there were a number of incongruous but noteworthy things about this article. The first was its timing. As of when it ran, the American economy was in fact not looking so "fabulously successful." Nineteen seventy-eight began the period of virtual stagnation in national wealth, and, as cited, it was also the year when the evident erosion of America's middle class was statistically confirmed.

Then there were the anomalies attendant upon the so-called entrepreneurial boom. Was it a coincidence that entrepreneurship began being touted as the talent that would save the country along about the time it became widely understood that the *last* thing that would save the country—the service economy—was in fact leading us down the tubes? Suddenly the deepest obeisances were being made to the visionaries who went off and founded fresh pasta and over-priced cheese stores or who marketed lines of apparel that featured the logos of best-selling soft drinks. Maybe *they* would be the epic figures who would rescue us, who would somehow replenish the storehouse of more.

These guys made for lively copy, but it was hard not to suspect that the applause for the entrepreneurial boom was louder than the boom itself—to wonder if perhaps the applause existed to cover the thinness of the music. True, a record number of new companies were starting up; a record number were also going belly-up. True, new businesses were the single most fertile source of new jobs; but the majority of those positions were the sort of junk jobs—low pay, no benefits—that were better to count than to hold. And while entrepreneurship touched a mythic nerve and conjured images of frontier daring, the notion, for almost everybody, was finally a fantasy. Not only would more than 99 percent of all Americans never start substantial enterprises, they didn't even *want* to. It was a daydream on the same order as meeting a great-looking woman on the flight to Omaha and having sex with her standing up in the bathroom. The concept was swell, the logistics just too daunting.

But the oddest and most telling thing about the "Romantic Hero" article was the fact that it appeared at all. *Saturday*

Review was not a business magazine. It was a general-interest publication that concentrated heavily on literature and the performing arts, had a generally critical tone and upper-middlebrow readership, and billed itself as a cultural journal.

What was just beginning to happen by 1978, however, was that business was *becoming* culture. The office was starting to be regarded as a stage on which worthy dramas were performed, and the players in those dramas were presented as capable of edifying and perhaps heroic acts. Perversely, though, this was happening precisely at the moment when, in the *real* theater of business, the drama was turning into an unfunny farce in which we all got pie in the face. Inflation was high. Unemployment was high. Anxiety was high. Morale was low. The emergence of the business drama as a staple feature in popular culture, then, was hardly a "realistic" presentation of what was happening out there; it was more in the nature of a tribal incantation meant to ward off evils and bring on a rejuvenated prosperity, on the belief that chanting something fervently enough would bring that thing to pass.

Now, just as Wall Street is not America, so a cabal of editors, journalists, publicists, and network programmers should not be taken as perfectly reflective of American attitudes and preoccupations. Still, far more than media fashion was involved in the 1980s' elevation of business, money, and the people who had it to the status of culture and of news. The romance with business came from a grassroots need to believe that the machine was still working and that someone was in charge. This was the need that transformed Lee Iacocca, for example, from America's biggest welfare case to a national icon, and that made Donald Trump a celebrity just because his deals got done and his buildings got built.

Under the banner of that need to believe, business movers came to be fawned on in the 1980s as they had not been since before the Great Depression. An old phenomenon was making a comeback, and the 1980s version of it conformed almost perfectly to "a new way of flattering the wealthy" first described by G. K. Chesterton in 1908:

> In more straightforward times ... a poor man wishing to please a rich man simply said that he was the wisest, bravest, tallest, strongest, most benevolent and most beautiful of mankind; and as even the rich man probably knew that he wasn't that, the thing did the less harm.... The safety of this method was its artificiality.... But the moderns have invented a much subtler and more poisonous kind of eulogy. The modern method is to take the ... rich man, to give a credible picture of his type of personality, as that he is business-like, or a sportsman, or fond of art, or convivial, or reserved; and then enormously exaggerate the value and importance of these natural qualities. Those who praise Mr. Carnegie do not say that he is as wise as Solomon and as brave as Mars; I wish they did. It would be the next most honest thing to giving their real reason for praising him, which is simply that he has money.

Through the 1980s, praising people for having money became almost a national reflex. Moreover, it mattered less and less how the money had been gotten, partly because, in an age of eroding values, every dollar was taken to be the same as every other, whether earned, embezzled, or inherited from a spouse who had died under dubious circumstances; and partly because the field of kissing-up-to-the-rich had become so balkanized that different outlets specialized in different aspects of it. The narrow-footed ladies of Greenwich still had *Town & Country,* of course, and beefeating capitalists still had *Forbes.* But now there was also

Vanity Fair, which premiered in 1983 and, resolute in its European pretensions, favored personages whose fortunes had been grubbed together by an ancestor—though it might occasionally feature someone who worked for a living, if, like Ralph Lauren or Calvin Klein, that person had style, filled ad pages, and was deemed sufficiently photogenic. *Manhattan, inc.,* on the other hand, which bowed in 1984, featured only people who worked, trafficking in the day-dreams of business-as-adventure, business-as-glitz, business-as-sex. So enraptured with business bigs did *Manhattan, inc.* presume its readers to be that the editors once saw fit to devote nine pages to Donald Trump's view on world peace.

If *Manhattan, inc.* might usefully be thought of as the fashion magazine about money, then *M,* published by the producers of *Womens Wear Daily,* might be described as the money magazine about fashion. *M* aimed at the older male audience, and, supported almost exclusively by cloth-ing ads, it had as its mission to take the silver-haired CEO type far beyond the strictures of the three-piece suit and the red silk tie. *M* wanted its aging, no longer flat-tummied readers to feel that, graced by wealth and rendered leonine by power, they would cut a stately and not an idiotic figure in jodhpurs, hand-embroidered smoking jackets, and baggy linen suits.

Even the sober *New York Times* saw opportunities in the rather sudden national obsession with the Successful Busi-nessperson. By far the longest article published in recent years in the *Times Magazine* was a 1985 profile of Avon CEO Hicks Waldron—twenty-five pages of breathless present-tense prose that must have had thousands of administrative assistants reaching for their highlighters so that their bosses might peruse a more condensed version. In 1986, as if an entire business section every day of the week did not suffice, the *Times* first published a twice-yearly Sunday supplement called *The Business World.* In addition to the usual mix of profiles, polls, and boardroom dramas, the editors of the journal of record found it newsworthy to report on "Executive Fun and Games" and to note in another article that fly-fishing "has long appealed to many at the upper end of the financial spectrum."

If the sheer proliferation of stories about people with money suggested a national mythologization, the images that went with the copy further supported the argument. No longer were chairmen of the board photographed sitting at their desks, a sterling pen set in front of them and a globe at their side, their collars immaculate and their expressions somber. Now business stars were photographed—literally—sitting in the lotus position, towering over skylines, standing on their heads. Secure in their celebrity, they could be portrayed as regular guys, pictured in crewneck sweaters, with their canoes, their pedigree dogs, their tennis rackets. Sometimes they were backlit, which seemed to give them halos; sometimes they were stroboscopically spotlighted so that they seemed enveloped in an aura of cosmic energy that pulled them out of their dim environment and transposed them to some higher plane of being.

In 1986 the origins of this "new business photography" were correctly traced back to the hyped-up, eroticized portraiture pioneered by Annie Leibovitz in her work for *Rolling Stone* in the 1970s. The culture-hero status formerly accorded to rock stars was now being ascribed to dealmakers, moneylenders, bond salesmen. (As in seventies rock 'n' roll, it might be observed, the glamour portraiture in business was overwhelmingly male. That the American workplace had been forever altered by the wholesale entrance of women was universally acknowledged, and the female middle-manager in tailored suit and mid-heel shoes had become a stereotype; but where were the superstar female images in the high end of the new business iconography? Who would be the business world's Madonna?) In the 1980s, the real fan magazine was no longer *Rolling Stone* but *Fortune.*

Among the media, probably the biggest beneficiary of the burgeoning interest in business was *The Wall Street Journal,* which saw its domestic circulation go from 1.2 million in 1970 to well over 2 million in 1987. Like the guy who had never stopped wearing skinny ties, the *Journal* carried itself through the eighties with a quiet sense of having been vindicated, of having waited in silent rightness for fashion to come to it.

The paper itself, in fact, with its no-nonsense typeface and distinctive line drawings, had become a central icon in the business mythology, and as such it was the recipient of a great deal of exposure at other people's expense. Cologne ads no longer showed their product next to a muddy rugby shirt to make the point that wearing perfume didn't mean a guy was a wuss; now the bottle was perched on top of a copy of the *Journal,* an accoutrement for the no less manly playing field of business. When airlines, wooing the business traveler, claimed they had the roomiest seats, they clinched the point by showing a passenger with his *Journal* opened wide in front of him. And in revivals of the old visual cliché about the married couple who just don't talk anymore, it was now not one but two copies of the *WSJ* that provided the interpersonal armor at the breakfast table—or, more likely, at the breakfast counter, since eighties couples were presumably too hard-driving to waste time sitting down for orange juice and coffee.

By mid-decade, the *Journal* had become such a name to conjure with that it spun off a radio feature, carried on nearly a hundred stations nationwide. *The Wall Street Journal Re-*

port will stand as one of the 1980s' strangest yet most characteristic phenomena, a little jewel of compensation-by-hype. Three or four minutes long, the *Report* featured quick bursts of economic information sandwiched between business-to-business advertisements—competing long-distance phone systems hawking their corporate rates, computer companies proclaiming their compatibility, and, of course, *The Wall Street Journal* itself telling media buyers why they should advertise in *The Wall Street Journal.* As to the editorial content of the *Report,* the evening installments provided a wrap-up of the day's market activity, coupled with a galloping "analysis" of why the movement had been plus or minus.

Less clear, however, was the rationale for the factoids dispensed on the *WSJR* during other parts of the day. At 9:00 A.M., for instance, it might be announced that durable goods orders for the previous month had been up two-tenths of a percent, which was less than hoped but more than feared, and compared somewhat favorably, but not all that favorably, with the same period a year ago. At eleven it might be reported that official government estimates for the quarter's economic growth, discounting defense contracting, had been revised downward by a tenth of one percent, bringing it back to where it had been before a week of heavy car sales had caused a cautious optimism. (Optimism, by the way, was always hedged with caution, just as concern was always ennobled by being "serious.")

Now, what was odd about these quanta of information was that the handful of working professionals who really needed the data would already have had them from more direct sources, while the overwhelming majority of listeners, even if they could follow the mumbo-jumbo, would have no practical use whatsoever for the stuff. So why was precious air time being lavished on it?

The answer becomes more apparent when the editorial

content of the *WSJR* is considered alongside probably the most talked-about ad campaign featured on it, the "Wang Makes It Work" series. In these commercials for Wang office systems, listeners eavesdropped on pairs of excited yuppies swapping war stories about how they sold customers on Wang's "heavy connectivity" and "SNA networks," how "MIS guys" were using "nodes" to link "VSes."

It was not an accident that these spots sounded like a Danny Kaye double-talk routine. Bemusement and wonder, not knowledge, were the real objects of the exercise—as they were in the reportage on "durable goods orders"—and this, in turn, was part of the larger pattern: people told themselves they were cleaving to reality by being business-like, when in fact they were merely subscribing to a mythology that, while internally consistent and certainly useful, was, like all mythologies, finally a construct. People told themselves they were getting information, and hence being active, with-it participants in the information age, when in fact what they were getting was a dose of business abracadabra, a fix of hocus-pocus that had less to do with rational discourse than with a kind of secular prayer. Obscure business news was oddly soothing, and inscrutable business ads were oddly confirming, because attending to them made people feel they were plugged-in members of the business congregation.

The question that remains, however, is why so many people, and especially young people, were so eager not just to join that flock, but wholeheartedly to adopt its creed. Maybe it was a cadre of specialists who shaped the new business journalism and contrived the pseudo-rock-star imagery and decided that mumbo-jumbo business ads were the way to go; but there seemed to be some tens of millions of civilians out there who ate the stuff up, who saw their own yearnings reflected in it. Why?

Over the previous four decades, Americans had grown radically suspicious of virtually every institution from the Pentagon to the PTA, chary of every redemptive vehicle from political activism to psychedelic drugs to jogging to romantic love. It was as if, as life got tougher for many and the game got meaner for all, a savvy skepticism had become the last bastion of defiant pride: we might be abused, we might be beaten, but goddammit, we wouldn't be fooled.

Why then was virtually no one voicing the suspicion that maybe all this stuff about the glamour and excitement of business was one more form of ephemeral ballyhoo, one more decade-long fantasy about life's true guts that ultimately would not satisfy?

///// THREE

Let's give credit where credit is due.

In large part, the new business mythology went largely unquestioned and uncriticized through the 1980s because the business rah-rahs—the flacks, the copywriters, the Chamber of Commerce toastmasters, the high-energy journalists who turned their adaptable skills toward the warm spot in the marketplace—did a damn good job of keeping the mythology compelling. In its service, they developed a language that the novelist E. L. Doctorow has described as "high-tech baroque, the kind of diction that is self-insulating and self-ennobling ... very often lyric and almost always metaphorical. It suggests something is there when in fact nothing is there at all."

Everywhere you looked in the 1980s, business was being cloaked in the cadences of high adventure, gamesmanship, and, not infrequently, of frank and remorseless aggression and even violence. A brokerage firm called Fidelity USA urged the public to "consider it[s services] advanced weaponry in the struggle for riches." The company offered "an entire arsenal of financial instruments," and observed that while "the struggle for wealth will always be bitter . . . with Fidelity USA, you can enter it armed and dangerous." If you really wanted to get combative about it, you could read the 1987 book *The Corporate Warriors,* which posited the quaint idea that everything an executive needed to know had already been thought of by the "great war thinkers"; this how-to peppered its pages with aphorisms from Machiavelli, Sun Tzu, Clausewitz, Julius Caesar, and Alexander the Great.

Sadly, war has losers as well as winners; and so does business, as was made plain by a 1987 *Manhattan, inc.* story called "Soldiers of Misfortune," a piece about "two wild and crazy ad men" whose agency was on the skids and who for some reason agreed to be photographed in shredded camouflage fatigues, with greasepaint powder burns, an arm sling, and a crutch. Perhaps these scarred veterans, hamming it up in the year of *Platoon,* would have benefited from the battlefield savvy of Lee Iacocca, who, in his autobiography, describes himself as a "general in the trenches" almost as often as he reminds the reader of his immigrant background. Or maybe the soldiers of misfortune just lacked "the right stuff," the famous Tom Wolfe coinage originally applied to fighter jocks and astronauts, more recently apostrophized in unblushing reference to accountants, salespeople, and trainees in banks.

If military allusions played off the conceit that business was deadly serious, then sports metaphors were intended to suggest that it was grand and rollicking fun, orderly and hygienic. A series of commercials for the financial services firm Paine Webber, for example, showed Jimmy Connors being run ragged on the tennis court—until he enlisted the help of Paine Webber's "professionals," who, strange to tell, all kept racquets on their desks and were always ready with a backhand retrieve or overhead smash, the impedimenta of jackets, ties, and wingtip shoes notwithstanding.

In eighties business-myth parlance, companies didn't merely compete in keeping with market mechanisms, they had "slugfests." An executive who made an error of omission had "dropped the ball"; one who flopped by trying too hard had "gone down swinging." Sitting in the office all night in front of a computer screen sounded less tedious when described as "putting on a full-court press," and endless rounds of meetings sounded cozier when characterized as "huddles." In what was perhaps the most hackneyed and at the same time pathetic simile of all, managers were forever being likened to quarterbacks (who, in turn, were likened to generals); at least one real quarterback, Fran Tarkenton of the New York Giants and the Minnesota Vikings, read the downfield opening and came off the bench as a consultant, lecture-circuit commentator, and best-selling author.

Since business and sports were so closely identified in the 1980s, and since it was fashionable to flatter the wealthy for being wealthy, there followed the curious assumption that successful businesspeople must also be talented athletes. In 1986, *The New York Times* passed along the news that "many top executives . . . when they are not trapped in a whirl of conferences or making phone calls from the corporate jet . . . are likely to be off blasting ducks out of the sky or swatting a golf ball three hundred yards down the fairway." Apparently top executives never missed the ducks, and apparently the upper echelons of American business were happily free of duffers who swatted the ball 120 yards, seldom down the fairway. Sedentary klutzes, it seemed, had no place in the new business pantheon. Every corporate biggie was presumed to be good at some sport, if only croquet, which the *Times* reporter celebrated as "chess on grass," feeling compelled to point out, as well, that "the balls are much bigger" than commonly believed.

Buried amid all the military and athletic imagery, all the scattershot evocations of competition and conquest, was an unmistakable undertone of rigorously sublimated sex. The business rah-rahs, of course, cultivated the idea that enterprise was sexy, but the "official" version of the business erotic had to do with the heterosexual appeal of power. On Wall Street, the trinity of "bimbos, limos, and lines" neatly summed up the mythic relationships among luxury, license, and the real or imagined enhancement of prowess. A recurring motif in successful woman's sex-and-shopping novels was the perk of being able to keep, and dominate, a younger man. Business achievers of either gender were presumed to engage in heavy petting that felt particularly good when performed behind the smoked-glass windows of a stretch Mercedes.

That, as we say, was the more or less official view of the sexiness of money and clout. The species of sex that actually filtered through the business rhetoric, however, was of a rather different sort. It was essentially sadistic and implicitly homoerotic, since, for all the obeisances made to equal opportunity, the *agon* of business was still presented almost entirely as a spectacle of men doing things to men. Someone bested in business was said to have been "fucked," or "screwed," or, in a more genteel description of the same transaction, to have "been had." People "sucked up" to the boss. People "kissed ass" in the hope of being treated indulgently. Among peers in the upper echelons of business, the imperative was to be "top dog." As with Olympic wrestlers in polymorphously sexual Athens, the mythic content of business struggles ultimately came down to the paradigm of men grappling naked in public.

At their most extreme, the rituals of businessmen, and

most apparently of businessmen-at-play, blurred the lines among enterprise and war, sport and violence, libido and cruelty, in ways that smacked of the macabre. A high-level aerospace industry club, for example, that modestly called itself the Conquistadores del Cielo, held an annual outing whose climactic event was a "fast-draw" contest. Executives faced off against each other, armed with electronic "pistols." At the critical moment they reached for their holsters and fired at each other's hearts. A galvanic sensor recorded who'd had his aorta blown off. Thus, in the electronic age, there were sporting and sociable ways in which hetero executives could simulate the frontier myths of the Wild West while getting harmlessly "fucked," "killed," or both.

/// FOUR

But these are sophisticated times, times in which it is widely understood that the word is not the thing, that symbolic gestures do not draw blood, that metaphors of war and sport and sex may be colorful and sometimes incisive but are not to be taken literally.

Or are we really that sophisticated?

If we were, why would we swallow so much of the eighties business mythology that plays precisely off those metaphors, and that asks us to accept a version of the workplace so plainly out of line with how things really are?

Why would we gobble up characterizations of business as swashbuckling, dare-all battle when it is not exactly news— John Kenneth Galbraith said it in 1958—that "modern business enterprise can be understood only as a comprehensive effort to reduce risk"? Risk is for amateurs. Professionals traffic in the sure thing. When business is done as it ought to be done, there is no suspense and no "battle" whatsoever. Further, on those occasions when something does go dreadfully wrong and business "generals" march off to disaster, they don't fall on their swords or commit *seppuku.* They are bid adieu with a "golden parachute" that sets them up quite handsomely until the next job comes along.

Similarly flimsy are the actual correspondences between business and sports. Indeed, the qualities of sport that refresh the spirit are precisely the qualities that seem ever less present in the workplace. We admire teamwork, yet in what has been dubbed an "era of me-first management," with job-hopping at an all-time high and job security at a post-Depression low, teamwork is more a nostalgic notion than a functional one. We delight in the merciless but crystalline rules of sport, while in business, a broadly perceived crisis in ethics has unmoored us from the comfort of boundaries and standards. We relish the peak effort of sport, but how often, amid the general sequence of routine chores, does business really stretch us? We revel in the conclusiveness of sport, the fact that when the whistle blows there is a winner and a loser, something has been settled; how often is anything really settled in business? Companies merge, change names, disappear entirely; strategies are revamped with every tremor in the interest rate or every change of mood in Washington or on Wall Street; the frustration of never quite seeing something through to the final whistle is endemic.

As to the presumed sexiness of enterprise, in 1987 *Penthouse* commissioned a survey on the private lives of entrepreneurs, designed to trace the connections between the professional and erotic drives of those wild and charismatic "romantic hero[es] of American business." Suffice it to say that in matters of marriage, divorce, affairs both on and off the job, age at loss of virginity, overall number of sexual partners, and frequency of lovemaking and masturbation, the entrepreneurs were found to be breathtakingly average.

If the survey result was somewhat anticlimactic, then the

same might be said of the entire process of juxtaposing 1980s business myth with business fact. The rhetoric and the imagery were more grand and gripping than they had ever been, but they tended to dwarf the reality in pizzazz, in drama, in titillation. The thing being celebrated all but disappeared in the flash and excess of the celebration.

But perhaps that was in keeping with the real agenda of the business rah-rahs—not exactly to persuade people that business was as momentous as war and as cleanly exciting as the Millrose Games, but simply to distract them from what was perhaps the last remaining insight about business that might be deemed subversive.

It was no longer subversive to point out that American business wasn't working very well. That had been an acceptable and even redundant thing to say since at least 1980 or so, the heyday of theories X, Y, and Z, and a time when a former Harvard Business School professor could go public as advocating the shutting down of business schools.

It was no longer subversive to argue that American business was bankrupting the future by allotting its greatest rewards to raiders, arbitrageurs, investment bankers—people who shuffled assets and skimmed a vigorish while seldom adding value. So what? The government was also mortgaging the future, as were millions of individuals in debt to the eyeballs.

It was no longer subversive to make noise about the business community's quiet renege on affirmative-action promises made to women and minorities; apparently no one much cared.

No, possibly the only subversive realization left was the simple observation that business really wasn't all that interesting.

Take away the battlefield imagery, the gridiron metaphors, the barroom slang, and what did you have? A job. A place to go between breakfast time and winter dusk, and, presumably, a way to pay the bills. You didn't have a radar scope, you had a computer screen; you weren't trying to hit a home run, you were trying to sell somebody something. This wasn't called epic combat or an Olympiad, it was called making a living, and while it had its satisfactions—even, sometimes, its excitements—the Super Bowl it was not. It was simply a necessity for most folks, as everyone had known since the expulsion from Eden.

Through most of the 1980s, though, nobody just came out and said it like that. Instead, in keeping with the syndrome of compensation-by-hype, the business rah-rahs kept up a steady clamor of supposedly inspirational tales, worked at creating a cultural context of motivational fibs. The irony was that, in trying so hard to glorify work, the tactic in fact degraded it. Wasn't *work itself* sufficiently noble, without making it sound like a guerrilla war or a boxing match? Couldn't the labors that men and women responsibly performed to earn their keep be looked at and respected simply for what they were? What had become of the value of the task itself—the task construed not as metaphorical sport or metaphorical anything, but simply as the honest and concentrated application of thought, skill, and muscle?

The business rah-rahs came across as awfully cocky in the 1980s, but apparently they weren't truly confident about what they had to sell. The new mythology of ambition and striving, they seemed to think, would only fly if it was propped up by references to jazzier arenas. The job itself, the actual *doing* of it, didn't seem to count for much. No wonder people got confused. They were being asked to accept the equations of "businesslike" with "realistic," "professional" with "responsible," just at the time when business was pulling on shoulder pads and six-shooters, doing everything it could to cloak itself in fantasy.

7

A Sickness
Called
Success

*Among democratic nations, ambition is
ardent and continual, but its aim is not
habitually lofty; and life is generally spent in
eagerly coveting small objects.*

—*Tocqueville*

ONE

Not that people were simply suckered into accepting the business mythology of the 1980s. No, people chose to believe it because they thought the belief would have a payoff; in this they were like most people who believed most things.

The samurai says to his code: I will cleave to you, and you will bring me glory. The conventionally religious man says to his God: I will worship You, and You will guide me into Heaven. The enduring power of the Faust legend lies in its distillation of the notion that all of us cut deals with our demons—the angelic demons no less than the devilish. We steer our efforts in accordance with a given set of promises, promises so fraught with wishing that they seem of necessity to hold an element of magic; and whether or not we reach the fulfillment of those promises, the pursuit of them determines our course.

So it was with the widespread will to believe in the new business mythology. To adopt that credo was to cut a deal, and the deal went something like this: I will believe that the pursuit of wealth is in itself exciting, and engrossing, and fashionable, and worthy of the best part of my time, my attention, and my passion, and in return the pursuit of wealth will make me a "success."

"Success," to an extraordinary degree, was the constant target of will and exertions in the 1980s, the glittering but indistinct Oz toward which aspirations strained. What, precisely, did the word mean? No one seemed to know, but it didn't really matter. Success didn't need to be defined or examined; it was enough merely to invoke it, to intone the magic word. Success was invoked more often and with far greater assurance than was self-fulfillment in the seventies; it was pursued by far greater numbers and with far greater heat than were peace and love in the sixties. Those other credos, after all, set themselves up, if not in opposition to, then certainly in tension with, conventional self-interest; some part of their vigor was squandered on resolving that tension, on trying to wrestle that tension to the mat while keeping one's values intact.

The credo of success, eighties-style, on the other hand, *was* the credo of self-interest. It was old-fashioned economic Darwinism dressed up in new clothes. Success eighties-style was survival-of-the-fiscally-fittest padding the jungle in running shoes. It was primal aggressiveness slaking itself not on blood but on cold-pressed virgin olive oil. It was the unchastened acquisitive impulse, the primal appetite for more, legitimized by social fashion and summarized in the deceptively mild war whoop, *go for it.*

But in fact there was nothing at all mild about the eighties quest for success. That quest, rather, was feverish and a little hysterical, carried out in a kind of trance. The thing was to *get there*. Getting there was in the nature of a personal dare, and once you'd accepted it, you neither rested nor asked questions.

Just as the business rah-rahs dragooned the language of sport and war into the service of buying and selling, so the success gurus injected momentous phrases and biblical cadences into the earthbound processes of making it. Motivational best-sellers—*In Search of Excellence, What They Don't Teach You at Harvard Business School, What Color Is Your Parachute?*—glutted the bookstore racks nearest the cash registers. For the television generation, there was a line of videos called "Watch Your Way to Success." The bottom-line message of the motivators was appropriately summarized in 1986 by the critic Benjamin DeMott: "Go," they were saying, "go where Americans have always gone for fresh nourishment. . . . Not to religion or art or controlled substances, but to where the action is. Go to the can-do world of business." The can-do world of business, as we have argued, was in fact becoming a sort of religion, in keeping with "the attempt of some new image makers to transform the corporation into a church." Like any church, the corporation was obliged to offer up some version of salvation, and success itself seemed to serve the purpose neatly.

Success as salvation—or at least as the surest evidence of salvation—had of course been a very respectable concept around four hundred years ago. John Calvin dined out on it often. But could financial success possibly be passed off in the late twentieth century as grace-made-manifest? For that matter, were there, in our skeptical time, ways of getting rich and powerful that would not seem *ipso facto* in conflict with prevailing versions of virtue and decency?

It is worth recalling that in the not very distant past—just before the eighties socked in, in fact—it seemed there were.

In those more confident economic times, it was credible to posit a future in which technology would combine with Aquarian consciousness to produce a species of success by which everyone could be affluent, happy, and fulfilled: America as one big Apple computer, back in the days when that was an exciting and euphoric company, or as one big Celestial Seasonings, getting both rich and healthy on Red Zinger tea. This vision of success came, so to speak, from a counterculture to the counterculture—a group that took seriously the priorities of the sixties, but who saw nothing the least bit wrong with making oodles of money, nothing necessarily stultifying about organizations, nothing so irredeemable about the system that it couldn't be worked with. This bright-eyed and halcyon version of ambition was driven not by greed but by the desire to be independent and the best, not by selfishness but by the gratification of making good things happen. Under its banner, values and advancement would never conflict, talent would never be wasted, politics and institutional neurosis would never prevail over an enlightened disbursement of just deserts.

For a brief time—very brief—this ideal of success seemed to be pointing the way toward a green and temperate future. As the actual future slunk in, however, with its threats, anxieties, and disappointments, the Aquarian version of making it came to seem a shade too genteel if not too soft-headed to cut it in the new and meaner arena. *Not* everyone could have a niche. There were always shakeouts. Some years it seemed there was less money up for grabs; some years it seemed there was more. Either way, there were always too many hands reaching for it, and, explain it however you like, some of those hands were going to come away empty. Far from being more nurturing and benign, the

workplace was becoming dicier and more nakedly competitive; a more armored notion of success was needed to deal
with it. If your textbook was *The Greening of America,* you
were going to have a damn tough time when tested on
Looking Out for Number One.

The change in substance was neatly mirrored by a change
in image: from Steve Apple founder Jobs, sitting lotus-style
on a bare floor in an empty living room, to a twenty-
three-year-old banker in a yellow tie and a suit that looked
too big for him, trying valiantly (a) to keep his cigar lit and
(b) to make a good show of pretending to enjoy it. The new
successful person, that is to say, was supposed to look not
like a reconstructed hippie but like a dusted-off embodiment of successes past.

Was it the implicit harking back to Calvin that gave success
eighties-style such a musty, retro look and feel? Or was it
simply the coming back into vogue of whiskey-and-pocket-
watch capitalism as it existed around the turn of the century?

In either case, as the eighties progressed, it became clear
that a new sort of status anxiety was taking hold, and
"success," therefore, was being measured increasingly by
what showed on the surface. After at least two decades in
which "status symbols" had fallen into disrepute and were
taken as signs of Neanderthal taste and arrested social
development, visible tokens of standing came roaring back.
CEOs driving their own little cars and looking for a parking
space like everyone else? The hell with that. Now it was
limos, and signs as big as movie marquees that said
Reserved for the Boss. Hierarchy was back in style. Symbols
of preferment were back in vogue.

Since the impulse for the new version of success was
essentially nostalgic, it didn't hurt at all that the "new status"
symbols were in almost every case clichéd. Macanudo, in a
brilliantly simple marketing ploy, claimed that its big black

stogies embodied "the sweet smell of success," and suddenly people were sucking Macanudos as if it were the
1920s. Chivas Regal Scotch made it sound almost like the
historic duty of the successful person to drink a brown
whiskey aged twelve years. The obviously expensive watch
made a stunning comeback in the 1980s, becoming as much
of a totem as it had been in the heyday of the hand-etched
clamshell case. The new generation of "power" watches
boasted extra dials for keeping Tokyo and London time,
showed the phases of the moon, in case their owners
couldn't spare a second to look up at the sky, and promised
to be waterproof to three hundred feet, though chances
were they would never be sunk deeper than the bottom of
a Jacuzzi. In the 1980s, successful people held sincere and
even doting conversations about their watches, spoke of
them rather in the way they might have talked about their
dogs, except that having a dog was too much of a commitment. Who manned Fido's poop-scoop when you had to fly
on short notice to Singapore?

Then, of course, there was the car, the most hackneyed
yet compelling status symbol of them all. Between 1978 and
1987, U.S. sales of BMWs more than tripled. Jaguar increased
American sales eightfold between 1980 and 1987. And
between 1986 and 1987 alone, Mercedes, already the leader
in high-end imports, added another 14 percent to its U.S.
market.

Yet there was something poignant about the Mercedes
boom. Americans tended to think that in purchasing a
Mercedes they were "growing into" European taste and
appreciation of quality, whereas in Germany, according to
Joseph Epstein in *The American Scholar,* a Mercedes was
thought of as "a sign of high vulgarity, a car of the kind
owned by Beverly Hills dentists or African cabinet minis-
ters." Besides, even in America, a Mercedes couldn't really

provide success-security. It could always be aced out by, say, a Rolls—a fact diabolically exploited by a 1986 Rolls-Royce ad: a Rolls and a Mercedes are stopped side by side at a red light. The Mercedes is eclipsed by the taller, more muscular Rolls, and the driver of the smaller car is made to look moony, hangdog, invidious, craven, ashamed of himself. Confronted by the six-figure auto, the toy he doesn't yet own and presumably cannot yet afford, he realizes he is not yet truly successful, in spite of how jaunty he felt on the day he drove his 560 SL out of the showroom. Suddenly he feels small.

This tableau suggests something odd and terribly fragile that was at the center of success eighties-style—or rather, something that was where the center would have been, if success eighties-style *had* a center. But it didn't seem to, and that was the problem.

What was this new sort of success *in itself*? You couldn't really say; you could only illustrate it by holding up the things that went with it. You couldn't really say what success was made of, or why it was a worthwhile goal, except by pointing to the things it bought. Talking about success in the 1980s was like trying to speak a foreign language through the use of flash cards. You could name things, but not explain how they related, because you only had the nouns, you didn't have the grammar. The grammar should have been provided by a web of personal values. Values should have provided the structure, the syntax, in which the individual tokens of success would fit together to tell the story of what success had to do with the *person* who was successful.

Without those values, however, success became nothing more than a bunch of stuff with price tags on it. People pointed to a summer house and said: success. They held up the flash card of a car phone, a condo, a designer baby off to pre-nursery school, and said: success.

But those things weren't success. They were by-products of success. They came after, and all they meant was money. Success itself could not be defined by the reward, but only in terms of some achievement that earned the reward. In the absence of a working grammar of personal values, people in the 1980s didn't seem able to make that link. And they didn't even seem to realize that some integral connection that should have been there, wasn't.

/// TWO

But something was missing, some basic hunger was going unfed, and although the deficiency hadn't been pinpointed, it began to be noticed as the eighties progressed that something about success—the species of it that was in fashion and the way it was being sought—was making a lot of people sick. Moreover, in keeping with the notion of cutting deals with our demons, it seemed that people were being rewarded in the marketplace for being sick.

In 1985 the American Psychological Association held a symposium on a newly described syndrome known as "the impostor phenomenon." Broadly speaking, "impostors" were men and women, generally in their twenties and thirties, who were successful in their careers and yet felt like bluffers, vulnerable at any moment to exposure and disgrace, even dissolution. So fragile was their self-esteem, so airy their sense of real accomplishment, that the smallest thing—a question they couldn't answer, a small gaffe at a meeting—could send them plummeting into anxiety and depression.

University of Pennsylvania Medical School psychologist Joan Harvey had identified several species of "impostors"— and these types, in turn, seemed to describe a fair proportion of ambitious young Americans. The "workaholics," in

Harvey's schema, threw themselves into killingly long hours as a way of compensating for their self-perceived lack of innate talent or intelligence. The "charmers" resorted to socializing, flirting, and flattering, thereby undermining their chances of ever really knowing if their success was based on anything substantial, anything germane to the job at hand. "Magical thinkers" subjected themselves to spasms of cramming and fits of anxiety, imagining that the only way they could possibly succeed was by first enduring a masochistic ritual of dread. "Shrinking violets," though they might be aching for praise and secretly hating their colleagues, wilted in the face of compliments and were always finding ways of deflecting recognition from themselves.

Though couched in the suspect language of pop psychology, the discussion of the impostor phenomenon was based on interview-driven research and did seem to point up a significant truth: among the tens of millions of young people embroiled in an apparently straight-ahead quest for success, there were many for whom the process was surprisingly ambivalent, many for whom the tokens of making it did not translate into the confidence and contentment that, according to the business mythology, went with job promotions and a hefty paycheck.

In stark contrast to the stereotype of the self-satisfied yuppie, these were people who *didn't* simply assume they deserved their champagne and ripened cheese. To their credit, and their deep discomfort, they were self-candid enough to be bothered by a gnawing sense of inauthenticity. And while feelings of inauthenticity were hardly new to the eighties, there were two things about the eighties version that may have been unprecedented.

First, there was the sheer extent of it. The psychologists who identified the impostor phenomenon claimed that as many as 40 percent of young succeeders suffered from the private belief that they were faking it. For the sake of argument, let's say the shrinks exaggerated by half; that still left one person in five essentially lying to him- or herself every hour of the business day.

Moreover, the impostor scenario cut across such a broad swath of the career and demographic spectra that it seemed clear the syndrome derived not from pressures specific to any given field or group, but from the pursuit of eighties-style success, period. Studies were done on lawyers, on middle managers, on women, on blacks. The findings were consistent. Up and down the line, people had bought into a version of success that turned out not to satisfy. Whether or not the impostor phenomenon said much about the eternal verities of the human psyche, it did seem, like Freud's studies of hysteria in *fin de siècle* Vienna, to say a great deal about how people were driving themselves crazy in a given place and time.

The second new wrinkle in the impostor phenomenon was that it affected people who *claimed* not to be alienated from their work.

Alienation from work, of course, was a complaint at least as old as the industrial revolution. Observers as diverse as Adam Smith and Karl Marx agreed that the concentration of capital and the division of labor would make people less at one with the means by which they earned their living, would pave the way for rootlessness and anomie. This prospect, once nearly as traumatic as the death of God, was, by the mid-twentieth century in America, accepted with a resigned shrug and another can of beer or another dry martini. It was one of those things about modern life that was less than ideal, but it had its compensations. If you didn't love your work, at least you had your leisure. If the divvying up of labor reduced individual jobs to functions that didn't make a whole lot of sense in themselves, at least that seemed to be the most efficient way of churning out *more*. Besides, alienation, while it was no picnic, had the benefit of forcing you to develop other resources, to conjure other comforts, to will other things into mattering. The bottom line was that a job was something you did. Your real self, like the clothes you liked to wear, was reserved for evenings and weekends. It came out when you played the piano or puttered in the workshop or smoked grass or made love, it had its shining moments on vacations that had better turn out to be terrific, because an otherwise toxic concentration of longing was riding on them.

By the ethos of 1980s-style success, however, that detached stance in regard to work was no longer acceptable. Not that work, for the overwhelming majority, had gotten any more satisfying or any more expressive than it had been in the sixties or the seventies. But the simple economic need to do it had become more compelling, and social fashion had shifted accordingly. Competitiveness, both national and personal, was the word of the day; and alienation—*acknowledged* alienation—had again become a fringe attitude, as it had been back in the fifties, when Maynard G. Krebs, America's television beatnik, would shriek at the mention of work (*"Work?!"*) as though the syllable carried some dread disease. No, in the eighties, people were supposed to approach their jobs—their Careers—with the utmost seriousness and involvement, the highest and sometimes most exclusive commitment. For the true fast-trackers, as the journalist Ellen Hopkins observed, "leisure, health, relationships, happiness itself—all [were] secondary to work." In the eighties, people were supposed to bring their real selves to the office, and the office, in turn, would provide the backdrop against which those real selves could strut their stuff.

The problem was that it was precisely the people who

identified most strongly with work and success who seemed most prone to feel like impostors—and this led into an emotional and philosophical cul-de-sac, a logical impasse with hellish implications. After you'd settled for a definition of success that equated it merely with money and the things that money bought, and after you'd cut the deal that brought those things your way—if you had *gotten there* and *still* didn't feel authentically successful, what then?

⫻ THREE

The impostor phenomenon, in broad outline, was easy to identify and easy to describe. A subtler question, however, was *why* the whole issue of success created emotional turmoil in so many people, why a version of making it that had been so avidly embraced was turning out, for so many, not to work. On this issue, a revealing and remarkably fast-shifting debate developed through the middle years of the 1980s.

As a point of reference, consider a 1984 *Newsweek* article called "The Pursuit of Unhappiness"—a piece that neatly summarizes what has already become the "old" way of looking at success crises. The story was about some people's tendency to sabotage their own chances of making it, and it began with a vignette about a patient telling his therapist how well he's doing at his job. "I may even be in for a promotion," the patient says, a forced enthusiasm imperfectly masking his anxiety. "They're really beginning to reject—I mean, respect my abilities there." Two days later, the fellow contrives to have a blow-up with his boss and forfeits his chance to get ahead.

Why did he do it? According to the conventional wisdom as of 1984, the drama was essentially Oedipal. The success-avoider shot himself in the foot as a cockeyed way of "protecting the self-esteem of an unsuccessful father," or hiding from himself what might appear "an angry mockery" of the parent, or trying to "ward off the envy of siblings." In the Freudian canon, these were, of course, male dynamics; how they figured in women's self-willed failures was never quite explained.

But that was only one of many things that went unexplained, and even unexamined, in traditional approaches to the psychodynamics of success and failure. Indeed, maybe the most striking thing about the conventional wisdom on the subject was the range of assumptions it allowed to go unquestioned, the number of circumstances that were accepted as givens.

It went unquestioned that "success," however it was defined at a given historical moment, was necessarily and unambiguously good, and "failure" was automatically bad.

It went unquestioned that "failure" had to do with some "flaw" in the individual, rather than in some possible lack of subtlety or discrimination or justice in how the "successes" and the "failures" were sorted out.

And it went unquestioned that the "flaws" that made some people fail had their origins in early childhood development, and could not, therefore, be viewed as reasoned, adult reactions to what may have been unwholesome or unnatural circumstances in the workplace.

In 1986, with America's preoccupation with success at perhaps its very peak, the focus of the discussion abruptly and radically shifted.

A growing number of psychologists seemed to be coming to the simultaneous realization that it made little sense to discuss the meaning of success and failure in the individual without also essaying a psychological critique of success in the culture. In the vanguard of this new school was a therapist named Douglas LaBier, whose work, most basically, was premised on the notion that "work can, quite literally, drive people crazy."

LaBier started from the clinically observed paradox that there were "people who appear[ed] to be sick [i.e., ineffective in terms of work] but [were] normal," and "people who appear[ed] to be normal [i.e., able to become successful] but [were] sick."

The only logical way to resolve this paradox was to acknowledge that there were apparently widespread instances in which the "career environment, in effect, require[d] disturbed attitudes." Those attitudes included hyper-competitiveness, habitual mistrust of one's colleagues, and, most profoundly, a willingness to suspend or even defy personal values in favor of the demands of the organization; *those* were the demons that needed to be dealt with in the name of success eighties-style, and dealing with them took its toll. In LaBier's experience with fast-track patients, the side-effects of "successful" adjustments included "feelings ... of entrapment, guilt, and self-betrayal, which [left] the person feeling out of kilter, off-balance, and unfulfilled, despite his or her success."

Talk about subversive. Implicitly, LaBier's formulation took the traditional value judgments about success and failure and stood them absolutely on their heads.

It used to be assumed that success made people happy, and failure made them sad, and that, moreover, people who "succeeded" had a predilection for gladness while those who "failed" were predisposed to making themselves miserable.

Now, however, it was proposed not only that success could *make* people disturbed, but that it was often disturbed people who had the most insistent and unexamined need of success to begin with. No longer did the "failures" have a lock on character defects. The "successful" could also be seen as compensating for developmental glitches and real or imagined inadequacies, pursuing "power as a magical solution to vulnerability and helplessness." Those who "failed," by getting off the fast track or choosing never to get on it, might do so because, emotionally speaking, they could afford to; their better-balanced egos allowed them to make "difficult but rational decisions" about what they truly valued.

Further, while it had long been an American axiom that "success" called for sacrifice, the real nature of what people gave up was being reexamined. The old wisdom had it that the sacrifices were unambiguously admirable—one sacrificed leisure time, self-indulgences, play, and that was all to the good. But what about the *other* sacrifices that making it often seemed to demand: the sacrifice of independent judgment; the abdication of a vision if it happened not to fit in with one's paid function. Was it admirable to sacrifice one's peace of mind to advance, say, in a company that polluted? Was it admirable to sacrifice a vocation as a playwright to "succeed" as a churner-out of soap operas? And did it make moral or social sense to reward those sorts of sacrifices, to hold them up as cultural ideals?

In a way, the revised clinical thinking about success and failure was only a formalization of what was already a widely held understanding: that there were plenty of mean, sick bastards out there who were making it, and who were fundamentally miserable anyway. And while that didn't mean that success was bad, it suggested pretty clearly that it wasn't necessarily a function of virtue and mental health, either. What the work of LaBier and others accomplished was to establish an intellectually respectable framework in which the neurotic side of eighties ambitions could be discussed with greater candor than it ever had before.

Once success-malaise was out of the closet, talking about

it took on rather the character of a collective catharsis. Far from pooh-poohing the subject, both the very conservative *Nation's Business* and *Fortune* addressed it as a real and serious problem. Almost overnight, dealing with the pathology of success became a recognized psychiatric specialty in the major cities. *The New York Times* devoted a lead article in its Sunday business section to the phenomenon of people who "hit bottom when they reach the top." Personal disasters ranging from cocaine abuse to sundered marriages to alcoholism to suicide were ascribed not to the stresses of failure, or even the stresses of *seeking* success, but rather to the disillusionment that came with success itself, the puncturing of "a false fantasy of what success would bring." Love, serenity, self-esteem—these were thought to be part of the deal, and when they turned out not to be, the sense of having been duped could be ferocious. There were still those nagging questions: *What next? What for?*

Those questions wouldn't go away, and when success-malaise was at its most virulent and unremitting, there seemed only one way to answer them: more of the same, in ever larger doses. By 1987 it was being observed that there were people who got "high and hooked on money in the same way that others [became] addicted to alcohol and cocaine." An "injection" of funds made these people feel "secure, victorious, strong, loved, proud and sexually attractive." The difficulty was that, like other kinds of addicts, the dollar-junkie would do just about anything to meet the inexorable demands of his habit. For that reason, it could be argued that regarding white-collar crime and other ethical lapses merely as a function of greed—a moral concept—was inadequate; a "clinical ... framework" should also be brought to bear, because these people had fallen beyond the pale of personal responsibility. Deprived of their shot of money, they might have "a reaction . . . every bit as extreme as that of a heroin addict denied his fix."

This analogy, while dramatic and not unpersuasive, had one major flaw—a flaw that, if you thought about it, made money-addiction an even more unsettling notion. The mere possession of heroin was a crime, after all, while the possession of money was not. Not only was it not a crime, but in an age that flattered the wealthy for being wealthy, possession of money was *ipso facto* good. And among people who were more comfortable counting up *more* than making judgments as to quality, possession of a *lot* of money was *ipso facto* better. So where was the line between admirable ambition and unseemly grasping, between healthy striving and ugly obsession, between "getting used to a successful lifestyle," as the vomitous jargon went, and becoming addicted to dollars?

That line was awfully tough to locate, because the money-junkies weren't after some gutter drug that self-respecting folks would have no truck with. They wanted the exact same thing that *everyone* was being persuaded to want in the 1980s: success as measured by the rewards for success.

The only difference was that the sick ones wanted it a shade more badly.

//// FOUR

Between 1970 and 1983 the suicide rate among white males in the "success years" between twenty-five and thirty-four increased by nearly 32 percent.

In 1966 an American woman was one-twentieth as likely to have an ulcer as was an American man. By 1986, thanks to the blessing of much broader participation in the success sweepstakes, she had fully half as much chance to end up with a perforated stomach.

Through the 1980s, job-hopping among the privileged young was epidemic, with tenure in certain fast-track industries averaging as little as eighteen months. The usual explanation was that people changed jobs to accelerate their movement to the next raise, the next promotion. It was at least plausible, however, that they also job-hopped in search of some meaning, some gratification beyond the paycheck, that was lacking in the job they held before. They dodged emptiness by courting novelty, and didn't simply pursue success, but also fled the recognition of success's limitations.

Those limitations applied at the national as well as at the individual level. In 1984, *New Republic* columnist "TRB" argued that prevailing economic policies and social attitudes had "made success in America more successful, but . . . [did] nothing to make it more productive. . . . [Was society] getting value-for-money from its highly paid investment bankers and lawyers; from corporate executives . . . [and] speculators[?]" Or did the cult of success, with its glorification of wealth for its own sake and unavoidable consequence of widening inequality, invite "invidious comparisons" which tended over time to "rend the social fabric"?

No one was answering those questions in the 1980s; hardly anyone was asking them. And hardly anyone asked them because they were embarrassing. They demanded that success be looked at *in context,* and a sense of context is precisely what the contemporary version of success was lacking. Christopher Lasch, in his prescient 1979 book, *The Culture of Narcissism,* had argued that in the America then developing, "the new ideal of success . . . [would have] no reference to anything outside the self. . . . Success equals success."

Commensurate only with itself, success eighties-style was chillingly isolated from the life that went on around it. And the "successful" people who started off full of drive and purpose and ended up feeling like impostors, or became money junkies, did so because at some point they could no longer avoid noticing that they had come unmoored. Success was a floating island. It didn't connect with anything; it was discontinuous on every side.

It was discontinuous with the movement of the nation at large, a movement characterized not by giddy spurts and quick scores but by the steady and momentous effort of tens of millions of men and women trying to hold their dignity while trying, as well, to hold their ground.

It was discontinuous with virtually every thread of recent social history, which had stressed growing equality rather than growing disparity, the enlightened use of leisure rather than a conspicuous obsession with work, informality rather than hierarchy, the sexiness of sex rather than the sexiness of power, and the value of time more than the value of money.

And, perhaps most insidiously, it was discontinuous with the notion of substantial, self-chosen achievement. Asked what they wanted to be when they grew up, kids used to say "a doctor," "a teacher," "a scientist." In the eighties they learned to say "a success."

But *success* is a different kind of noun. It isn't something you pick. It's something that happens—or should happen—because of the inherent quality and value of what you do. Skip that connection, as it was skipped by the faulty moral grammar of the 1980s, and success comes unglued from what it ought to mean. It loses its solidity, its whiff of the grand, and ends up meaning simply having money.

Still, having money is pleasanter than not, and for many if not for most, succeeding by the standards of the eighties was easier than groping toward a new definition of success. So be it, people seemed to conclude. If success boils down to dollars and the things that dollars can buy, then bring on the bucks, and bring on the gewgaws.

8 ///

A Tyranny Miscalled Taste

In 1958, a Frenchman named Baron Marcel Bich bought the moribund Waterman pen company and began marketing a new product modestly called the Bic.

The Bic wrote very well. It had a clear plastic casing, so you could see when you were getting low on ink, and a cap with a flexible clip that fit securely over the lip of a pocket. It was hexagonal so it wouldn't roll off your desk. It was durable enough so that, as the commercials showed, it could be shot from a high-powered rifle through a heavy-gauge slab of plywood, and though the casing could be seen splintering in ultra-slow motion, the pen would still write. The Bic cost nineteen cents—less if you bought it in a multi-pack.

The Bic was a flawless example of modern design. It was simple. It looked like what it did. It took advantage of available technologies and employed appropriate materials. In keeping with the social vision of the original modernist theorists, it was a democratic commodity, within the reach of all. It was a people's pen, the right pen at the right time, and in 1967, 480 million of them were sold.

By the middle 1980s, the Bic was as out of fashion as bell-bottom jeans. Plenty of them were still being sold, but now they tended to be office-issue, dispensed in anonymous dozens, and written with when no one was looking. When people *were* looking, the pen of choice had become the Mont Blanc. Between 1981 and 1987, the sales of Mont Blanc pens increased in America by roughly 30 percent a year.

The Mont Blanc wrote at least as well as the Bic, and had a similarly convenient pocket clip. But the Mont Blanc was partly made of gold and cost up to two hundred dollars. This meant, among other things, that when you lent someone your pen you made damn sure you got it back; with the Bic, you'd shrug it away as you would a pack of matches, and the pens would circulate. You could always get hold of one for the purpose of, say, making out a deposit slip at the bank or jotting down a phone number in a bar. But the Mont Blanc was not passed so readily from hand to hand; it was a possession, an *objet,* a thing of worth. It was owned and prized, and if, for instance, it fell out of your pocket and vanished down a subway grating, you would be depressed.

So why did people want a two-hundred-dollar pen in the first place, a pen that would be one more thing to worry about?

No doubt there was a range of answers. The Mont Blanc felt good in your hand. There was a certain elegance in writing with a fountain pen. It was satisfying to own something that, in theory, would last a very long time. All these were good reasons, though whether they justified buying a pen that cost a thousand times as much as other pens was moot. What seemed to clinch the decision, however, was not a reason, exactly, but an invocation: people bought the Mont Blanc pen because of its "quality," which testified, in turn, to their "taste."

Nineteen cents might buy you something to doodle with, it was suggested, but it took two hundred clams to purchase a "quality" writing instrument. A plastic ballpoint might suffice for transferring ink to paper, but "taste" demanded a handsome accessory for the pocket of the hundred-dollar business shirt or the lady's worsted suit. It was all a matter of sensibility, according to the mostly urban well-to-do who had adopted what might be termed the curatorial approach to their possessions.

Now, quality is concentration embodied, and taste is one of the hallmarks of an alert existence; together, the two notions are among life's solaces. The only problem is that, much of the time, the people who thought they were talking about taste and quality weren't. Taste and quality were bandied about in the eighties in much the same way that "success" was; they were words that felt good in the mouth, that made one feel in step, notwithstanding that the syllables had been largely emptied of their content.

Ever have a heart-to-heart talk with a pen salesman? Mention quality as the reason people bought Mont Blanc pens, and he'll laugh. The real reason people bought them was that they cost two hundred dollars, everybody *knew* they cost two hundred dollars, and there were only so many people who could or would lay down two century notes for a pen. The Mont Blanc sent a message, but the message had virtually nothing to do with taste and everything to do with money; the real delight in owning one lay in the knowledge that most people couldn't afford to, and that the people who counted would know enough to be impressed.

Vogue, in 1987, made it official by dubbing the Mont Blanc "the status pen," installing it alongside such well-worn consumer clichés as "the status handbag (Louis Vuitton)

[and] the status loafer (Gucci)." They might also have included the status leaf (radicchio), the status panties (Hanro), the status vinegar (balsamic), the status athletic supporter (Le Jacques), the status tennis racquet (the Prince Custom, $1000), and, in what *The New York Times* called "the age of designer water," the status H_2O (Evian).

In virtually every product category, there was an item or a brand that proudly, even defiantly, set out to be more expensive than all others. This brand, almost by definition, would then become the standard of "taste" and "quality" against which less esteemed items could be measured. No one seemed to notice that a basic tenet of market capitalism was being turned upside down: price was dictating value, rather than vice versa.

And money didn't just buy, it signified. In the 1980s, goods carried the sort of price tags that couldn't be removed at the cash register, price tags that persisted, as it were, in code. "Sensibility" eighties-style thus had less to do with connoisseurship as to the intrinsic excellence of pens or lettuces or shoes or cars, than with an adeptness at learning the codes surrounding them, knowing which stuff was the right stuff, which stuff would be recognized, approved, and envied.

This, to be sure, was one version of taste. It was shoppers' taste—a taste that applied only to things that could be bought, and that defined sophistication essentially as the knowledge of what things cost. Under the banner of this version of taste, the ancient but lately dormant tendency toward conspicuous consumption staged, in the 1980s, a conspicuous revival.

//// TWO

Conspicuous consumption was as old as Babylon, but it took the Gilded Age in America, a time not unlike the 1980s, to give it a name.

The phrase was coined in 1899 by Thorstein Veblen, economist, social critic, author of *The Theory of the Leisure Class,* among other books, and one of the most implacable misanthropes and pessimists who ever lived. At his death in 1929, Veblen, by then a famous man, left strict instructions that no memorial services or eulogies should attend his passing. This was motivated not by modesty, but by malice, and by the satisfied conviction that there was nothing left to say. He'd spent his life arguing that mankind was not just greedy—a fact that people were perfectly willing to accept and even felt oddly flattered by, as when accused of being oversexed—but also primitive, irrational, self-deluding, and ultimately self-destructive in its greed. The stock-market crash was Veblen's vindication; the Great Depression would be his monument. If ever a man died with the happy words "I told you so" still tickling his lips, it was Thorstein Veblen.

"Conspicuous consumption of valuable goods" was a notion at the very heart of Veblen's social theory. "To gain and hold the esteem of men," he had observed, "it [was] not sufficient merely to possess wealth or power. The wealth or power must be put in evidence." Obvious consumption— which required a general awareness of what things cost in order to *be* obvious—thus became "a means of reputability."

But what made certain goods valuable in the first place? Rarity, of course, was a factor in commodities like gold and jewels. But that did not explain, say, why a frock made by dressmaker *A* should cost twenty times as much as one of similar materials made by dressmaker *B,* or why the succulent but common oyster should be considered a poor man's staple by one generation and esteemed a great luxury by the next. To a large extent, it seemed, what made many things valuable was nothing more than a rather arbitrary consensus, also known as fashion. How the consensus got started, especially before the age of advertising, was something of a mystery.

Once established, however, consensual value fed on itself and became tyrannical over time because of people's blind and, as it were, tribal insistence on imitating each other.

"The propensity for emulation," Veblen believed, "is probably the strongest and most alert and persistent of the economic motives." Conventional "good taste" was thus the dull child of the desire to show off and the fear of not conforming.

In America, the drive toward emulation had other implications as well. In a supposedly classless society where, as we have seen, the upper crust was basically the bourgeoisie grown rich, money was the main if not the sole vehicle of social mobility. Class was as class spent; and so the tendency was to emulate "up." The idea was to stay at least abreast of economic peers while pretending to the style and usages of the class above—assuming there *was* a class above. A three-ring circus of waste and anxiety ensued: The wealthy, to impress each other, flaunted things they didn't need but could afford. Middle-class folks, trapped in a pattern of scrimp-and-splurge, decked their mantels with gimcracks they didn't need and couldn't afford. And the poor seethed in envy, exacerbating their material lacks by a humiliation that was partly self-inflicted.

"The pecuniary life" was thus a many-tiered pageant of folly featuring hierarchy without order, symbols without referents, a lavish mimicry posing as sophistication, and, much as in our own time, an idol of "success" that had to be known by its surface because no one ventured to guess what it might be made of underneath.

Veblen arrived at this dim view not by abstract thought but by a shrewd and merciless observation of the life going on around him—a life of gross inequality in which, for example, Andrew Carnegie's untaxed income was more than twenty thousand times as great as that of the average workingman, William K. Vanderbilt lived in a house with forty-five bathrooms and a garage for one hundred cars, and American moguls were pillaging the churches and piazzas of Europe, bringing home booty to bolster their imperial pretensions. Moreover, the 1890s, like the 1980s, were a period of plutography, when newspapers routinely published accounts of the banquets of the rich—published the *menus*—chronicling consumption down to the last bottle of Madeira and breast of canvasback duck. No small part of the pleasure of being wealthy was the knowledge that one would be publicly flattered for being so.

And how grandly flattered. In the 1890s, Darwin's theory of evolution—*The Origin of Species* had been published in 1859—was still a hot intellectual property. It had spawned all sorts of metaphors, framed a whole new way of looking at the world. One of its bastard offspring was called social Darwinism, a schema based on the notion that the marketplace was as legitimate a theater for the survival of the fittest as was the African savannah, and that the predatory pursuit of wealth and power was a fitting and even glorious aspect of the spectacle of life on earth. Social Darwinism flattered the wealthy in a way that makes all other flatteries seem niggling by comparison: it suggested that the rich were not merely winners by our ephemeral reckoning, but that they were on the cutting edge of evolution itself, carrying forward by their sanguineous drive and cunning the very possibilities of the race.

This, finally, was too much for Veblen. This was the point at which ordinary human vanity crossed the line into the bizarre. The dainty predacity of bankers standing in for the noble violence of tigers? The chicanery of corporation lawyers being equated with the graceful murderousness of hawks? No. As soon as competition was institutionalized, Veblen argued, it not only no longer served evolution but impeded it. In one of history's more breathtaking negations, he summed up the relationship between economic institutions and evolutionary advancement as follows: "What is, is wrong." Institutions were by their nature conservative, protective of the status quo. "The tendency of the pecuniary life," far from carrying humankind to new frontiers of ingenuity and dignity, "[was] to preserve the barbarian temperament" by rewarding what Veblen regarded as the less evolved traits of greed and aggressiveness.

As it was with the amassing of wealth, so it was with wealth's deployment—which brings us back to this curious business of "taste." The practitioners of conspicuous consumption might flatter themselves as being at the pinnacle of refinement, the very models of "civilized sensibility," yet they were, ultimately, slaves to ancient and primitive rituals of *more*. Folks had dressed to kill in Sumeria. There were influential show-offs in the age of Genghis Khan. Persian harlots wore their jewels in their belly buttons; the matrons of Newport pinned theirs to their bodices or hung them from their ears. How much difference was there? The captains of industry might one year favor sloops and the next year buy up steam yachts—rather as the 1980s well-to-do might one season flock to Porsche and next season go for the urban Jeep—but ultimately it all came down to the flaunting of wampum, to putting wealth in evidence. "Taste," in this version, came down to wampum. "Success," reckoned this way, came down to wampum. Fashionableness came down to wampum. The only problem was that wampum, that frail calculus of beads and shells, was never meant to bear the burden of so much desperate significance.

//// THREE

This is neither to deny nor knock the enjoyment that people have always gotten from their possessions. What people are buying, after all, once you get past the bare necessities, is the promise of pleasure, and insofar as there is real gratification to be derived from having things and appreciating their utility, beauty, and quality, amen to it.

But an odd thing seems to happen during periods when conspicuous consumption is in vogue. During those times people spend a great deal of money on things beyond the things they need. They invest, as well, a lot of caring, a lot of ego, a lot of anxious thought. And so they ask a lot—too much—of their possessions in return.

A certain line gets crossed. People look to their goods not just for pleasure but for meaning. They want their stuff to tell them who they are. They ask that inanimate things, mere objects, serve as stand-ins for momentous notions. Not just pretty flowers but a built-in serenity is taken to exist in the pattern of a Laura Ashley wallpaper. Not just style but stateliness of person is presumed to be made manifest by a Ralph Lauren blazer. "Taste" becomes a sort of cult by whose expensive magic such eminently human traits as sensuality, dignity, even humor are transubstantiated into consumer goods; and since those traits are taken to exist in such readily accessible and uncomplicated form on store shelves, there is less reason to search for them in other people or even in oneself. People disappear into their clothes. Their conversation becomes merely a part of the ambience of the restaurants they frequent. The pen they write with is taken to be more revealing than what they might scrawl.

Certainly this was true in the 1980s, a time when people pointed each other out as *the guy in the Armani jacket* or *the woman with the rose-colored Saab,* when "shopping [was] the unifying principle by which ... [some people] struc-ture[d their] days." Priorities, it seems fair to say, had gotten a little out of whack when a mother would tell "her tiny daughter shopping stories at bedtime," and a young girl, upon her religious confirmation, would choose for herself the name Imelda, as in Marcos, "patron saint of shoppers." Though perhaps this should not have seemed surprising at a time when 93 percent of teenage girls testified that store-hopping was their favorite activity, way ahead of dating, exercising, or even going to the movies.

Shopping, for some, had become a macabre detour in the otherwise unstylish quest to find oneself. Consider the "Sonia Sisters"—women who frequented designer Sonia Rykiel's boutique at Henri Bendel in Manhattan, and who, according to the floor manager there, "gradually ... be-c[a]me obsessed with acquiring all the right pieces" and took on a "spooky resemblance to one another." For them, the clothes became a sort of exoskeleton, which, as in the case of insects, was the sole protection and support of the gelatinous and trembling critter inside. When you bought "taste," you bought yourself a personality, and it was that, over and above the much-blabbed-about "quality" of the goods, which justified the price.

But what justified the price, say, of an eight-hundred-dollar pair of shoes? Nothing short of a fairy-tale magic presumably contained in them. That, at least, would seem to be the conclusion to be drawn from the comment of a salesperson at the ultra-expensive Susan Bennis/Warren Edwards store. "You can almost hear [the customers] think-ing," she said, "if I had those shoes, what wonderful things would happen to me?"

Well, what wonderful things *would* happen? Who knows? But chances are they would be things that gave a few more spins to the wheel of getting-and-spending-and-spending-and-getting. In the 1980s, one dressed for success so that one might earn more money (and/or latch on to someone who did) so that one could shop again for the accoutrements of success. If the process seemed to have no end-point, that was not by accident. Back in 1971, Charles Reich, in *The Greening of America,* had identified a dynamic he called "impoverishment by substitution." What consumer society tended to do, Reich argued, was to withhold such basic gratifications as a sense of purpose, of community, of simply being comfortable in one's skin, and to offer up in place of those things the whole glittering panoply of stuff that could be purchased. The impoverishment came from the fact that while feeding one's life on consumer goods might distract one from the more basic hungers, it could never really satisfy them—and the basic hungers didn't go away. If you tried to satisfy them on a diet of empty calories, it was hard to stop eating, notwithstanding the dim awareness that you were getting stuffed but not nourished.

Given that dynamic, it was not surprising that one of the 1980s' characteristic emotional maladies was "compulsive shopping"—a phrase that moved into widespread clinical use in 1984. Compulsive shopping was the flip side of money addiction—a dysfunction, so to speak, of the output mode rather than the input mode. There were people out there who literally shopped till they dropped, who spoiled their marriages, wrecked their finances, and occasionally committed felonies because they simply could not stop buying. There was the young woman who would "do anything" to get shopping money, and who hoarded skirts and blouses "until finally the rods in her closet came crashing down." There was the wife who resorted to the subterfuge of "slip[ping] dry cleaners' bags over her new clothes" so her husband wouldn't know she'd been binge-ing again. Not that compulsive shopping was the sole domain of women. Men might be less likely to go haywire over clothes, but there was no shortage of males who simply could not stay out of, for example, electronics stores, upgrading the three-thousand-dollar speakers to a five-thousand-dollar pair, whipping out the wallet-warm Visa card for a high-tech television with more dots in its screen.

Now here, at the societal as well as the individual level, was a situation that did not make a great deal of sense. You had billions of dollars being spent on advertising and promotion, encouraging just the sort of material competitiveness and display that Veblen had described almost a hundred years before. You had millions if not tens of millions of folks who had bought into the fashion of rabid consuming and who looked at spending money as perhaps the most consistently enjoyable thing they did. Yet, in sum, you had a situation that seemed neither to be making most people happy nor functioning in such a way as to promote the well-being of the system itself.

At the macro level, economists were bewailing high levels of personal debt and low levels of saving, claiming—and backing the claim with comparisons to Japan, West Germany, and Korea—that the pattern discouraged meaningful investment in new growth; more now, that is to say, meant less later. In 1986, around five dollars were owed for every dollar that was being saved in America, and interest payments alone—not counting mortgage interest—accounted for nearly as big a chunk of average household expenditures as did health care. Where was the pool of capital that would feed expansion?

If that pool wasn't where productive industry could get at it, it wasn't in the pockets of individuals, either—since individuals had used it, often before they actually *had* it, to buy stuff. This led to a number of unappetizing paradoxes. People bought for pleasure, then suffered the pain of debt, pain that often outlived the enjoyment of what they'd purchased. They indulged their "taste" for the "quality" of goods, only to find that those goods connected only incidentally with the quality of their lives. In buying whatever they felt like buying, people thought they were freely exercising their economic options, yet in fact they were hamstringing their options over time; future money was pre-allocated to past purchases, and the proportion of money already spoken for kept rising.

On the other hand, the Reagan "recovery," as has been argued, was basically a recovery in spending. It was a false euphoria, but in the near term it was better than no euphoria at all. Pull the plug on conspicuous consumption, and you pull the plug on the rebound. At the very least you short-circuit the rising numbers that were a balm to the habit of more.

So what was the "right" degree of acquisitiveness? What was the "healthy" level of craving stuff? Where did "responsible" and even patriotic spending—the sort that kept the machinery cranked up—cross the line into compulsive and repulsive shopping-mania?

That point was awfully difficult to locate. For one thing, as in the case of the money junkies, the cravings of the obsessive spenders were not foreign to the rest of us. 'Fess up—we all wanted the cashmere and the leather and the pewter and the oak; the out-of-control ones were just a notch or two more avid in their hankering.

Then there was the confusing tendency, as we have seen, to regard what is "healthy" in terms of what is "normal." What were taken to be "normal" spending patterns in America in the 1980s, however, probably hadn't seemed normal since Germany in the days of the Weimar Republic. In most other times and places, people went into hock in the face of catastrophe, not each time they wanted a new pair of boots. A virtually universal consumer indebtedness, in most times and places, would have signaled crisis. In America it was business as usual. Or usual, at least, at a time when people would give up almost anything—security, purpose, peace of mind—sooner than they would go without the things that came with price tags.

//" FOUR

If the border between healthy and pathological spending was hazy, the focus of the eighties buying spree was clear: prestige items at the high end of the market.

That focus was established as early as dreary 1981, when it could breezily be observed that, although inflation was 10.4 percent and almost 8.5 million people were unemployed, "there [was] no recession in the luxury market." In New York, "Russian sables starting at $40,000" were selling briskly, and in Texas, silk sheets were "being snapped up" at $1,500 a set. Leg of lion was being sold in Washington for $19.99 a pound, and in San Francisco, gold belts were moving well at $30,000. Neither excuses nor illusions were offered about the overall economic context in which this binge was taking place. It was reported, for example, that "in the Detroit area, where layoffs in the auto industry have led to an unemployment rate of 11.4 percent, luxury sales have never been better." What "you're seeing," commented one economist, is "the moderate and lower-income American going down the tubes, while other groups of households are doing well."

Under the selective umbrella of Reaganism, those "other groups of households" did even better as the decade progressed, and they seemed ever more intent on flaunting it. Between 1983 and 1984 alone, sales of stretch limousines doubled. As of 1977, the average age of a first-time fur coat owner was fifty; by 1987 it had tumbled to twenty-six. While overall sales of alcoholic beverages were flat, American consumption of French champagne increased by more than 50 percent between 1984 and 1986.

These trends were not wasted on marketers, who abruptly turned their attention away from the middle class—the hot sector since the fifties—and back toward the carriage trade.

Through the eighties, the most affluent consumers were pursued with a singlemindedness probably not seen since the institution of the progressive income tax. Thanks to the new device of zip-code marketing, promotion could be pinpointed toward wealthy neighborhoods; fat, splendiferous magazines crammed with ads for Belgian chocolates and German cars appeared free of charge in the mailboxes of the rich. Those on the statusy mailing lists were bombarded with catalogs hawking everything from gold-plated dumbbells at $1,500 to suits of armor at $3,800 and up. By 1985 it could be categorically stated that dealing in "luxury items and services put firms in the right niche."

But moving one $75,000 set of alligator luggage wasn't like moving a thousand seventy-five-dollar pieces of Samsonite. A different approach, a different psychology, pertained, and by 1986 this psychology was deemed of sufficient interest to warrant a primer on "the art of selling to the very rich." How did you go about cozying up to what the reporter N. R. Kleinfield identified as that "plentiful number of very wealthy, sometimes very young, Americans for whom a simple Cadillac [wouldn't] do and a Bloomingdale's gown [was] unthinkable"?

Curiously, perhaps, when the practitioners of this art were consulted, "taste" and "quality" were words that didn't come up very often in their expert analyses. The hot buttons, rather, seemed to be flattery, novelty, visibility, extremity.

"Wealthy individuals want . . . wacky stuff," said a designer of what he himself called "oddball limousines," cars that might feature, for example, a Jacuzzi and/or a putting green.

Said a representative of Bijan, the ultra-expensive men's designer: "Our customers, because they're rich, famous, powerful, don't need anything. . . . So [we] have to impress them . . . by that brass railing with no fingerprints on it."

The founder of a high-end cruise line averred that his marketing breakthrough consisted in the realizations that "the rich didn't like mingling with ordinary people," and that if passengers requested, say, accordion-style drinking straws to sip champagne through, "you don't ask questions, you just give them what they want."

The head of the North American Watch Company, whose top-of-the-line Piaget retailed for three million bucks, bluntly acknowledged that people bought his doodad not for its presumed excellence but "to show their station in life." Asked why he spent half a million dollars a year to sponsor two polo teams, he responded, "When you have the most expensive product . . . you have to approach . . . people more intellectually."

Non-polo players might perhaps be excused for not recognizing polo as primarily a cerebral activity, or for imagining that the game's intellectual burden fell mainly on the horses. But then, money, in the 1980s, was presumed to indicate sexiness, athleticism, dignity—why not throw in intellect as well? For that matter, why not just categorically define money as *everything good,* and stop messing around with small distinctions?

In a sense, that is precisely what eighties social fashion did. For all the nattering about taste and discrimination, what pertained, in fact, was an auctioneer's sort of sensibility, a sensibility that had no choice but to ascribe all good qualities to anything expensive. *Top-of-the-lineness* was the operative criterion, whether the object in question was a space-station Hamptons dune house, or a ballroom-sized Boukhara rug. On the surface, eighties taste appeared eclectic, since it embraced such seemingly disparate elements as "the man's diamond"—which de Beers was trying to rehabilitate from its long-standing association with pimps and mobsters—and old Bordeaux wines, a newly widespread fancy for which had driven prices through the roof. In fact, though, eighties taste was not eclectic at all; it had a well-defined and even tyrannical framework based not on style but cost. Consider: the sixties had Pop, which reveled in the ironic use of inexpensive, kitschy artifacts from mass culture; the seventies had cheap chic, with its Fruit of the Loom T-shirts and its five-and-dime-store tennis shoes. Can you think of *one* inexpensive thing that was fashionable in the 1980s?

With price as nearly the sole signifying measure by which various objects were judged, eighties taste came near to being a perfectly airtight system, a code with references only to itself. Yet there were two small glitches, two places where the seams showed.

The first flaw had to do with confidence. If an awareness of what things cost supposedly sufficed to indicate sophistication and security, why did people so often seem to be trying a bit too hard? Multi-carat gemstone rings replacing simple wedding bands; irreplaceable vintages being quaffed on occasions where six-dollar Beaujolais would really have done better—this was just bad form.

The second flaw was more depressing: eighties taste seemed to peter out precipitously as soon as you left the shopping mall and entered the realm of the museum, the library, the concert hall. It was as if people had used up their whole stock of discernment on the all-important question of their purchases, and had no discrimination left. The brainless, stupid books read between the satin sheets in the silk pajamas; the appalling music played through the thirty-thousand-dollar sound systems; the jewels worn to the opera where no one knew or cared to know the opera: these were evidence of a great canniness as to who was who, combined with a remarkable ignorance of, and indifference to, what was what.

This sort of taste, of course, was nothing new. It was the taste of the *arriviste,* and it had existed in Thorstein Veblen's time, as well as in many times and places before. It tended to flower during periods of social disarray—times when a sense of shared purpose was absent, when a meaningful consensus as to the content of a well-lived life was missing, and people, quietly desperate to figure out where they stood, looked to noisy sorts of display to tell them.

⫻ FIVE

In 1980s America, most people were getting function-ally poorer, the middle class was splintering, there was be-ginning to be a broad suspicion that the system was well past its peak, and the *arriviste* was being hailed as "a patriot."

This actually made perfect sense if you considered not the substance but the symbol. It didn't matter that the new fortunes, as in the case of the corporate raiders and greenmailers, tended to come at the expense of other people's jobs or stockholders' interests, or, as in the case of certain real-estate developers, that they cost some people their homes, neighborhoods, or small businesses. More important, apparently, was the vicarious pick-me-up the new rich provided in "demonstrat[ing] what we all want[ed] to believe—that America is indeed the Land of Opportunity." Maybe it was no longer the land of opportunity for *most;* second chances were growing rarer, and maybe opportunity was becoming something more in the nature of a spectator sport. Still, it was reassuring to see that not everyone in America was getting hammered by changed circumstances, that some people could still wring princely rewards from the system. Nouveau riche, far from being an insult, had now become "a compliment, a testimony to one's genius."

Since gobs of money were taken to suggest both patrio-tism and brilliance, it followed, as the financier Felix Rohatyn observed, that sufficient wealth could now "buy social status immediately." In this regard, it should be understood, the 1980s were far more gilded, far more mercenary, far more narrowly defined by bucks, than even Veblen's Gilded Age.

In the 1890s, only nine of the ninety richest men in America were thought classy enough to be included in Lady Astor's Four Hundred. In the 1980s, the "Four Hundred" that the broader public chose to fawn on—the list compiled by *Forbes*—*were* the four hundred richest. Personal wealth was the only measure. "Class" had nothing to do with it. And this had real implications for the tenor of the time. Remember the trickle-down theory? Well, as it turned out, wealth did not trickle down very far, but manners and morals did. And *arriviste* manners and morals, like *arriviste* taste, were not especially pretty.

The hegemony of old money—old, that is, by American standards—had hardly been the best of all worlds, but it did have certain things to recommend it. To old money, it was axiomatic that wealth carried with it responsibility; the word, so thoroughly out of fashion now, was *stewardship*. Old money fostered an ethic of service—an ethic that *new* money tended not to have time for. It harbored the idea of giving something back—a notion that didn't quite compute with those still actively amassing their fortunes.

Old money promoted a code of decency that held, according to the writer Holly Brubach, "that the haves are in some way beholden to the have-nots ... [that] moderation was more becoming than lavish trappings ... [and that] publicly reveling in one's wealth ... [was] vulgar. ... There used to be the admonition, so self-evident that it rarely needed explaining, that to go about advertising the vast extent of one's wealth to people who were not as well off was arrogant and rude."

That admonition, of course, presupposed that arrogance and rudeness were bad, but under the hegemony of *new* money, it was not so clear they were. People still *said* arrogance and rudeness were bad, but in practice they could be pretty handy social tools: what simpler way to demonstrate that one could afford to offend people? What neater shorthand for announcing that one had moved into a higher sphere, where one could not be got even with? A "high society" centered on the newly rich didn't do away with snobbery and a penchant for exclusion. Hardly. With money standing as the sole criterion for who would get past the red velvet rope, it was more crucial than ever that one's credentials were in order; wealth and power, as Veblen phrased it, had to be put in evidence. A simple gesture like leaving the Mercedes double-parked on Rodeo Drive while the liveried chauffeur ran in for the packages and other traffic had to go around had a pleasant shoring-up effect on one's self-importance.

Though perhaps the eighties' most characteristic and most pernicious form of arrogance was arrogance-by-omission, rudeness-by-declining-to-recognize.

In 1962, the novelist Ralph Ellison wrote a book called *Invisible Man.* The title came from Ellison's contention that the humiliating and enraging thing about being black in America was not so much that white folks treated you badly, as that they acted as if you weren't there at all. Well, through the 1980s, something like that was coming to be the situation of Americans of any color who were outside the top echelons of consumption.

In 1986 it was observed in *Fortune* that "in the metaphysics of the market, only those who buy and sell truly exist." And as the market became ever more narrowly defined by its top end—that is to say, the more tyrannically entrenched eighties "taste" became—the closer to nonexistence came anyone who couldn't spring for the choice labels and the choice materials: the "quality" goods. Retailers no longer courted that customer. Service people didn't particularly care about his trade. Magazines didn't even want his subscription, as it watered down their demographics. To those whose business was *more,* the people who had less simply didn't matter. By the metaphysics of the market, the little guy could drop dead.

Not that the typical "moderate and lower-income American" was barred altogether from enjoying the eighties spectacle of the consumption of new wealth. He could watch it on television. In the splendor and unchastened excess of the Ewings, the Carringtons, the Colbys, the average joe and the average joanne could glimpse the intoxicating richness of a life in which people solicitously asked each other if they were enjoying their caviar, in which handsome patriarchs asked to have the limo, not the car, brought round, and in which women wore strapless gowns to brunch.

That the prime-time soap operas offered up an imbecilic parody of what it meant to be wealthy was widely acknowledged; but then, being wealthy was getting to be a parody of what it meant to be wealthy. Perhaps the capping silliness of eighties taste, in fact, was that real-life rich people—people who'd gotten wealthy so fast that they hadn't had time to learn the social graces—studied television to learn how the rich should act. Life imitated art, except the art was the hack work of scriptwriters who no doubt regarded the whole well-paying business as a hilarious exercise in intellectual slumming.

Less hilarious, however, was the stance of the non-wealthy in regard to these circuses of conspicuous money. Theirs was a nose-against-the-windowpane perspective on a scene that was a stage set to begin with: a fantasy of a fantasy. Those who could not spend in accordance with what in the 1980s passed for a fitting lavishness were at a double remove from what used to be called the American Dream; and they seemed to be getting more distanced from it all the time.

9 ///

The War Between Life and Lifestyle

/// ONE

The American Dream was not the only good thing to be shut away behind the glass of storefronts and television screens in the 1980s. Something even more basic was being distanced, repackaged, made into something to be looked at rather than embraced.

It was called life.

Or rather, it used to be called life, until people began realizing you could charge more for it if you called it "lifestyle."

But what was lifestyle, exactly? The word did not appear at all in *The Random House Dictionary,* 1966 edition. Nor was it listed in the 1971 version of *The Oxford English Dictionary.* Webster's *Third New International,* 1976, noted the term's existence but did not bother to define it, merely sending the reader from "life" to "style," leaving him to infer the composite meaning for himself.

Not until 1980, fittingly enough, did the word seem to be regarded as worthy of the efforts of lexicographers. In that year the updated *Random House College Dictionary* described *lifestyle* as "a person's typical approach to living, including his moral attitudes, preferred entertainments, fads, fashions, etc." In 1981 the *Grolier International Dictionary* defined the word as "an internally consistent way of life ... that reflects ... attitudes and values." In 1983 *Webster's Ninth New Collegiate* more flatly described *lifestyle* as "the typical way of life of an individual, group, or culture"; it also gave the date of the term's coinage—incorrectly—as 1946.

Now, the dictionaries did more than simply trace the entry of "lifestyle" into common usage. They also hinted at a shift in the meaning of the term—really a drain on its meaning—that seemed to be happening from year to year. Consider: in 1980, "moral attitudes" had been the first-listed component of lifestyle; lifestyle, went the inference, flowed from those attitudes. That primacy no longer pertained in the 1981 definition, though "values" were at least "reflect[ed]" in a lifestyle's patterns. But what had happened by 1983? By 1983, lifestyle was being simply, noncommittally, defined as a "typical way of life." Maybe it had to do with values, maybe it didn't. Maybe it flowed from moral attitudes, maybe it was just a collection of "fads, fashions, etc." Like "success," like "taste," like "quality," the word *lifestyle* was being defined ever more narrowly by what showed on the surface. Why make judgments as to what was, or wasn't, underneath?

Evidence of this devolution in meaning could be seen in other places as well. Between 1978 and 1983, if you looked up *lifestyle* in the *Reader's Guide to Periodical Literature,* you would be referred to the rubric Conduct of Life. *Conduct of life*—this was a phrase with some guts and some grandeur to it. It suggested active choice on things that mattered. The category, in turn, was subdivided into such value-laden sections as Altruism and Public Service, along with basic areas of commitment like Marriage and Education.

As of 1984, *lifestyle* was no longer cross-referenced that way. The term became a heading unto itself, and it no longer seemed to cover the sort of issues that defined the moral texture and quality of a life. Now it served as an umbrella for articles about decorating, vacations, garden parties, skirt lengths, time-share condos, Dove Bars, the return of the debutante, and Tofutti.

What was happening, essentially, was that the two components of the term *lifestyle* were having a nasty little war, and style was winning it. Mere life—life unadorned by trends and purchases—was losing ground. How much could you say about mere life, after all? Life was what it had always been, a matter of work and ambivalence and suffering and occasional deep joy. Style, on the other hand, was a great deal more diverting. It changed almost every day. *Nouvelle* went out, *bistro* came in, black clothes were hot, marijuana was not. Style flickered by about as fast as you could flip the pages of a glossy magazine, and it provided the illusion that consumption was always interesting and that a progression, if not progress, was taking place.

That lifestyle was coming to be identified with the superficial and the ephemeral was ironic, however, because the term had been invented to denote precisely the opposite.

It was coined in 1929, by the psychiatrist Alfred Adler. Alder had broken with Freud, his teacher, over the latter's insistence that early childhood traumas left a person psychologically scarred forever. For Adler, this notion was too deterministic and too bleak; why go through all the sweat and strain of becoming a responsible adult if the early damage could never be undone? No, the Freudian schema left too small a role for insight and for courage; it allotted an insufficient payoff in the struggle to live well and truly.

Adler argued, therefore, that while a person could never erase the hurts of infancy and toddlerhood, he or she could transcend them through the vehicle of lifestyle—defined, broadly, as the sum total of values, passions, knowledge, meaningful deeds, and eccentricities that constituted a person's uniqueness. Lifestyle, in Adler's usage, was as individual as breath and went as deep as bone. It was also momentous, comprising nothing less than a person's vision of how to make peace with a sometimes intransigent world.

Until the 1960s, the word *lifestyle* was seldom heard outside the psychoanalytic ghetto. Then, curiously, when the term began to be used in a nonclinical sense, it tended to be applied only to people whose behavior digressed from the norm. You didn't have a lifestyle unless it was an "alternative lifestyle." You might have a "gay lifestyle" or a "hippie lifestyle," but you wouldn't have an "average middle-class heterosexual white person's lifestyle."

The implications of this usage seemed to be two-edged. On one side, America was not ready simply to let different-ness slide by uncommented upon; yet a somewhat forced tolerance was the order of the day. One was supposed to be benign, and expressing differences in terms of lifestyle had a benign ring to it. It suggested that these " 'others' who seemed so alien were presumably living lives like the rest of us"; only the trim, so to speak, was different.

In fact, that was not quite true, nor was the impulse toward putting it that way really all that tolerant. It smacked a little of some-of-my-best-friends-are-black/gay/Jewish/ radical. "Lifestyle" differences, in gut matters like sex, race, religion, and politics, mattered plenty, and the greater moral challenge lay not in trying to make the differences safe by downplaying them, but in meeting them eyeball to eyeball. In any case, the point is that, while lifestyle was already being watered down from Adler's all-embracing meaning, it was still seen as having to do with basic choices as to how one would live.

It wasn't until the 1980s that lifestyle became primarily if not exclusively a function of what one bought.

Living the "active lifestyle" in the eighties, for example, didn't necessarily mean a person was active, but that he or she purchased "active wear." The "executive lifestyle" didn't necessarily have anything to do with being an executive, but with buying a lot of airline tickets and putting a lot of meals on a credit card. Lifestyle still had to do with choices, but now the choices were whether one would own or lease a car, buy fresh or frozen orange juice, velvet drapes or vertical blinds, cotton or polyester shirts. As taste was being reduced to a knowledge of what things cost, so lifestyle, formerly a map of one's adjustment to the world, was coming down to questions of where one scrimped and where one splurged. The word, by mid-decade, had become "the property of mass-marketing."

Lifestyle, it was beginning to be noticed, was not only a descriptive tool but could be used as a predictive one: tell us what a person's lifestyle is—or what he likes to think it is—and we will tell you what that person will buy. That this formulation should have come about just at the time when "targeting"—the zeroing-in on a select bloc of potential customers—had become the marketing strategy of choice, provided a windfall for those social scientists and consultants who'd had the foresight to set up shop as "lifestyle experts." Targeting by lifestyle, after all, was a subtler process than targeting by the old demographic categories of age, education level, or household income. It required interpretive savvy and was a job for specialists.

Prominent among these were the members of a California research group called SRI International, who, in 1978, had launched a massive social-trends study called Values and Lifestyles—VALS for short. In 1983, the study bore fruit in the form of the book *The Nine American Lifestyles,* and by 1984 more than 150 business concerns were paying up to thirty thousand dollars each for the benefits of SRI's data and advice.

Now, the substance of the SRI study need not concern us here. In broad outline, however, the evolution of that project provides a concise illustration of what happened to lifestyle once the notion entered the parlance of the marketplace.

First of all, what had become of the "values" that had been part of the original SRI study but had somehow vanished from the title of the book? Typically, that element, with its troublesome abstraction and potentially subversive hint that maybe human behavior couldn't, or shouldn't, be reduced to consumer choices, had been purged. On the other hand, one could not but admire the precision with which the experts had determined that there were neither eight lifestyles nor ten, but nine. Silly old Adler had believed there were as many lifestyles as there were people trying to make their way decently through the universe; *he* would never have cut it in marketing, where the aim was not the celebration of individuality but the divvying up of humankind into identifiable blocs of disposable income. In the hands of the marketers, lifestyle, "once an expression of tolerance and respect for idiosyncrasy ... [became] a rhetorical slug more evocative of conformity."

Moreover, once the lifestyle-grouping habit spilled over into popular usage, there were virtually no limits to its power to stereotype. Whether they liked it or not, people who bought condos were now presumed to be "living the condo lifestyle." It was presumed, further, that they would resemble, or at the very least fit in with, others who had also bought condos. On the other hand, those who lived the "second-home lifestyle" probably wouldn't have a great deal to say to those who led the "RV lifestyle," much less to those who followed the "day-trip lifestyle." Those who enjoyed the "skiing lifestyle" were clearly differentiable from those who led the "bowling lifestyle." Lifestyle, that is to say, was coming to be an acceptable back-door euphemism for the word that could not be spoken in America: class. And the things one bought to define one's lifestyle were becoming tokens that made it ever clearer who was in a given club and who was not.

As lifestyle came to be defined ever more narrowly as a function of spending patterns, the word's relation to life itself—life beyond the marketplace—became so tenuous as almost to disappear. "Moral attitudes" had been squeezed out even as connotations of the term; "values" had apparently fallen out of the bag on the way to the cash register. Lifestyle had less and less to do with what one thought or believed or felt or was. By the final years of the 1980s it could be said that lifestyle was to life as Hamburger Helper was to hamburger. It was the package without the meat, a dead product trying to market its way into animation. It was a boxful of contrived ingredients standing in for something that used to be made of blood and muscle.

/// **TWO**

This leaching out of the meaning of lifestyle was more than just a philological accident. It had causes and it had consequences.

Some of the causes have already been suggested here: the

hoarding impulse that kicked in when the hunger for more collided with the realization that *more* was getting harder to come by; the new insecurity of the middle class, which made people scramble to preserve the appearance that they were moving up, not down; the materialism that necessarily went with a definition of success that centered not on accomplishment but on reward; the readiness, at a time when business was fashionable, to adopt the priorities and the jargon that the business world proposed.

As to the consequences, one aspect of them was neatly summarized in a 1987 *New Yorker* cartoon.

A youngish man in shorts, sneakers, and visor cap is leaning back against his convertible sports car. At his side is a tennis racquet and a can of balls. In the passenger seat, a woman wearing sunglasses and a big straw hat gives forth a broad and self-contented smile. A palm tree and what appears to be a luxury high-rise loom in the background; in the distance, boats are going by. The fellow is talking to another racquet-toting couple in sunglasses, and his face is slightly troubled—though less troubled than it ought to be, considering what he is saying: "I despise my life, but I'm in love with my life style."

This was perhaps the perfect statement of a quintessential eighties bind—the conflict, almost never openly acknowledged and perhaps seldom even recognized, between a well-accoutered and seemingly "successful" image, and a self that was not the least bit satisfied thereby. Unhappiness seeped in from the edges where lifestyle left off—and lifestyle, like eighties taste, always left off somewhere. When it did, it threw a person back onto the sort of inner resources that too often had gone undeveloped. Lifestyle was fine as long as the stores were open, as long as the restaurants were serving, as long as there was someplace to go in the car. But how about when there wasn't? In even the most assiduously "styled" life, there'd be times when there was no stuff and no activities to hide behind, times when you'd be doing nothing naked. That's when life itself would rear up and demand to be recognized, awful in its unembellishment and as jarring as a sudden face in a nighttime window.

In the war between life and lifestyle, lifestyle's strategy was to stave off that recognition as long as possible. The trick was to keep life so well dressed and entertained, so encrusted with nice things, that it would cease to know itself—or would even come to despise itself—without them. Lifestyle advanced by substituting false needs for true ones, and it conquered, finally, by making of itself not a set of chosen pleasures but an addiction.

/// THREE

Addiction, as we have argued, is a dangerous metaphor, a metaphor that spews blame in all directions. Still, how else can one characterize such late-eighties phenomena as "feeling poor on $600,000 a year"?

This, according to *The New York Times,* was the dilemma of a certain group of financial professionals who had "sort of reduced [them]selves to an equation where net worth equals self-worth," and who had bought into a lifestyle whose customs and demands were nearly as rigorous and expensive as life at a royal court. These people *had* to live in certain neighborhoods, *had* to send their children to certain schools, *had* to eat in certain restaurants, *had* to vacation on certain islands. Except by climbing to what was, by the brittle consensus of their own circle, the very pinnacle of the lifestyle pyramid, they had no way of determining how they were doing. They had no other standard of value; they had no other life.

By all the fashionable criteria of the eighties, these people were winners. They had hot jobs, they made big money, the media sought them out. Yet it seems clear that their "feeling poor" was not simply an economic matter, but had to do with less quantifiable deprivations as well. They were hungry for something, hurting for something. But what was it that was being withheld from them?

In part, it was a sense of the purpose of their work, a satisfactory grasp of the end result of their talent and their brains. If they couldn't *see* the end result, then their blustery confidence turned fragile. For bankers and brokers especially, but also for tens of millions of others who worked in the service-and-information economy, work was becoming ever more abstract. People did not "save lives or . . . produce spark plugs or house paint." Talking on the telephone, making entries in a computer, they dealt increasingly in wealth *as such.*

Working at this level of abstraction could be highly efficient—it eliminated the step between product and profit, since profit *was* the product—and if you were in the right spot it could make you quite rich quite fast. But the streamlining did not come without a cost. It left some riddles dangling. What did all that abstract money represent, if not the reward for actually creating value? What, finally, determined the worth of a day's work, if not the beauty or usefulness of something you could hold in your hand?

These were questions that could not readily be answered in terms of life—life, that is, outside the marketplace. They could only be answered in terms of lifestyle, because lifestyle and the marketplace, so to speak, were family. They shared a certain viewpoint, a certain hothouse logic. What did the money represent? It represented the ability to buy stuff, the ability to fly first class. What was the value of a day's work? Exactly what the marketplace would pay for it, not

one penny more or less. By definition. Lifestyle thus provided modern, pragmatic, easy answers to the difficult
questions raised by life, and so people found it convenient
to dodge the demands of the latter by immersing themselves
in the prerogatives of the former.

Easy answers, however, are seldom final answers, and the
mere embracing of lifestyle didn't settle the issue. When did
you have *enough* lifestyle? Never—because the object of the
exercise was not to meet this or that goal, but to stay abreast
of whatever was going on. Whatever was going on, meanwhile, kept getting more expensive. In keeping with Veblen's idea of emulation, people had a way of "chasing the
same things," and therefore driving up prices on "co-ops,
houses in Southampton, art ... [apartments] in Aspen."
People liked to think that, as they got wealthier and
participated in a more rarefied segment of the market, they
would do their business in a more discreet and dignified
atmosphere: the hushed showrooms of Cartier rather than
the crush of Joe's Jewelers. In fact, however, the operative
model of the high-end lifestylers was not the boutique but
the auction, in which the pace was frenzied, the spending
unabashedly competitive, and where the object was not
simply to get the desired item but to knock the other son of
a bitch out of the bidding.

This emulative element of lifestyle, in turn, let the air out
of one of the 1980s' biggest and most convenient lies: that
money equaled freedom.

Just as people invoked "quality" when they were really
talking about price, so they invoked "freedom" when what
they really meant was privilege. Freedom sounded so much
better, after all, and it could be applied to almost anything.
A desire, say, for a very expensive pair of cufflinks might
seem petty, even crass, whereas reveling in the freedom to
go into the store to buy the cufflinks seemed more in the

spirit of 1776. It was as if, in America, if you could portray your greed as a greed for liberty, it wouldn't count as greed at all.

Liberty, however, is not a category that shows up under the rubric of Lifestyle. Privilege is. Privilege is a marketplace idea, a comparative notion. One is always more privileged or less privileged, relative to someone else. Freedom doesn't work that way. One does not compete at being true to oneself; if you're worrying about what the next guy is doing, you've given up your freedom before you start.

The people who felt poor on $600,000 a year were leading a very privileged lifestyle that wasn't a free life at all. They weren't free to work less. They weren't free to work *more* at something they might like better but would pay them less. They weren't even really free to buy what they wanted, since the sort of things that went with their lifestyle constituted a rather narrow and conventionalized catalog, a menu of luxurious clichés. They were stuck with the Baccarat, the beluga, and the black-tie Saturday evenings, and they couldn't give them up without, God forbid, seeming to be slipping. True to the wisdom of the Chinese curse, there were people whose hard fate it was to have gotten what they wished for.

⫻ FOUR

Not that you had to be a millionaire to qualify as a casualty in the war between life and lifestyle.

The battle was being waged in the heart, mind, and bank account of every man and woman who had to make trade-offs between self-chosen goals and social fashions, between following a star and following a trend. Though the choice, of course, was seldom so clear. In fact, probably the most common injury in the war between life and lifestyle was a sort of numbness, a paralysis of will, in the grip of which one truly didn't *know* if one was choosing for oneself or simply being swept along, if one wanted certain things because of a real conviction that they would enhance one's life or because one was slavishly following the conventions of the day.

Consider the extreme but not atypical tale of "the woman with $1,200 worth of pots and pans in her kitchen who [ate] every meal in a restaurant." This woman, it seems fair to say, was a little benumbed, a little confused. Presumably she loved to cook, and presumably derived from cooking the sort of intimate satisfaction that is very much in the province of life. Yet the demands of lifestyle—and not, as in the recent past, of gender politics—barred her from her own kitchen.

First there was the New Work Ethic, to which she had to cleave in order to spring for the French copper in the first place. This ethic, as we will argue, had less to do with actually accomplishing anything than with arriving at a visible and socially approved state of exhaustion; there was little energy for slicing and dicing at the end of the day. Then there was the lure of the bistros and the trattorias, the shrines of the "new pastime of 'competitive eating.' " Restaurants were culture in the 1980s, and not to go to them made one culturally deprived. The bottom line seemed to be that you broke your butt in order to afford things—like wonderful cookware—you would then not have leisure to enjoy; and so you substituted for them *different* things—like eating in nice restaurants—that were pleasant enough, but were less personal, less creative, less your own.

The war between lifestyle and life, as this suggests, often boiled down to the conflict between money and time. There simply weren't enough hours in the day to earn a living *and* go to the health club *and* do the shopping *and* eat the mahi-mahi *and* dabble in the kitchen or the workshop or at the keyboard or the easel. Something had to go.

What went? Increasingly through the eighties, what went were the things that took time without, on the one hand, making money, or on the other hand, costing money in ways that conferred status. Things like friendship. Things like romance. Things like sitting around doing nothing, except maybe looking out the window. Private things whose value you alone determined.

Given the tendency of human beings to try to make virtue out of fashion, there was a fair amount of rhetoric during the decade to the effect that this was not simply how things were, but how they ought to be. One avid young lifestyler, purportedly speaking for his friends and colleagues, ticked off the things "we're willing to perhaps sacrifice," as if these sacrifices were evidence of great self-discipline, maturity, and character: "marriage, families, free time, relaxation." The suggestion, apparently, was that those things were mere fripperies being renounced in favor of some higher aim. But what *was* the higher aim? What could *be* the higher aim? Buying an apartment? Getting a raise? Eating in more restaurants?

Values, it seems clear, had gotten exuberantly out of whack, and it didn't take the stock market crash to plant the notion that a reconsideration was coming due. Already in 1984, it had been predicted that the not-too-distant future would give rise to "the biggest wave of midcareer crises this nation has ever seen," as people reassessed the relative worth of what they had seized and what they had let slip. Spearheaded by the noisy and number-dominant members of the baby boom, that reassessment, moreover, was not likely to be a subtle, well-behaved affair, but would be entered into "with the same flamboyance with which [many of these same people had] bec[o]me hippies and Yuppies."

Seventy million relatively young adults, give or take a few, coming to yet another collective shift of consciousness? The prediction, even if just *slightly* true, even if true for three people out of a hundred, was both unsettling and bracing. Such a broad rethinking of what was worth it would bring about a ferment carrying with it both turmoil and a whiff of redemption. What, after all, was a midcareer or midlife crisis, if not the plain and ancient claims of life finally asserting themselves against the frilly and relentless demands of lifestyle?

FIVE

The question that still gnaws, though, is how had lifestyle, through the eighties, come to seem more important than life in the first place? How had money become more valuable than time; how had the tokens of success come to seem more crucial than truly choosing one's own future?

The answer, paradoxically, would seem to be that money *didn't* become more important in the eighties. Other things were allowed to become less so. And this is what accounted for the decade's particular form of impoverishment, its blandness and vacuity.

Consider, as one example, the idea of service. It used to be believed that giving something back to the community—something in the form of time and sweat, rather than a check—was important, a substantial element in a balanced and well-led life. It broadened one's sympathies while making one more appreciative of one's own good fortune. In the eighties, community service seemed to be thought of as something you did in place of jail time if convicted of a white-collar crime. What should have been regarded as a life-affirming privilege was viewed now as a penance.

Or take the notion of personal development. In the sixties

and seventies, the self was seen as an evolving and elastic entity, clay to be shaped and reshaped. Making a fetish of personal growth, of course, could and sometimes did lead to excess and absurdity; but the impulse itself was founded on some pretty good ideas—the idea that study was a lifelong activity, the idea that there *was* such a thing as spiritual development, and that the quest for it didn't end on the day you finished *Siddhartha.* In the eighties, personal development became, literally, a matter of silhouette, the outline of one's flesh in the mirrors of the aerobics room. There was muscular development and there was career development. Development of what might quaintly be called the inner person was allowed to slip into unimportance. Nobody could see the inner person, after all.

Then there was the hoary old concept of national purpose, with its power to give meaning and coherence to the lives of individuals. That idea, too, seemed to become unimportant in the eighties—and this was strange, because the case could be made that America now had a clearer and more pressing mission than at any time since the depths of the Cold War: to accept with grace the obvious truth that our economic hegemony was over, and to move with dignity, realism, and alertness into a changed world where nations would deal more closely as equals—and where individuals would learn the knack of being content with what they had.

The business rah-rahs wouldn't put it that way, of course, any more than would the politicians. They'd rather yammer about America coming back and about the stockpiles of more being endlessly replenished. But that wasn't purpose, it was nostalgia, and while it sounded patriotic, it in fact derived from an unadmitted spasm of national self-blame: We must have lost the ancient virtues if these other countries have caught up to us, if our standard of living has leveled. Rather than cultivating *new* virtues that would serve us better, we should mortify ourselves by bearing down all the more narrowly on precisely those things that weren't working.

This, finally, was the oddest thing of all about the 1980s—the decade's perverse insistence on making obsessions of precisely those things that were causing people to be anxious, unhappy, fretful. Like a kid sucking at a loose tooth, people just couldn't turn their attention away from the part that was bleeding.

Money worries were driving people crazy, and so it was decided that money was the measure of all things. Business was getting leaner, meaner, harder to break into and easier to fall out of, and so by consensus business became the worthwhile arena. The financial sector was letting the country down, and so it came to be imagined that the financial sector *was* the country.

At the same time that the nervous-making things were being exalted, the things that might have provided some perspective or relief were being ignored. Introspection, for example, was utterly out of fashion, as if it had been introspection, rather than active greed, that had put a sickly cast on everything from Wall Street to college basketball. The choice *not* to strive was seen as totally unacceptable, although it was the addiction to more, and not the willingness to have less, that was discredited by dicey circumstances. "Failure" was anathema, a word people could barely bring themselves to say. But it wasn't the "failure" of those who let the allure of fast times pass them by that contributed to a widening and demoralizing inequality; it was the "success" of those who grabbed on.

And it wasn't too much life that had led to a situation where values were unmoored, intimate choices were dictated by social fashion, and people too often couldn't figure out why they were chasing what they were chasing. It was too much lifestyle.

Part III

BEYOND
THE WISDOM
OF THE
MARKETPLACE

Civilization and the graces of life flourish best
where there are dedicated and intelligent
people . . . who prefer dignity, fame,
authority, prestige or ease of
conscience to mere money.

—Luigi Barzini

10 ///

The
Jargon
of Active
Choice

/// ONE

"Is it because of the baby?" asked Sally Collier's soon-to-be-former boss, pointing at her belly.

"Yes and no," she said.

"Because if it is," he went on, "there are things we can do. We can always stretch things. Some extra leave. Assignments close to home. We'll try to work with you."

"I appreciate that, Bob," said Sally. "I really do. But it isn't just the baby."

"Well, what is it then?"

Sally, of course, had an answer rehearsed. She'd talked it over with Benno, with friends, with colleagues. A strange process, talking over a big decision with a range of people. What everyone told you, really, was what they wished *they* were doing, and their reasons partly became your own. You borrowed a smart-sounding explanation from one person and a good excuse from someone else, and before you knew it you had an edifice of logic supporting what you plain and simple wanted from the start. Sally cleared her throat and, from habit, moved to cross her legs. She kept forgetting they wouldn't cross. She chucked the airtight answer. "Bob, this used to be a great job."

"Yes, it was," he said. A veteran of twenty-four years at the network, Bob Edwards had been through much of the development of television news and television politics, been through the days of wild growth and lavish spending, as well as the days of takeovers and cutbacks and the stomachache Fridays of telling people they were fired. He was not what you'd call a company man, and yet he had a personal code, unusual in the media, that said you didn't badmouth the people who paid your salary. On occasion he bit the inside of his lip until he tasted blood.

"It's still a *good* job," said Sally. "Relative, I mean, to other jobs. But, Bob, I've been here since college. Since I was a kid. I mean, sure, having the baby is part of it—I'm seven months and I'm feeling all the standard instincts. But I was getting antsy before. I really think free-lancing is the way I want to go."

Edwards swiveled in his chair, looked out the window at the lean stone fortress of Rockefeller Center. Up until a couple of years ago, if an employee he didn't want to lose talked to him about free-lancing, he'd give that person the security pitch. *Think about what you're giving up,* he'd say. *I don't just mean the paycheck; I mean the chance to grow with the job.* That argument had broken down, of course, and not just at the networks. It used to be that the really terrible people got fired, the really great ones moved up very fast or quit, and the great majority in the middle stayed on track. Now the firings and the quittings just seemed to sort of happen. Am I getting inattentive, Edwards wondered, or is it true that things are getting more random?

"I think I really decided during the strike," said Sally, calling him back from the view. "The strike was the first time since I was twenty-two that I'd wake up in the morning and not know what I was doing that day. It reminded me of school vacations or of my first few months in New York, before I got hired. It was a feeling I'd almost forgotten: you wake up and there's a kind of anxiety. You don't want to *admit* it's anxiety, because we all like to imagine we're so resourceful and there's so much we'd love to do if we only had the time. But face it, it makes you nervous. So I'd have some coffee, look at *Today,* and then I'd have to decide, for myself, right then, what I wanted to do. Go out? Not go out? See people? Be alone? Read? Write? Find some little project around the house? It was a challenge. More of a challenge than the job has gotten to be. And it was satisfying. Just seeing what would happen next was satisfying. And that's why I don't want to work full-time anymore."

"I understand," Bob Edwards said. "And with Benno doing so well . . ."

Sally Collier stiffened slightly and scanned her boss's face. Was he getting in a last little dig, airing his resentment that some people had the prerogative of leaving and others apparently did not? He looked tired, grayish around the eyes, older somehow than she'd noticed before, and she decided not to take offense. "Just for the record, Bob," she said, "Benno isn't doing well at all just now."

/// TWO

In early 1988, history in certain ways seemed curiously suspended.

No doubt the lame-duck presidency of Ronald Reagan had much to do with the feeling of a dead spot in time, as did the failure of the men campaigning to succeed him to put across an inspiring or even a credible agenda as to what should happen next. Economically, following the market crisis of October '87, there was a sense of waiting for the other shoe to drop, for the crash to be reflected in the broader world; but the suspense existed, so to speak, without the devices of suspense—no heartbeat music on the soundtrack, no slow pans to a ringing telephone, just a bunch of numbers plodding along without a clear direction. Trade figures waffled and wavered, interest rates ticked upward and receded. It was tough not to yawn. And while it could persuasively be argued that the eighties were already over, it was hard to find evidence that the era destined to be called the nineties had yet begun.

When *would* the nineties begin, and what would the new phase look like?

Those questions were just beginning to be seen as grist for conjecture, the stuff of dinner-party chitchat and the stock in trade of pundits eager to say something, anything, first. The nineties, it might be suggested, would be a time of quiet but thorough reform. Or the new day might look a great deal like the old day.

The nineties might feature a stepping back from greed, if not because human nature had reformed, then because there'd be fewer gobs of money floating loose in space. Or the decade might see an even greater institutionalization of greed, as the disgust-threshold moved higher and railing against avarice became passé.

The new decade could see a heightened emphasis on domesticity, as the baby boomlet of the late eighties became the nuclear-family boomlet of the years beyond. And/or the development of an AIDS vaccine could bring about a mood of sexual expansiveness and there'd be coition in the streets.

The arts and sciences would revive, as young people realized that neither law school nor business school was a sure ticket anymore. Then again, a new hot specialty might come along, and the conventionally ambitious would flock to it as lemminglike as before.

A "Europeanization" would kick in, as Americans gradually, grudgingly, accustomed themselves to the idea of a steady-state economy and making the best of what they had. Or the habit of more might grasp and scramble through yet another generation, financing itself with yen and deutsche marks as it tastefully furnished an ever deeper hole.

Thus the range—part of the range—of prognostications. But crystal-ball-gazing was one thing, advocacy was another. What *should* happen? And how should those things be brought about? Putting it in those terms clearly raised the stakes of the discussion. Being wrong now meant not just missing one's guess, but being *wrong*. Besides, talking about what should happen next required, by necessity, some of the same vocabulary used to describe things that had happened before; it was tough to make clear that one was reaching toward something new, not falling back on something quaint.

Take money. It was easy enough to say that money, relative to other measures of value, should become less important as we slouch toward the millennium. The catch was that, as soon as you said anything that could remotely be construed as anti-money, it sounded like the sixties. The very words smelled of reefer. They conjured images of bearded vegetarians in flannel shirts, and hippie chicks who didn't shave their armpits. They opened one to that most damning of charges: not pragmatic.

The trick, then, was to make it clear that the gripe was not with money—not at all—but with the wholesale adoption of the wisdom of the marketplace as an adequate wisdom. The gripe, to put it simply, is with the assumption that everything can be assigned a price. The gripe is with the idea that a thing's value—whether that thing is a pen, a watch, or the thought, labor, and time of a person—is solely and reasonably determined by what someone else will pay for it.

During the 1980s, the marketplace way of determining worth became so deeply entrenched that people almost stopped noticing how big a part it played in their thinking. Since virtually everything was looked at in marketplace perspective, no one thing stood out as being so, and the version of life offered by that perspective seemed unassailable, self-evident.

In 1986, by way of illustration, the financial writer Andrew Tobias gave an account of an unintentionally surreal dinner party he'd attended with a group of young investment bankers. At this gathering, people straightfacedly swapped tales about twenty-five-year-old bond salesmen making two million dollars a year, while hundreds of thousands of their coevals were still struggling to pay off school loans; and about a kid two years into working life getting a nearly 1,000 percent raise one day, boosting his annual paycheck from $70,000 to $600,000, while median household income languished in the mid-twenty-thousands.

Suddenly, one of those present had a moment's glimpse beyond the marketplace perspective: had what passed in the eighties for an epiphany. "It's crazy, isn't it?" he said.

The others, Tobias reported, "seemed not to grasp" what he was talking about.

Those stories, after all, had been generated by market mechanisms, and market mechanisms were rational mechanisms. "Crazy" things, by definition, didn't happen in that realm. If something *appeared* crazy, it was the observer's viewpoint, and not the thing itself, that was askew. That viewpoint, again by definition, was insufficiently hardheaded, not sophisticated enough, befogged by value judgments that only confused matters and caused unease.

The best way to avoid confusing matters—so the wisdom of the marketplace suggested—was not to have a viewpoint at all, but simply to let the marketplace decide. The marketplace would distinguish winners from losers, successes from failures, good moves from bad moves.

This was the dominant, if generally unacknowledged, strategy by which America sought to make sense of itself in the 1980s—and it was a strategy that pertained up and down the economic scale. Whether, in a given instance, someone was trying to justify the fact that new lawyers were hired at three times the salary of new teachers, or a blue-collar worker was trying to reconcile himself to his layoff, or a child was trying to figure out why Mommy and Daddy were at the office so long, the wisdom of the marketplace was presumed to offer an adequate and final explanation. That explanation might be couched in highfalutin business terms, or might be boiled down to the tautology *because that's how things are.* Either way, it was the marketplace talking, standing in as reality *in toto,* silencing protests and quashing doubts.

Letting the marketplace decide—that was a relief, as abdicating personal responsibility is always a relief. It simplified decisions. It imparted to choices an easy neutrality. It seemed to make all things comparable. Through the device of the marketplace, apples could be played off against oranges, good deeds could be measured against hack work, since all could be reduced to some value measured in money.

The problem, however, is that it *was* a reduction, and the factors that were canceled out to make the equations easier were among the essential factors. Take the example of teaching versus lawyering. The marketplace would factor into that choice what the two careers paid, the sorts of advancement they offered, perhaps the number of hours on and off the job. It wouldn't factor in the judgment that society needed good teachers more than it needed additional attorneys. It wouldn't presume to ask if one had a real talent, much less a calling, for either field. It wouldn't even deal with the issue of what one would rather do. Those factors constituted, so to speak, the flavor of a choice, and to the marketplace it was all vanilla. Marketplace wisdom, in its staunch refusal to issue verdicts as to *better,* could only indicate where there was *more* vanilla. And those who adopted the wisdom of the marketplace as their own wisdom simply let themselves be channeled in that direction.

There was thus an unadmitted passivity—both a moral and an imaginative torpor—in the eighties tendency to go where the pay stubs beckoned. To mask this passivity, to hide the essential blandness of it, the decade evolved a jargon of active choice: *going for it, grabbing the ring, shooting the moon.*

Sounds exciting, eh? Well, there *was* excitement, sometimes, in the fulfillment of the choice, in the work and competition of following through. Still, the choice itself was passive, almost fatalistic: I will let the marketplace tell me what to do. I will let the marketplace tell me what to be. I will let the marketplace tell me if I'm doing well or badly, and in the end I will let the marketplace tote up, in vanilla dollars, what I'm worth.

/// THREE

Benno Collier's mother had been nonplussed when, in 1984, her son quit practicing law. She'd grown accustomed to thinking of her boy as an attorney, introducing him as one, bragging about him as a member of a recognized profession. "What do I call you now?" she'd asked.

"Mom," Benno had told her, "I'm a salesman."

A salesman. This Mrs. Collier had a hard time getting used to. *Lawyer* conjured images of gold watch chains looped across handsome blue-gray vests, weighty, freshly polished shoes, and elegant pronouncements uttered in complete grammatical sentences for all the world to hear. Salesman? *Salesman*, to her, suggested pudgy men in cheap suits, wrinkled behind the knees, bending over the trunks of their cars to get their sample cases; ill-shaven daytime drinkers with diner chicken salad on their breath, telling dirty jokes to try to get their customers to like them. "Benno, why would you want to be a salesman?"

"Mom, if the word bothers you, you can say 'stockbroker.' Same thing. And the reason is money."

"A salesman makes more than a lawyer?"

"Watch me," Benno had said.

He recalled this conversation now, because with three months accounted for in 1988, it appeared that he would make something less than half as much money as he'd made in 1987. This was nothing to panic about. The rumors of mass firings had pretty well died down, and even a third of Benno's '87 haul was more than enough to live on.

But the cut threw him back onto thoughts of different people's way of reckoning, different people's hierarchies, different people's snobberies. His mother had a kind of snobbery based on what jobs were called and on what people wore when they did them. Doctor, attorney, executive: those were the nice jobs, the jobs nice people did while looking nice. Sally's journalist colleagues had a rather different snobbery. Theirs seemed to revolve around "talent," defined not merely as a knack one would be paid for, but as the ability to produce work admired by one's peers, and around "integrity," which, as Benno saw it, meant essentially managing to be simultaneously in and above the swirl of events; "integrity" also seemed to mean having loud fights with one's boss and getting fired at least once in one's career.

The snobbery Benno had bought into, he acknowledged, was based on income, pure and simple. It was not, he believed, fundamentally different from other snobberies, nor was it better or worse. It had its own pluses and minuses.

On the plus side, it was the clearest-cut and in some ways the most democratic hierarchy of them all. An ugly guy with a Brooklyn accent, no matter how brilliant or well-heeled he was, could never rise very high in Benno's mother's view of things; he'd always be a *schlump*. A sincere but ungifted woman would have a tough time getting very far in Sally's; the absence of talent was cruel and unfixable. In Benno's scheme, anybody could conceivably hit pay dirt. Not that, in the race for money, everyone started even in America, or that everyone had an equal shot. But insofar as sheer wealth was the object, it didn't matter where you started, only where you ended up,

Still, there was a drawback to that way of reckoning—the same drawback that pertained to the markets that gave rise to the wealth: volatility. Benno's mother's scheme was stable. If you were a surgeon, you were a surgeon; your practice might go a little better or a little worse, but the prestige of your profession stayed with you always. Sally's hierarchy assigned a central importance to control of one's destiny; you might get bounced around the industry, but ultimately it was up to you whether you were true to your talent, whether you shepherded your integrity or betrayed it. The hierarchy based on money was both unstable and largely out of one's control. If the markets went stinko, you went stinko with them, and while there might be such a thing as a poor but successful doctor—a researcher, say—or a poor but successful artist, a poor but successful stockbroker was a ludicrous conception, a bear's face on a bull's body, something not to be found in nature.

In law school it had been drummed into Benno Collier that an argument might be good or an argument might be bad, but it had, at a minimum, to be consistent. This turn of mind had stayed with him, and so the volatility of wealth was something he had to wrestle with. If you bought into the idea that income was an adequate measure of success at a time when things were humming, what justified cashing out of that belief just because the markets now were creaking? No one, obviously, went around saying, *Hi, I've just become sixty-six and two-thirds percent less successful.* But what *did* one say?

It wasn't, Benno admitted, just the money. Not really. Even among the guys who claimed most vigorously, even defiantly, that they were just there to get rich, it wasn't quite that simple. It was also that people outside were paying attention. The market guys were where the action was, their doings were the lead story on the evening news. There followed, as one of the guys in the bullpen put it, the hard-on of fashionability. But that, too, it seemed, was fading in the long suspended moment since the Crash. Business news? What really qualified as business news in comparison with the near-shutdown of the world financial system? How did you follow that act, except by changing the subject? The media, it seemed, were backing off a bit. Public preoccupation was growing less intense.

Benno's job, meanwhile, was getting relatively easier. The phones rang less, there were fewer balls to juggle, the hours were becoming almost normal. The timing, he told himself, was really pretty fortunate, what with the baby on the way.

He told himself he should be grateful that his life was calming down.

/// FOUR

In 1986, a popular brand of laxative made a bold departure in its radio advertising.

Gone from the airwaves were the familiar slow and mellow voices that conjured images of grandparents sitting on a porch, dealing gracefully if wistfully with the hard fact of life's processes becoming problematic. Now a new sort of sufferer was telling the world of his intestinal woes. This new voice seemed to belong to someone around thirty years old, and far from sounding sluggish, the voice was clipped and harried; the implication was that here was someone whose bowels had come to a standstill because he was just too busy to exercise them. Speaking as though in the confidence of the proctologist's office, he relates the crux of his complaint. It isn't that he doesn't feel well. It isn't that he worries his impaction may be symptomatic of some deeper trouble. It's that "when I'm constipated, I'm not as good at my job."

Now here was a hero for the 1980s.

Here was a man who had taken the priorities of the time into his very entrails. For this man, full and avid participation in the marketplace, come what may, was the thing that mattered most. He'd made his choice: To function in that realm was to live. To allow for success in that realm was the purpose of health. A little thing like one's bowels should not be allowed to impede one's progress.

Forget that chances are work stress was what was knotting his insides in the first place. Forget that if his life was in better balance, his digestive system probably would be too. The point is that, in the 1980s, optimal on-the-job performance seemed a perfectly reasonable pitch to make for a medicine. And if, on reflection, the approach seems a bit perverse, it fit in neatly with a larger pattern.

In the 1980s, advertising tended not simply to push specific products but to promote the primacy of the marketplace *in toto*. All those many ads that took the *you deserve it* tack—what they were saying, in effect, was that you've paid your dues *to* the marketplace, you've earned your gratifications *from* the marketplace. That there were pleasures and satisfactions *beyond* the marketplace had come to seem a rather exotic notion, and certainly not one that marketers would promulgate. In a sense, all ads promoted all commodities, because what was really being sold was the commodity turn of mind, the whole culture of earning and spending. Only through the marketplace could the exchange of rewards for achievement be effected. Making money/buying stuff—that was the only transaction that counted, and the eighties message was that there was nothing more important than elbowing in on the table where that game was being played.

It seems surprising at first glance that this wholesale selling of the marketplace ideal should have succeeded so dramatically. By the 1980s, the members of the baby-boom generation had become the heart of the American economy, and this was a group that had long prided itself on its independence and its skepticism, its resistance to being bamboozled. You wouldn't catch these people buying the Populuxe crap their parents had been so easily seduced into craving. No electric knives for this crowd; no ultra-modern plastic dishes with pictures that scraped off on your food. This, as commentators never got tired of observing, was a sophisticated group.

But all "sophisticated" seemed to mean, in this connection, was that they had seen all the old tricks, and so would have to be sucked in by way of new ones. The new trick of choice—embarrassingly transparent, once you thought about it, but effective nonetheless—was passing off consumer culture not as a vast machine fueled by people's money and their labor, by their cravings, their envy, and their social anxieties, but as a wonderful club they were privileged to join. Just as, by the jargon of active choice, people became persuaded that the career toward which the marketplace channeled them was their own self-selected road, so, as consumers, they accepted the notion that being able to pick item *A* as opposed to item *B* was evidence enough that they were choosing freely. Buying was voting with your wallet.

Won over by that variously phrased and oft-repeated message, the baby-boomers, for all their presumed autonomy, put themselves perhaps more utterly in the thrall of marketing than had any generation before them. The array of goods they had to choose from was, after all, impressive. You could have the blue sedan or the red convertible, the velvet sofa or the linen or the chintz. You could have your burger grilled or fried, and you could pick how many calories you wanted in your beer. Amid such a luxury of options it was easy to overlook the fact that no matter what sort of upholstery or razor blades you bought, you were choosing something that someone else had already chosen for you. As defined by the marketplace, the pursuit of happiness had a very clear-cut boundary: it went just as far as the limits of someone else's inventory.

///// **FIVE**

Department stores have windows for looking into, but none for looking out of; casinos have no clocks.

Under the strictures of the wisdom of the marketplace,

America in the 1980s came partly to resemble Neiman-Marcus and partly to resemble Harrah's.

On the earning side, it was the casino model that pertained. Returns on investments, as John Kenneth Galbraith argued, "no longer [had] any relation to underlying circumstance." More money was to be made by putting companies "in play" than by running them. A "hint of unreality," as Andrew Tobias maintained, "[had] crept into" scales of compensation. When it came to acquiring wealth, you rolled the dice and waited to see if you came up lucky.

On the spending side, there was no suspense whatever, because, as in a department store, almost everything in America seemed to have a big red price tag on it. Nor, as we have noted, did the price tags come off when a purchase was made, because in our "sophisticated" time everyone knew what everything cost.

So it was not surprising that 1980s America, like a department store, provided few reminders that there was a universe beyond the selling floor, and, like a casino, few reminders that time was inexorably passing, that the supply of it was finite. As the marketplace became ever more solidly, seamlessly installed as a world unto itself, it took an act of will and imagination to remember what life was like beyond its boundaries—to remember there *was* life beyond its boundaries.

It took imagination and alertness to recall that marketplace logic, while consistent, persuasive, even elegant in its way, did not adequately address the way people actually functioned or what they actually needed. The market model reduced things to a comforting simplicity: more money, more happy. Too bad life wasn't quite that simple.

The attempt to make life *appear* that simple could only lead to conflicts, confusion, lies both intentional and systemic. You could argue from today till tomorrow that market mechanisms were rational; that didn't change the fact that pay scales were "crazy" and speculation was "insane." You could prove that human acquisitiveness was necessary to make the machinery go; that didn't undo the unpleasant truth that white-collar crime partook not just of greed but of pathology. Unsatisfied hungers would always make people sick, and the focus of the sickness would be the thing society held up as most important. In 1984, *Esquire* magazine could make the odd but not ungrounded assertion that "if Freud were alive today, he'd be writing about money instead of sex."

And if Jesus were alive today, one imagines He would be reiterating His message to "render unto Caesar that which is Caesar's," but to avoid the confusion of realms that fostered the illusion that Caesar's domains—or those of the marketplace—constituted the universe entire. There were legitimate aspirations beyond the bazaar. There were choices that could not be reduced to the choice of buying or selling.

That confusion of realms, finally, was what made the apotheosis of the marketplace a grim prospect. The encroachment by the marketplace definition of worth on the broader notion of worthiness; the annexation of the whole realm of values by the marketplace version of value—those were reductions that made life poorer. They were reductions, too, that limited people's options. No matter how many choices were offered within the marketplace, no matter how freewheeling the jargon made those options sound, the selection was sparse and predictable in comparison with the untamed varieties to be found beyond the selling floor.

11 ///

Ghettos
of the
Conscience

/// **ONE**

Typical of the narrowing of perspective that went with the acceptance of marketplace wisdom as an adequate wisdom was the 1980s attitude toward ethics. By 1987 it was widely acknowledged that America was in the midst of a "sleaze wave." So many wealthy businessmen were in jail that one minimum-security prison had been dubbed "Club Fed." Shareholder suits against nest-feathering managements had become routine. E. F. Hutton had been caught kiting checks, and the Bank of Boston admitted laundering money. Evidence abounded that the betrayal of client confidences and fiduciary obligations, once all but unthinkable violations of professional principle, were becoming almost standard strategies for gaining that crucial edge.

The eighties response? The eighties response was to imagine that this widespread moral malaise could best be dealt with through the vehicle of "business ethics"—as though, if we could only come up with a set of guidelines pertaining to our handling of money, everything would be all right.

Wrong. Everything would not be all right, since the problem, at its most fundamental, was not one of mere greed but of an awful want of respect for the rules, for each other, and for ourselves. Cheating in business was one expression, but not the substance, of that lack of regard. Wealth, when it was dubiously acquired, became a measure of our contempt, a way of thumbing our noses at a system that could make us prosperous but not exalted. Well, O.K., if not esteemed for our merit, we could at least be fawned on for our bucks; if not secure in our purpose, we could at least be arrogant in our power. Money, as we have suggested, comes to seem more important as other good things are allowed to become less so; arguably, then, the eighties' narrow focus on ethics as right behavior in the getting of dollars was as much a symptom of the problem as a part of the solution. Didn't right behavior matter equally much in *other* spheres as well?

To be sure, ethics needed to be dealt with somehow, as even the most cursory rundown of some of the decade's low points will attest. Wall Street's leading arbitrageur, Ivan Boesky, was shown to be a felon and a fraud, whose self-vaunted clairvoyance depended on inside information provided by millionaires from the highest levels of investment banking; as in bad movies, Boesky paid for his dope in cash delivered in briefcases. A *Wall Street Journal* columnist, R. Foster Winans, was convicted for selling proprietary information about the stocks to be featured in his column. A defense contractor billed the Pentagon $1,118.26 for the plastic cap on a stool leg, and Cartier falsified sales records so that jewel buyers could welch on sales tax. Manville went

Chapter 11 to avoid paying damages to the people it had poisoned with asbestos, A. H. Robins was accused of a cover-up on the dangers of its Dalkon Shield contraceptive device, and Eli Lilly somehow forgot to tell consumers or the government that some people who took its drug Oraflex were keeling over dead.

Meanwhile, back on Wall Street, members of the so-called Yuppie Crime Ring were hoping their complexions would be clear on sentencing day, and New York columnist Ron Rosenbaum was advising young bankers to put aside their hallmark red suspenders. "Throw them out, fellas," he advised, because donning them was like "wearing a sartorial scarlet letter that says: I BELONG TO A SHAMEFUL PROFESSION. I AM PROBABLY A CROOK."

Delinquent behavior has always been a fertile field for speculation, and as the eighties progressed, there seemed to be almost as much theory about the widespread corruption as there was corruption. The sociologist David Riesman, author of that testament of anomie, *The Lonely Crowd,* laid the blame on the growth of a "transaction mentality," in which a sense of responsibility or consequences did not extend beyond the current deal, caper, or scam. The historian Maury Klein said we were living in "an age of Hessians," when loyalty was nil and the mercenary impulse ruled supreme. One pundit exhumed the Greek writer Polybius in likening eighties America to famously sleazy Carthage, a place where "nothing that results in profit [was] regarded as disgraceful." Essayist Myron Magnet observed that "as if trapped by a thermal inversion, the ethical atmosphere of business ... [was] growing acrid," and argued that the inhalation of those pernicious vapors could only lead to ever worse behavior.

How might the process be arrested? How might the downhill slide be stopped? For all the tsk-tsk-ing and all the learned phrasemaking, no one seemed to know. And—in

one of the eighties' oddest and most telling incidents—
when someone contributed $20 million of his own money
to the effort to find out, the general reaction was more one
of skepticism, resentment, and mockery than of gratitude.

The donor was a man named John S. R. Shad, who, in
March of 1987, announced a pledge of $30 million to the
Harvard Business School—two-thirds of it to be given by
himself, the other third to be raised by subscription. The gift
was earmarked for the promotion of the study of business
ethics, and it made headlines as by far the largest donation
ever made to any business school. Noteworthy, too, was the
fact that Jack Shad was no mere sermonizer or starry-eyed
do-gooder, but a man who, as then-outgoing chairman of
the Securities and Exchange Commission, had had a front-
row seat on market malfeasances and had pronounced
himself "disgusted" by them. As a former vice-chairman of
E. F. Hutton (he left well before the check-kiting scandal),
Shad had strong feelings about how business ought to be
done, and one of the things he got for his 20 million bucks
was a public forum in which to air his conviction that "ethics
pays" and that "the marketplace does reward . . . integrity."

The reaction to Shad's gift, as we say, was curious in the
extreme. *Business Week* wondered if the pledge was "a case
of throwing money at a problem that money helped
produce." *U.S. News & World Report* questioned whether
Harvard was "merely paying lip service to a widespread
business problem." *The Wall Street Journal* tartly observed
that "business ethics [has become] a growth industry, its
fortunes rising as the ethics of business appear to be
declining." And *Fortune* was downright sarcastic in raising
"a few sullen questions for John Shad. . . . Does any empir-
ical research perchance underlie the proposition that 'ethics
pays' . . . ? [And] have any B-school graduates gone to jail just
for being unethical? We rather had the impression that most
of those in trouble actually broke some law or other."

Now, journalists are paid low salaries to be cynical, so the press reaction, in itself, was perhaps not surprising. But much the same tone was struck by members of the business and academic communities as well. Andrew Sigler, chairman of Champion International and head of the Business Round-table's corporate responsibility task force, averred that he'd "be fascinated to see how they spend the money. If they just hire a professor and give him a chair, that won't do much good." John W. Rosenblum, dean of the University of Virginia's Darden Business School, admitted to being baffled at the fact of "a university which hasn't decided what to do in ethics get[ting] $30 million." And while professional jealousy may have informed *his* comments, it was harder to ascribe that motive to personnel at HBS. "They still have to sell this to one hundred tenured faculty," said one junior prof, "who think the whole discipline is garbage."

What was going on here? Some of the snideness, no doubt, derived from simple envy that anyone should have a spare 20 million bucks to give away; and it was true that business ethics had yet to prove itself as a substantive academic field. Still, what were people getting so hostile about? The virulence of the responses suggested that something was getting to people under the fingernails.

Whatever else a $30 million pledge meant, it meant that the study of business ethics would be able to marshal more resources and gain more visibility than it ever had before. It might even mean that, over time, the subject would actually be taken seriously. This apparently made a lot of people nervous.

Where was the threat in the prospect of business ethics outgrowing its status as Chamber of Commerce buzzword and academic orphan? The threat was this: If business ethics was really taken seriously, if it was pursued to its roots, it would have to be acknowledged that the subject didn't begin or end at nine or five or with elementary matters like insider trading or padded expense accounts or fibbing in negotiations. If the subject was really taken seriously, it would have to be acknowledged to pertain beyond the marketplace, it would have to be regarded in context with the rest of life. People backed off from this as they did from an open window when they were standing there naked and a stranger went strolling by.

At a time when money mattered greatly, and when the career was the closest available thing to a quest, people found it much less exposing to compartmentalize morality, to regard business as a sort of ghetto of the conscience, a bad neighborhood for values, but one that could be avoided in the evenings and on weekends. People liked to pretend they had a work self and a real self; the two met occasionally in the elevator, and like colleagues having a secret affair, they tried not to let it be noticed how intimately they knew each other, that in fact they shared a pillow after hours.

But the liaison couldn't be hushed up forever. Eventually it would become clear that the work self and the real self commingled. The way the work self acted didn't affect only how much money the real self had, whether the real self got promoted or fired. No, on-the-job behavior affected sleep, health, peace of mind. It apparently affected potency, fertility, and who your friends were. It affected the person the real self was, and it profoundly affected the quality of one's life. Take business ethics seriously, and it ended up being ethics, period. It was really that simple.

/// TWO

That was the scary part. That was why many people apparently preferred to keep the field of inquiry called "business ethics" small, parochial, manageable.

Talking about "business ethics" kept the debate scudding comfortably along the surface of what happened on the job, limited discussion to questions answerable by the wisdom of the marketplace. Talking about ethics, insofar as the subject *included* business behavior, opened a window on a far wider world. In that wider world, *more* and *better* were not interchangeable concepts, "success" did not necessarily stand as a dignified end in itself, "growth" in dollars did not necessarily mean that something good was happening.

As conventionally regarded, "business ethics" swallowed whole the premises of business itself. It had to. The discipline had a rich parent, called business, and a poor parent, called ethics, and was more intent on the approval of the former than of the latter. The field was bankrolled by true believers, and it needed to be made palatable to young people who didn't go to business school because of a burning interest in moral philosophy. Business ethics, therefore, stopped short of the radical self-examination that any body of thought must go through on the way to becoming respectable. It hadn't spent its forty days in the desert—and as long as it pretended that the workplace occupied its own insulated moral ghetto, it never would.

Business ethics was rife with givens. The sanctity of profit was, of course, a given. Not just the reality, but the legitimacy of human avarice as a motivator, was also a given. Inequality was a given, since Darwinian competitiveness was a given, and on the savannah of business there would always be winners and losers, predators and prey. Even a certain amount of criminality was a given; no one expected universal virtue in a domain where success was defined solely by the rewards of success, where accomplishment was judged by counting.

So the question, finally, was this: Given all those givens, all those premises that business ethics *had* to accept, could the field really pass itself off as a meaningful and independent branch of moral inquiry, or was it just a high-sounding synonym for watching your ass on your way to the top?

Why, by the marketplace logic of "business ethics," should

one behave honorably on the job? Only because the threat of
punishment loomed—if not the immediate threat of the law,
then the threat of incurring disapproval that would hamper
one's progress. On the subject of more positive reasons for
behaving well—the keeping of a trust, the ideal of social
duty, the sense of work-in-the-name-of-something-bigger—
"business ethics," by itself, had nothing at all to say. You had
to look *outside* the marketplace for those sorts of considerations, and looking beyond the marketplace was precisely
what "business ethics" was disinclined to do.

Thus, an impasse. On the turf where "business ethics"
confidently strode, it did not have much to offer that was
beyond the realm of a rather defensive common sense; and
on the issues of business reality and marketplace behavior
where an ethics perspective might have had an impact,
"business ethics" didn't dare to tread.

Take, for example, the fact that, of all major industrial
nations, excepting only France, the United States has the
broadest discrepancy between workers' income and the
income of top management. It seems obvious that this is, in
part, a moral issue, but would "business ethics" regard it as
such? Absolutely not. The disparity was set by the marketplace, and marketplace logic is inviolable. Have any laws
been broken? Have any explicit codes been flouted? If not,
"business ethics" says amen to whatever degree of inequality the system will support.

Or consider the moral implications of corporate takeovers
and divestitures. Isn't there a valid distinction to be made
between people who build up enterprises and people who
rip them apart? To put it as unfashionably as possible: Isn't
someone who creates a new plant and new jobs behaving
more morally than someone who liquidates? "Business ethics" makes no such distinction, as there is money to be made
either way. It is by now widely recognized that the need to

protect themselves against takeovers forces companies to deploy their resources in ways that make them less efficient: isn't this, in effect, stealing from us all? Again, "business ethics" evades the question by simply factoring takeovers into its bland acceptance of "marketplace reality."

The irony in all of this is that those who are skeptical of business ethics' efficacy routinely claim that the discipline is too idealistic, that in its attempts to bring right behavior to commerce it is aiming too high. In fact, just the opposite is true. The ambitions of "business ethics" have been depressingly modest. The field doesn't traffic in ideas, but only in procedures. It hasn't challenged the marketplace, but only sought to justify it. Like a state religion, business ethics has in reality been a rubber stamp for the authority on which it is supposed to be a check.

⫻ THREE

The reason for business ethics' wimpiness is not hard to find: the field, strictly speaking, does not exist at all.

In terms of moral categories as old as the Bible and as central to Western civilization as Aristotle, there is no such thing as "business ethics," any more than there is such a thing as sports ethics or leisure ethics or sex ethics.

There is only one ethics, and it applies to all aspects of life. It cannot be stretched, molded, julienned, or custom-fitted to suit the trends and the jargon of every activity and every special interest that comes along. Ethics is of a piece. True, it has limbs, but the limbs are all attached. Try to divide ethics, try to water it down, try to fragment it, and something majestic turns into something trivial; something essentially simple turns into something impossibly complex; something exalted turns into something suspect. What the management guru Peter Drucker once said about business ethics applies equally well to *any* discipline based on special-case fragments: those partial ethics are to ethics "what soft porn is to ... love." They are the poses without the substance, the gestures without the passion, the attitudes without the emotional clout.

The fragmentation of ethics was rampant in the 1980s, and while "business ethics," in keeping with the decade's obsession with the mechanics of wealth, got most of the play, business was hardly the only neighborhood of conscience to become ghetto-ized. Almost every transgression, in fact, seemed to define a mini-ethics unto itself. In New York, a series of scandals in the Koch administration gave rise to much lofty talk about "local government ethics." The baroque schemes of the Iran-contra arms peddlers led to discussions about "covert-operations ethics." Gary Hart's apparent infidelity evoked analysis of "sexual ethics of candidates," leaving those with a taste for fine distinctions to argue whether this was different from "sexual ethics of televangelists." High school students were caught cheating on their SATs—did this suggest a decline in "multiple-choice ethics"? College students were busted for running a campus prostitution ring—did this signal a crisis in "tuition-defrayment ethics"?

What accounted for this paper-thin slicing up of ethics in the first place? Allan Bloom, the professor whose 1987 book *The Closing of the American Mind* was probably the decade's unlikeliest number-one best-seller, laid much of the blame on an educational system that wrongheadedly pulled back from making strong moral judgments, leading people to believe that *everything was relative* and that acts could only be measured on a case by case basis. The end result of this sort of education, to paraphrase Bloom, was a dangerous parody of tolerance, a pseudo-open-mindedness masking a moral vacuum that verged on being evil by omission.

But the problem was deeper than anything that could be ascribed merely to the shortcomings of formal education.

No one was inculcating a broad-spectrum sense of ethics—families didn't seem to be doing it, conventional religions didn't do it, the government certainly didn't do it. No one *presumed* to do it. In this, people thought they were being amiable and urbane, when in fact they were simply being wishy-washy. Just as there was a masked passivity in people's willingness to sign on with the program of the marketplace, so there was an abject lack of boldness in their refusal to assert that some things *weren't* relative, some things *didn't* depend, some things were simply right or wrong, in all times and in all places, and that's that.

To be sure, there were certain things about contemporary America that strongly militated against anyone's seizing the high ground of an all-embracing ethical viewpoint. One of those things was our peculiar obsession with credentials. Rather than listen to what someone was saying, our first impulse tended to be to ask who the hell this person was to be saying it. This impulse served a purpose, of course, as a first-line defense against demagoguery; but it had a downside as well: the emphasis on credentials necessitated an emphasis on specialization, and specialization, by definition, narrowed the range of inquiry. To be quoted in the news magazines or interviewed for twelve seconds on the think-segment of TV news, you had to have a tag like Consultant in the Ethics of Mid-Size Organizations or Professor of Conflicts of Interest in the Service Sector. Can you imagine an onscreen graphic saying JOHN DOE—MORAL PERSON? No, you needed a title, something that pinpointed what you knew. The title, in turn, coupled with the fact that you'd once been quoted somewhere, constituted proof of your expertise; in fact, it constituted the expertise itself. Just as there were people who were famous for being famous, there were people who were experts at being experts.

But there was no credential that identified someone simply as a person who thought in terms of fairness, reason, responsibility, compassion. There was no one certified, simply, as Concerned with the Big Picture. There was no one with an advanced degree and five years' clinical experience in holding convictions about what we owe to each other and what we owe to ourselves.

No credential, no authority; no authority, no exposure. And so the vast and integral field of ethics has been largely left to be nattered over by "specialists" in various little corners of it. These specialists have the vocabulary to speak convincingly about corporate cultures, accounting practices, business constituencies. As hired superegos, they serve a purpose. But no amount of procedural detail adds up to a map of the art of living, which is, finally, what ethics is about.

/// FOUR

The failure to take on ethics whole—this is a failure with consequences that are as real as crime and as palpable as unhappiness.

White-collar felons, one imagines, become so not because they one day take a headlong leap into badness, but because they become persuaded that they can live by one morality in their pursuit of wealth while cleaving to a different one in, say, how they raise their children. Public officials who betray a trust do not, one expects, suddenly renounce the ethic of service that brought them to their career, but find a way to accommodate that ethic to a different one that supposedly pertains in the realm of personal gain.

These moral accommodations used to be called hypocrisy, and it used to be clear that they were wrong. That clarity dissolves, however, when ethics is viewed in fragments, when anything unsavory can be explained away as the sort of thing that happens in a ghetto of the conscience. When ethics is chopped up into shards, people fall through the cracks between the pieces.

More basically still, the fragmentation of ethics leads to an unfortunate tendency to get the whole point of the subject exactly dead-backwards wrong.

As long as ethics is thought of as a hodgepodge of precepts parochially applied in isolated instances, it tends to be perceived as a dreary list of prohibitions put across by solemn killjoys who either fancy themselves above the fray or simply have nothing to gain from it.

What "business ethics" seems to be saying is, Thou shalt not make as much money as thou otherwise might. "Sexual ethics" seems to demand that thou shalt not avail thyself of erotic opportunities otherwise attractive. "Political ethics" prescribes that thou shalt not take the exercise of thy power or influence quite to the limit. Viewed in pieces, ethics, like the Jiminy Cricket version of conscience, seems to be essentially a brake, and no one likes to step on the brake when he can step on the gas.

But that is a dumb way of looking at ethics—dumb because it is removed from context. Looking at ethics that way is like complaining that in baseball you have to hit between the foul lines; if you didn't have to, your range of options on any given pitch would be wider, that's true—but there would be no ballgame. Ethics is what defines the playing field and makes the game possible, and, taken whole, it is therefore the most affirmative thing in the world.

Other peoples at other times have known this. It's why the ancients revered their lawgivers, and why orthodox Jews dance with the scrolls of the Torah in their arms. The embrace of the rules is what keeps things on track, what keeps the game from flying off into chaos. *That* is the sense in which ethics is pragmatic, and it includes but goes far beyond the marketplace notion of right behavior paying off.

The real payoff is in function, durability, range. Things work better when there is a broad and voluntary subscription to a certain set of guidelines, and to a scheme of values that underlies them; look at Japan if you doubt it. Shared values define the sorts of behavior and achievement—both within the marketplace and beyond it—that are considered worthy of esteem. Values allow the satisfactions of adventure, romance, service to be considered alongside the satisfactions of career, advancement, "success." All have their place; all carry their responsibilities within a general code of decency; all bring their recognized rewards. By positing a wider range of possible and legitimate goals, an integral ethics fosters the crucial belief that the fulfillment of those goals—whether of wealth, pleasure, prestige, or the hope of Heaven—is in some credible relation to effort, deserts, and personal choice.

In 1980s America, rewards came to seem egregiously *out* of proportion to deserts—and there are few things more socially corrosive than this. Too much glitzy, questionably earned, and vacuously defined "success" for too few; too little sense of meaningful progress or respect for a great many more; and the absence of an inclusive sense of values that would remind us that things other than money should be factored into our reckoning of who is doing well.

Thus, a fractured and enfeebled ethics leads on to a downward spiral: the ghetto view of conscience creates an atmosphere in which the bad guys can prosper. Denatured values, having lost their ability to balance money against other things that matter, allow this to pass for "winning." Under the perception that the bad guys are winning anyway, ethics loses even more of its already compromised authority.

What is the end point of this cycle? This is a question that marketplace logic does not suffice to answer, and that "business ethics" would prefer not even to ask. It seems safe to say, however, that the last stop on the trolley would not be a neighborhood where one would like to live.

12

The New Leisure Meets the New Work Ethic

⫽⫽ ONE

In the sunny and confident year of 1959, it was predicted that by 1975 American families would be flying around in personal helicopters, moving sidewalks would whisk tens of thousands of pedestrians through crowded downtowns across the country, and highway accidents would be eliminated by electronic sensors beaming vehicles down the road. Rockets would deliver mail, and enormous floating-city cruise ships serving cafeteria-style meals would cross the Atlantic in four days and charge a fare of fifty dollars.

These prophecies were gathered from a consortium of scientists, and put forth in a special end-of-decade issue of *Life* magazine. Called "The Good Life," it is a document that remains extraordinarily poignant not only for its rosy view of the American future but for its benign yet canny limning of what was then the American present. The year 1959 was one in which the postwar habit of more was still a fresh excitement and not yet an addiction, a time when one of people's great problems was figuring out what to make of their good luck. What to do with their unprecedented affluence; to what tasks to apply their boundless enthusiasm; how to fill their idle hours.

This last dilemma was particularly germane to 1959, as one focus of the time's optimism was the development of a "new leisure"—pastimes, hobbies, far-ranging interests, not just for those whom Veblen had called "the leisure class," but for all. After the Depression, World War II, and the frenetic stint of economic empire-building, America could finally breathe a little easy. But the rather sudden emphasis on recreation was a bafflement as well as a privilege. How *did* one relax? And what sort of recreation was appropriate to one's age, income, standing? The editors of *Life* broached these questions through humor in a piece called "How Do *YOU* Rate in the New Leisure?"

The premise of the feature was that in modern America, "your [social] placement [had] little to do with any of the old standards of class distinction—money, birth, breeding. What count[ed] [was] simply how you spen[t] your spare time."

It wasn't so much what you did as how you did it. Consider fishing. The Aristocrat, in keeping with his obsession with form and indifference to results, favored fly-casting with home-tied flies. The Upper Bourgeois, who could probably afford a small boat or who at least had a friend who could, tended to fish with plugs, thereby increasing his chances of bringing home dinner and being a hero to his kids. The Lower Bourgeois, skiffless but sociable in ways that smacked of the vulgar, typically went out on party boats, while the Peasant sat on a stream bank, brown bag at the ready, drowning worms. As to his taste in cinema, the Aristocrat, having nothing to prove and being intellectually torpid by nature, tended to go to horror movies, which he pronounced amusing. The Upper Bourgeois, just barely sophisticated enough to have a rudimentary sense of camp, favored B-movies, while the Lower Bourgeois, straining to fill the vast gaps in his education, gravitated to the high-budget costume sagas, thinking he was thereby getting a painless primer as to what life was like in biblical times. Peasants went to horror movies, which provided one of their few opportunities to sit next to Aristocrats.

While the recreation-status system could easily be played for laughs, the broader subject of leisure was in fact taken very seriously, regarded almost piously, in the late 1950s. Leisure was a frontier, one of those new domains opened up by general prosperity, a rich realm it was part of the national purpose to explore. America, it seemed, was now wealthy and secure enough to become cultivated, to blossom forth as a land of recorder players, watercolorists, tea rose hybridizers. Citizens, as in ancient Athens, could engage in philosophy and politics for recreation, and, as in Victorian England, businessmen might perform scientific experiments in the evenings and on weekends. The time and the money were there.

The average employed American of 1959 had fully twenty more nonworking hours per week than had his counterpart of 1900; in all, and not counting time for sleeping, the typical worker had roughly 3,700 leisure hours a year. In addition, he had more disposable income than any average joe had ever enjoyed, and a far wider range of options to spend it on—though of course most of those options diverged rather broadly from the contemplative forms of leisure that *Life* held up as the classical ideal. In 1959, six times as many people were enrolled in ballroom dancing classes as in colleges and universities. Florida's sport-fishing industry brought in more money than its entire citrus crop, and in California more boats were being sold than cars. In New York State on the Fourth of July weekend of '59, more people were killed in boating accidents than on the highways. America had more skiers than Switzerland, and spent as much money on dogs as on lawyers. In Skokie, Illinois, a bowling alley was employing a full-time sociologist to devise optimal means for melding the lanes into the life of the neighborhood.

The supposition underlying this last detail, of course, was that individual leisure *could* be melded into the life of the neighborhood; and this in turn suggests something essential and too easily overlooked about the ideal of leisure in the fifties: leisure was regarded as a public act. Maybe people weren't reciting sonnets or discussing current events in the public square, maybe they were just drinking beer and bowling, but still, there was a sense that the purpose of free time didn't begin and end with individual dabblings or solipsistic "self-improvement." Leisure, even if a given aspect of it was enjoyed in private and alone, was, no less than work, something one did as a member of a community.

After all, it had been not individual, but social, communal progress that had created the abundance of leisure time in the first place. No one person created the technologies that were making possible the enormous gains in productivity that were making possible the shorter and still-shortening work week. It was not individual success, but strong unions bargaining collectively and strong industries prospering that allowed employees to make handsomer livings while clocking fewer hours. The new leisure existed, that is to say, because America had created a structure that allowed for it;

enjoying spare time meant participating in that structure, weaving one's leisure through the social fabric.

By the optimism of the 1950s, the ever more enlightened use of leisure time was seen as a confirmation of the American way—an at least partial answer to the nagging question, *What's all that money for?* Family helicopters were a nice fantasy; rocket-mail might happen someday; in the meantime, using extra time and extra wealth to broaden life's scope was an improvement that could happen *now*. Leisure was perhaps the simplest means by which the stockpile of postwar *more* could begin to be translated into *better*.

⫴ TWO

But using leisure well was far easier said than done. It was a learned skill, it took practice. And learning it was difficult—in part because the new leisure carried with it strong components of guilt and of anxiety. Boredom loomed as a constant threat and a mark of shame. Not only did it seem vaguely immoral to expend time and energy away from work, but there was something wrong with someone who got bored even though there was an archery range and a pitch-and-putt just up the road, even though the public library stayed open late, the church was forming a Little Theater group, and the lawn was crying out to be edged.

New options breed new pathologies. The late fifties saw the rise of the "weekend alcoholic," the guy so flustered by his leisure that he could not stay sober off the job. Also identified as an object of fantasy—perhaps, who knows, she really did exist—was the bored housewife whose tasks had been made so quick and painless by her gadgets that she had no way of filling her days except by becoming a Miltown freak, sitting around in a nose-cone bra and waiting to seduce the guys who serviced the appliances.

What was happening was that the same new technologies that were making life "easier"—in the curious usage of that term which refers to a shifting of burdens from the physical to the psychological—also tended to make it less straight-forward and in some ways less secure. On the one hand, the celebration of the new leisure was a salute to American prosperity, relative equality, and ever-expanding opportunities. On the other hand, it was a defensive gesture, a way of putting a brave face on something that carried with it a good deal of terror. What happened when work got *too* easy, became inadequate as a means of self-definition and self-justification? Things were sliding that way already, and given the late-fifties penchant for grandiose predictions, there loomed the fear that before too long human labor would become outmoded altogether.

Automation was a word that made people swallow hard in the 1950s. Everyone knew it constituted "progress," everyone knew it made life "easier," but no one knew where it would all end. Automation conjured images of vast, sealed factories inhabited only by humanoid gizmos— riveters that clanked, sealers that hissed, mantislike robot arms that plopped the finished product onto trucks. These mythical factories, it was imagined, would employ exactly one guy to sit in a shed in front of what looked like a gigantic Cadillac dashboard, occasionally glancing over the top of his newspaper to make sure the lights were still flashing. In the famous phrase of the mathematician Norbert Wiener, the promise of automation was that it would pave the way for "the human use of human beings," that it would ennoble labor by eliminating drudgery. But what of the millions who'd formerly fed their families and, almost as important, filled their waking hours by precisely the sort of drudgery being eliminated?

The specter of personal obsolescence hounded not only

those engaged in manual work. What automation was to the production line, electronics was to the office—and white-collar paranoiacs would soon come to overestimate the self-sufficiency of the early "thinking machines" to roughly the same extent that labor leaders overestimated the ability of the "factory of tomorrow" to run itself. (The all-controlling computer, HAL, from the 1968 film *2001: A Space Odyssey,* would be the highest embodiment of this paranoia.) Cousin to the fear that a human hand would never again be called upon to turn a lathe was the fear that the human mind would never be required for another bit of arithmetic, another logical inference, another decision on a marketing plan.

From the perspective of the 1980s, it is difficult to realize that the focus of these fears was not exactly economic. Somehow, it could be believed in 1959, people would still be able to make their livings. The unions would protect the workingman, the corporations would somehow carry the bureaucrats. The system would provide. The anxiety centered, rather, on the emotional role of work, the part played by the marketplace in people's sense of what was fitting. How could a man—and in the late fifties it was men who would be affected by the workplace changes—justify his place in the home and the community, vent his vigor and strut his strength, without the sort of labor that demanded the best or at least the most he had to offer?

He would have to show his worthiness in other ways. He would have to be versatile, resourceful, good at bridge, woodworking, and entertaining his kids. Being a decent athlete would help enormously, as would having a green thumb. The compleat American would have to become a Saturday sort of guy, as the ethos of job-oriented singlemindedness evolved into the ethos of well-roundedness. Americans, those most Calvinist of peoples, were coming gradually to the privileged but unsettling realization that salvation might lie as much in play as in work.

⫽⫽⫽ THREE

Not that work and play were opposed.

Much of the fifties commentary on the new leisure, in fact, was aimed quite specifically at reminding people, after three hundred years of Puritanism, that they were not. *Life* quoted Aristotle to the effect that work and leisure were two aspects of the same drive toward excellence, the same yearning for meaningful activity. (The magazine's editors, well-practiced in their judgment as to how much the American public could swallow, soft-pedaled the philosopher's further contention that leisure was superior to work, and was its end.) Essayists pointed out that, ever since the expulsion from Eden, labor had been all but universally regarded as a vexation, the most basic of the necessary evils, and the aim of societies had always been to lighten the load—whether by technological advances, dragging home slaves to do the more disgusting chores, or simply attaining a certain standard of living and then saying the hell with more.

The notion that labor was in itself virtuous was, historically speaking, a very *nouveau* conception, and would have been hilarious if not appalling to the ancients—the Judeo-Christian ancients no less than the pagans. The Hebrews' rigorous observance of the Sabbath was based on the conviction that work was irretrievably earthbound, and that only at rest—freshly washed, wearing his most comfortable clothes, and with a large meal in his belly—was man fully fit to meditate on the Scriptures and celebrate the greatness of God. It took Saint Benedict, around the year 529, to make explicit the Christian linkage of labor and faith, in the motto of the order he founded: "To work is to pray." That may have been fine for monks, but another millennium passed before Calvin came along and framed the Protestant ethic in a form that applied to lay people as well.

Work, in the historical scheme, became noble only yesterday. Quite by coincidence, it became noble just around the time a frontier called America was beginning to be settled. Having grown up together, the United States and the work ethic were as intimately linked as twins, and, as with twins, it was sometimes hard to tell where the identity of the one left off and the uniqueness of the other began. Their destinies had perhaps become more intertwined than was good for them.

They were so intertwined that saying anything critical of the work ethic was a very tricky business. Insofar as that ethic was still construed as being integral to the Protestant faith, calling it into question came dangerously close to criticizing religion; work-as-worship was dogma, sort of, and as such it was off limits to lay pundits. Even in its purely secular aspects, the Protestant ethic had become so nearly synonymous with the national virtue that being less than gung-ho about it seemed unpatriotic as well. Callused hands; uncomplaining toil; sacrifice of self and, not infrequently, others; legitimate pride in earned wealth and standing—these were the things that had made America America. No one with a mainstream constituency was going to essay too basic a critique of them.

No one, for example, at least in the relatively polite 1950s, seemed inclined to suggest that certain Calvinist doctrines, while phenomenally successful as social engineering, were somewhat shocking as theology. There was a spectacular presumption at the heart of making a religious virtue of labor: it assumed that God needed puny little man to complete His work. According to Calvin, what made labor an act of faith was that it enabled humanity to toil along with the Creator in the perfection of the universe. Maybe this was credible at a time when human labor consisted of clearing wilderness to bring forth orderly and productive farmland. But did the Almighty really need Ralph Kramden to drive a bus and Ed Norton to unplug a sewer to complete His Grand Design? For that matter, was humankind helping to perfect God's world by decimating forests, stinking up waterways, and gashing hills to get at the coal and iron? And what about the American ideal of the *self-made* man—if work was truly an apprenticeship to God, wasn't that a contradictory and even a sacrilegious notion?

Questions like that were out of bounds in the 1950s. Which was too bad. The sacred-cow status of the work ethic made it very difficult to bring nuances into the debate; and the debate should have been all nuance: What *kinds* of labor were intrinsically spiritual? What could be done about the kinds of work that went *against* the spirit? When could *play* stand as a kind of worship? The idea, after all, was not to discredit work, but to bring our understanding of it into line with contemporary realities.

Simply equating labor with virtue carried with it as well the unfortunate corollary of equating leisure with vice. This attitude had made social sense when there was a continent to shape, when hunger loomed as a constant threat. Whatever the Puritans' ideas about getting into Heaven, it was survival in this life that they had in mind when they made pleasure a misdemeanor and disparaged laughter even in children. That bias made no sense in the affluent society of the 1950s, when the level of consumption, more than of production, was what determined the economic vigor of the nation.

Besides, in modern America, leisure had become a political and even a moral achievement. As in classical

Greece, aiming merely at survival was aiming far too low; that was for barbarians. The more fitting goal was—or should have been—culture, learning, quality of life, and in that context labor and leisure could be cogently examined only with regard to one another. Devalue either and you devalue both.

The contemporary problem, as the more prescient observers saw it, was that both *were* being devalued. The social critic Paul Goodman, as early as 1960, looked around at a society in which "a lot of people [were becoming] productively expendable," and arrived at the gloomy conclusion that "for most men there is no man's work, and also therefore no man's play." Goodman acknowledged that "the Calvinist Ethic is essentially true," at least as it pertained to the work side of the equation. "If a man doesn't give himself without timidity to a real effort that satisfies his best standards of honor, integrity, and utility, he is not in a state of grace." Without the peace that came from significant work, he was ill-equipped to pursue the "serious leisure [that] was the chief way a ... man grew in character," and would instead give in to "being drowned in canned entertainment and spectatoritis."

Sloan Wilson, whose 1955 novel, *The Man in the Gray Flannel Suit,* was one of the earliest testaments of postwar anomie, saw "a kind of madness in many of the chores and frantic distractions we invent for ourselves" in the name of relaxation. Feeling authentic neither at work nor at play, people tended to make one merely an extension of, rather than a complement to, the other. "For many men," Wilson observed, "a job is simply a tournament entered in order to finance another tournament. Such men try to get the highest salary at the office in order to buy the fastest boat on the lake." This literal or metaphorical speedboating, in turn, was a sort of pseudo-recreation that simply hauled the preoccupations of the marketplace—money, power, the semblance of danger—into the playroom. Thus, "the true leisure which is a rewarding, nourishing use of free time" gave way to "a feckless, aimless meandering" that accomplished little except to fill the vacant hours till Monday morning.

These travesties of leisure were the more unfortunate in view of the life that might have been lived if work and play had found their proper balance, if they had managed to become allies while keeping their respective dignities intact. Indeed, from the perspective of 1959, it seemed that the dual blessings of free time and disposable cash were about to usher in a platinum age that would make all previous golden ages seem squalid by comparison. "The opportunity is so unprecedented," wrote the editors of *Life,* ". . . that American civilization ought to be freer and bolder than the Greek, more just and powerful than the Roman, wiser than the Confucian, richer in invention and talent than the Florentine or Elizabethan, more resplendent than the Mogul, prouder than the Spanish, saner than the French, more responsible than the Victorian, and happier than all of them together."

⫻ FOUR

It was pretty to think so, and from the perspective of 1959, the exorbitant rhetoric did not seem totally off the wall. So what happened?

What happened was that over the next two decades the American psyche did indeed bring work and leisure into balance, but in a very perverse way. Rather than promoting leisure to a dignity commensurate with that of work, people demoted work to what had formerly been regarded as the indignity of leisure. Call it a backlash from three centuries of worldly ambition congratulating itself. Through much of the

1960s and 1970s, work was widely regarded as a bothersome necessity that distracted one from one's real interests and fulfillments. A job was essentially a waste of time one endured in exchange for rent, groceries, and gas for the car.

It would be a mistake, of course, to assume that this attitude was ever anything like universal. But it would be equally incorrect, and more misleadingly so, to pretend that it was a fringe phenomenon, the sole domain of a few tens of thousands of hippies, losers, and disillusioned flakes who fled the marketplace in favor of communes, crash pads, and national parks. No, what was going on was a far more general redefinition of the implicit contracts between the worker and the workplace, and between the workplace and the society. This rethinking was a direct reaction to the version of the work ethic that had gone before, and it needs to be understood as a link to the new version of the work ethic—the eighties version—that swept into fashion afterward.

Remember *The Graduate*? In that 1968 film, the young protagonist—hardly a hippie or a revolutionary, and in fact a bourgeois little twit driving around in a sports car (a red convertible "wop job," to be more precise) and trying to lose his overripe virginity—confesses himself to be "a little worried about [his] future." A half-drunk and smugly paternal friend of the family has one word for him: "Plastics." In those two syllables were contained all the fatuity, frustration, and killing dullness that the traditional work ethic seemed to offer in the later 1960s. It really didn't matter what you did, since work had been drained of its content. The only imperative was to go where the opportunities were—to let yourself be led by the wisdom of the marketplace—no matter how abject those opportunities might be, no matter how ugly, ersatz, or absurd the end product. As Mrs. Robinson was to sex, so the workplace was to destiny: a temptress past her prime, not without the power to seduce, but without the substance and the goodness truly to fulfill. It was only a slight overstatement to say that *The Graduate* "symbolize[d] an entire generation's disenchantment with the job options offered by the most diversified society in the world."

That society, it seemed by 1970, was in the grips of a "work crisis. . . . Increasingly, the reaction of the young to the establishment work scene [was] to drop out." The dropouts, moreover, tended to be exactly the bright and well-educated people the society needed "to assume the burdens of technology management." Thus, in barely more than a decade, America's paranoia about automation and computers had done a 180-degree turnaround: the fear now was not that self-sufficient gadgets would put people out of work, but that "we may find ourselves dependent upon a complex technology that nobody can or will run." America needed engineers, facilitators, *believers,* but "bright college graduates [were becoming] taxi drivers, waiters, and supermarket checkers. . . . Communes [were being] founded by renegades from Yale, Princeton, Stanford, Dartmouth, and Berkeley."

Why? There was a constellation of reasons ranging from Vietnam to environmental concerns to the demographic bulge that magnified individual adolescent rebellions into social history. There was also the simple fact that the halfhearted participation in the fat economy of those days was participation enough; one could get by. But another reason was suggested in Studs Terkel's introduction to his 1974 collection of interviews, *Working.* "This book," Terkel wrote, "being about work, is, by its very nature, about violence—to the spirit as well as to the body. . . . It is about ulcers . . . shouting matches . . . nervous breakdowns. . . . It is, above all . . . about daily humiliations."

Had work become more humiliating in 1974 than in, say, 1954? In itself, almost certainly not. What had changed, however, was that the assumed virtue had gone out of enduring the humiliation. Under the aegis of the traditional work ethic, the ideal man was the man who could take whatever the foreman and the bosses dished out, whether the punishment came in the blue-collar form of physical degradation and docked pay, or the white-collar version of endless hours of "voluntary" overtime and ideas stolen by one's supervisor. That was dues; custom dictated that you paid up and didn't bitch. Under the new ethic of self-fulfillment, the man or woman for whom a job was daily martyrdom was at best a victim and at worst a fool. Work wasn't the army; you could leave. The refrain of the working person with dignity intact was no longer "Sixteen Tons" but "You Can Take This Job and Shove It."

Again, we're not talking hippies here. Between 1960 and 1972, worker absenteeism at auto plants doubled; on Mondays and Fridays it was common for 15 percent of the crew not to show up. Between 1969 and 1972 alone, the proportion of people reporting themselves dissatisfied with their work increased by over 46 percent. Insurance companies had to refigure their worker compensation scales in the middle seventies, not because more employees were getting injured on the job, but because they were staying out of work far longer for the same injuries; what was there to prove by going back any sooner than you had to? By 1972, an AT&T spokesman acknowledged, the phone company was "run[ning] out of dumb people to handle those dumb jobs." Even with unemployment at a then-considered-high 5.5 percent, people were declining jobs "they consider[ed] menial or unpleasant," and Douglas Fraser, then a United Auto Workers vice-president, suggested that "maybe we ought to stop talking about the work ethic and start talking about the life ethic."

While Calvin was thus taking his lumps, another development was also helping to redefine attitudes toward and priorities within the workplace. That, of course, was the flooding in of women. Between 1965 and 1976 the number of women in the labor force increased by 50 percent—and for the new entrants, the outside-the-home work ethic had the appeal, at least, of novelty. Novel, as well, for many women, was the experience of being an active economic contributor to a household that had previously gotten by with a single earner. Among married women aged twenty to fifty-four, 41.5 percent had held jobs in 1967; by 1976 the percentage had swelled to 52.4 percent. An undeterminable proportion of those women went to work out of perceived necessity, but for many, entering the work force was discretionary.

Discretion, however, cut both ways, and along with the phenomenon of wives who felt proud and privileged to work for pay came the phenomenon of increasing numbers of husbands who felt proud and privileged not to. During the ten years ending in 1977, the number of men who neither held nor were seeking jobs increased by 71 percent. Some had become househusbands. Some worked sporadically as carpenters or handymen or drivers. An increasing proportion basked in the tax-free status of the underground economy, and the only thing that could be said about their labor was that it was *unaccounted for*.

These fellows had gone about as far as possible from the Calvinist idea of "grace made manifest" by worldly accomplishments. Manifest? So far as the realm of work was concerned, they were doing everything they could to become invisible.

//// FIVE

What was going on with the new ideal of leisure while the old ideal of work was losing its cachet?

It would be nice to think that the time and passion being withheld from paid labor were being channeled into the sorts of substantial and public-spirited recreation that *Life* had foreseen in 1959. In fact, however, the concept of spare time in America had been moving precisely the other way, becoming ever more private, self-contained, even solipsistic. Free time was time for hiding out.

The sixties argot spoke the unvarnished truth in its preoccupation with what went on inside people's heads, since not a great deal was issuing forth—or not, at least, going farther than the small circle of one's friends. Marijuana, the decade's hallmark drug, went a long way toward giving introspection a bad name. In the potted years, introspection was something you did *instead* of talking, *instead* of acting, *instead* of leaving your room; all but lost was the sense in which introspection is a preparation for action, a private getting ready to be publicly more effective.

When, in the seventies, the marijuana culture subsided and the fitness craze kicked in, it was the most solitary forms of sweat-and-strain that attracted the grunting millions; now even friends tended to be excluded from one's leisure. Team sports were fine for watching on TV, but one's own workout consisted of jogging, aerobics, stretching, Nautilus. America had never been leaner or lonelier. Riding the stationary bike, Walkman in place and newspaper perched on the handlebars, one could trim one's cellulite and enhance one's oxygen utilization while having absolutely nothing to do with anyone. Gourmet take-out and a movie on the VCR would make it a perfectly hermetic evening.

Not that there was anything wrong with solitary sweating, a dinner eaten alone, or home entertainment in the sublime comfort of one's PJs. But where was the glue that would bind those individual recreations together, that would make them more than a series of isolating diversions? Nautilus may have defined the quadriceps, but the purpose of leisure was to define the whole person in relation to the world around him or her; *that* sort of definition was being slighted.

And all of us were being impoverished by the slight. Collectively considered, a society's leisure constitutes a gigantic exercise in show-and-tell, a celebration of the attainments a citizenry has reached in excess of the mere business of survival. Leisure represents a society's surplus competence, surplus curiosity—even, at its highest, surplus genius. When that surplus is treated as a public kitty, civilization happens. When it is jealously held in private little stashes, all that comes of it is increased leotard sales and movie rentals, and a social aloofness that comes not from conscious choice but simply from the habit of staying snugly inside one's skin.

Through the 1980s, leisure became ever more atomized, each of us hoarding his little stock of it in precisely the same way we hoarded our money and our very personal ambitions as to our careers. The several forms of egoism were of course related, as work and leisure went public or private together. With no shared sense of the inherent value of work, there could be no shared sense of the value of play.

/// SIX

In the 1980s—so we have often been told, generally by people trying to sell us something—the work ethic staged an impressive revival.

"The Pride Is Back," one carmaker claimed, though it seemed dubious that morale had lifted in Detroit now that many of this company's cars were made in Asia. "Your Money Should Work As Hard As You Do," spieled a financial services firm, flattering its prospective customers for being driven as well as well off. Ads for Holiday Inn showed workaholics of all races, creeds, and colors converging on its hostelries, miraculously unrumpled even after monster days of travel, meetings, and triumphant sales calls. In 1986, "A New Take on Type A" was offered. The revised medical view was that previous findings on the links between job stress and heart attacks may have been skewed; now that work was virtuous again, the docs were saying that if you approached your career with joy and pursued your ambition with zest rather than hostile desperation, a regimen of sixteen-hour days probably wouldn't kill you, after all.

But what kind of work and what kind of virtue were actually making a comeback in the eighties? In fact, it was not the sort of work that went into making cars, and not the sort of virtue that inhered in being a proud part of an effective team, of pulling one's weight in an enterprise larger than oneself. The work ethic of the eighties, that is to say, borrowed the vocabulary and reached for the legitimacy of the work ethic that had gone before, but in reality it was a different animal.

The new work ethic was two-tiered, as work itself was becoming increasingly two-tiered. There had always been, as John Kenneth Galbraith put it, a "terrible class aspect of the work ethic"; traditionally, work had been thought to be "especially ethical for the poor and much less ethical for the rich." That, of course, was when the rich had been the leisure class.

But in the 1980s, in a development that must be regarded as epochal, that dynamic flip-flopped. Indolent millionaires were no longer in style. The fashionable wealthy were now the slaving wealthy—the people who negotiated through the night to close the deal, who were up before dawn to monitor the London exchanges, who were interrupted at dinner to revise a brief or stanch a flow of funds. That these truly hardworking people were, by any reasonable measure, egregiously overpaid for what they did, fed both their motivation and their fashionableness. It made them paragons of a new work ethic geared to traders, corporate lawyers, investment bankers, starters-up of companies taken public. This was an ethic that held out a dazzlingly fat carrot to the very small minority who might plausibly have a shot at getting to the economic top.

But it didn't say much to most of us. Most of us, however hard we worked, were not in line for the long green, the major money, and most of us knew it. Most of us were therefore immune to, if not resentful of, the new work-ethic pitch. In a 1968 survey, 58 percent of the public had agreed with the statement "hard work always pays off." By 1978 the figure had shrunk to 44 percent, and by 1983 it was down to 36 percent. That same year, only 13 percent of the work force believed that they themselves would be the primary beneficiaries of harder work or increased efficiency. As the sociologist and pollster Daniel Yankelovich put it, worker morale had deteriorated "because the American economy no longer seem[ed] to be delivering as reliably on the implied promise that hard work will bring material improvement." To put it another way, the typical American employee was not moved to great feats of dedication by seeing other jerks get rich.

Through the middle 1980s, with the economy purportedly recovering and the beer commercials lionizing those good old blue-collar guys, tens of millions of jobholders found themselves curiously unaffected either by prosperity or by the psychological boost that supposedly went with it. In each of the "good" years of 1984, 1985, and 1986, between 1 million and 2 million manufacturing jobs disappeared. Of the workers displaced, more than a third remained jobless beyond the time their unemployment benefits ran out. More than half of the rest took jobs that paid them 30 to 50 percent less than the jobs they'd lost. In 1987—the fifth

yawning and readily visible disparity between that group's prospects and everybody else's. At a time when the popular buzzwords were competitiveness and productivity, the message that was really being sent to most of America's employees was *Why bother?*

/// **SEVEN**

As the gulf—both economic and psychic—broadened between privileged work and grunt work, so the ideal of a public, socially bonding leisure receded ever farther into the distance. Those who were cut off from the opportunity for gratifying labor did indeed tend, as had been predicted more than a quarter-century before, to fall into a torpor that made them easy prey for "canned entertainments and spectatoritis." For them, "leisure" was the soaps and/or the sports page, and they were dissuaded from ranging farther not only by financial constraints but by a terrible and systemic dulling of their curiosity.

Those who had the good work, meanwhile, and who therefore subscribed most heartily to the new work ethic of the 1980s, took a very different approach to leisure—yet ended up at a point not so very far removed. Spurred on by the potential oversize rewards, eighties go-getters tended to work until there was simply nothing left. When they were finished dealing with people on behalf of the firm, they were finished dealing with people; when they were done giving to the job, they'd had it with giving. Leisure, for them, was recuperation and the chance to attend to themselves. It was not a realm in which to seek new challenges—other than, perhaps, of the cardiovascular sort—because they had challenges enough.

It was certainly not a realm in which to rub elbows with those outside their own social and economic circle. In a

straight year of economic growth—fully 40 per
employed Americans were earning less than $11,00(
and between 10 million and 20 million people—no
ing housewives, students, the disabled, or the retired
staying out of the job market altogether. The Labor
ment, in an uncharacteristically straightforward usag∈
these people "discouraged workers."

It was a peculiar sort of work ethic that could coex
and even flourish in the face of, circumstances such ∂
It was so peculiar that it was hard not to wonder if ∣
the term "work ethic" was being stretched beyond ∈
ity. The phrase *used* to embrace everyone in the labⲟ
Everyone should work hard; everyone could be ∈
materially as well as spiritually, by doing so. But no
itself was becoming elitist—far more so, really, than
As in the late days of Rome, when the idle or underen
masses were placated with bread and circuses, leisⵏ
what passed for leisure—had gotten as cheap as dir
the blessings of layaway and easy credit, only the tru
were unable to splurge on a VCR and a portable miⵏ
for making one-minute popcorn.

It was work—good work—that had become th
commodity, the luxury. Only a relative few could haⴱ
that called forth peak effort by affording self-esteeⲛ
chance at meaningful advancement. Only a relati
were really being courted by the marketplace,
relative few could honestly be motivated to buⵤ
humps. The eighties work ethic was a work ethic
seventy-thousand-and-over set.

It was nothing new, of course, that those who strⵏ
hardest were those who perceived themselves as haⴱ
most to gain by it. What was new, however, ⴱ
narrowness of the swath of population for whom har
seemed worth the trouble; new as well, in America, ⴱ

time of widening inequality, the workaholic elite and the underemployed masses were increasingly becoming a mutual embarrassment and a mutual rebuke. How, under those circumstances, could there possibly be such a thing as a "national" leisure?

And how had 1950s optimism erred so widely in thinking there *would* be?

Fifties optimism went awry, it seems, in presuming that imperial America would adopt as its ideal the classical notion of balance. It was assumed that, given a certain level of prosperity and security, people would *choose* leisure—as they had done, say, in Periclean Athens or Renaissance Florence. Everyone would come to see the virtues of cultivation, the value of rewards outside the marketplace, and people would therefore work less as they could afford to. The good work, it followed, would be spread around as those who'd made their pile stepped partially aside, and the trend could only be toward greater equality. Thus the ideal of balance in the individual life would automatically conduce to the reality of balance in the society at large.

What the formula failed to take into account, of course, was greed—not simply or perhaps even mainly the greed for money, but for the work itself, for the responsibility and power that went with the money and fostered the comforting illusions that one was indispensable and had a clear purpose. In the eighties, almost no one with good work slowed down if he or she could possibly help it; no one "wasted" time on leisure if that time could be spent staying ahead of the pack. Eighties greed was not essentially of the decadent or hedonistic variety—the era would have been more interesting if it had been; rather, it was a nervous, twitchy, looking-over-the-shoulder-while-running-full-speed-ahead sort of affair—and as long as that sort of greed was waxing, the ideal of balance necessarily waned.

Without the ideal of balance, the shining promise of the new leisure very soon turned quaint. The enlightened use of spare time competing for equal prestige with the doing of paid work and the making of money? No. Maybe for a brief time, when America's hegemony seemed boundless and the question of *What next?* took continuing prosperity as a given—maybe then that Renaissance stuff would wash. But not now. The notion of a public-spirited leisure had been added to that long list of luxuries we could supposedly no longer afford.

Which was too bad, because of all the manifold optimisms of 1959, the optimism of leisure was perhaps the one that didn't have to be disappointed. Rocket mail? With the government falling deeper and deeper into hock, no one expected rocket mail. Ten-thousand-passenger cruise ships? That had been an Edsel all along. But the idea that a nation could be enriched as much by its play as by its work—that idea did not depend on jazzy new technologies and it didn't have to cost a lot of money. All it took was a shared belief that building a civilization went beyond building an economy, and could only be accomplished by many pairs of hands.

13 //

The
F-Word

*I rated Wolfe first because we had all failed but
Wolfe had made the best failure because he had
tried hardest to say the most.*

—*William Faulkner*

//// ONE

Albert Einstein was a failure. He set for himself the task
of deriving a set of equations so spectacularly versatile that
they could account for every physical occurrence in the
universe, and he blew it. He had to settle for the theory of
relativity—to many, the most sublime construct in science,
to Einstein a mere piddling first step.

John Milton was a failure. In writing *Paradise Lost,* his
stated aim was to "justify the ways of God to man." He
flopped, as God's ways remain as inscrutable, and man as
unresigned, as before.

Beethoven, whose music was conceived to go one-on-one
with the clamoring of Fate, was a failure, as was Socrates,
who made a fatal losing bet that men could be persuaded

their true self-interest lay in being reasonable and just. For that matter, in our own time, everyone who has muddled toward a cancer cure has thus far been a washout, as has everyone who has flailed away at eliminating poverty. The moral of the story would seem to be that talent, passion, dedication, and even genius do not necessarily doom one to success. Aim high enough and you can always fall on your face.

Not that failure of this sort has been a widespread problem in America of late. The case can be made, in fact, that one of the 1980s' signal woes was a shortage of failures. Grand failures, that is. What failures there were—businesses going belly-up, people losing their jobs or (God forbid) stalling in their career tracks—were of the same stripe as the successes there were.

One guy makes partner, another doesn't; big deal. One guy gets a Christmas bonus and buys a European sedan, another guy doesn't and keeps his K-car another year. No doubt these things matter a lot to the people they happen to, and we should all feel bad for the guy who doesn't get the Jag. But we're not talking starvation here, nor are we talking breakthroughs of the soaring human spirit. We're talking varying possibilities within the gray area, the very gray area, lodged comfortably between. We're plotting points along a continuum of comfort and status, a continuum that, by consensus though not by necessity, gives both success and failure their meanings.

But there's a curious thing about this continuum. Out of linguistic habit, we speak of it as reflecting our "value system"—yet values, except for money values, have been virtually excluded from our reckoning of where a given "success" or "failure" falls. What gets factored in, other than income and job title? Does anyone get points for the intrinsic value of what he or she *tried* to do? Is it taken into consideration that some paths are simply harder than others? Is there anything, in short, that makes the terms *success* and *failure* more than pompous synonyms for well-paid or not? And if there isn't, isn't it a little embarrassing, doesn't it make you feel a little bit sucked in, to get so rabid about success?

Like work and leisure, success and failure become exalted or devalued together; trivialize one and you trivialize both. In the 1980s, both were trivialized.

Success, as we have argued, was reduced to a flash-card sort of language, a bunch of nouns with price tags on them. Paycheck; co-op; famous car—you connect the dots. If there was an integral relation between these buyable things and some substantive achievement that earned them, the relation was seldom explained. Usually it couldn't be explained, except by invoking the wisdom of the marketplace, and that wisdom comes down finally to a tautology: that's what it's worth because that's what someone will pay.

This particular view of success did not come to hold sway by accident; it has its advantages. For one thing, in the pseudo-flush years of the middle 1980s, there was enough slack in the system so that many more people could afford to be rewarded than would actually accomplish anything of consequence. For another, in a highly specialized world, understanding the guts of another person's achievement is difficult, whereas recognizing the consensual, Veblenian tokens of making it is easy.

But there is one great and terrifying problem with defining success in terms of the things success conventionally buys: those things can always be taken away. They can be taken away through no fault of one's own, and they can be taken away fast. The honeymoon ends in Silicon Valley, and the Mercedeses vanish from the new-age parking lots where not even the Big Cheese had a reserved space; have all the laid-off people who only yesterday were great successes, not only wealthy at a young age but part of an industry considered hip, gone instantly back to being computer nerds with pen-packs in the pockets of their badly fitting shirts? The millionaire-making firms of Wall Street start trimming fat in response to Meltdown Monday; the people who get axed will still have their tassel loafers and their Rolexes, but maybe they won't make it out to Easthampton this season—have these erstwhile whiz-kids suddenly become *schlemiels*?

These are not abstract questions, but lived dilemmas. This stuff happens—and it happens with special violence to people who have enjoyed the luxury, and suffered the peril, of imagining it couldn't happen to *them*. Well, it could, and it has; and the event has exposed the bankruptcy of yet another of the 1980s' widespread and convenient fibs: that people craved success not because they were greedy, not because they hankered for money or status per se, but because they wanted to feel that they were in control of their lives.

Well, who doesn't? But it is demonstrably, dramatically false that control of one's life consists in a fast-track job, a fat paycheck, and a hoard of possessions. To the extent that one becomes dependent on those things, in fact, one cedes control of one's destiny and puts oneself at the mercy of forces that no one seems to understand, much less be in charge of. The stock market falls five hundred points in a day, and no one has the faintest idea why. The company gets bought out, and vice-presidents read about it in the paper. This is being in control? No, this is staking one's sense of self on a dog race. This is banking on a gossamer thread of self-esteem that can be swept away by a pink slip. A kind of success that can be instantly squashed by the guy in the corner office is not the kind of success on which one ought to pin one's hopes.

Forget philosophy. Forget ethics and forget social concerns. Look at it purely in terms of the nakedest, most cynical self-interest: Why define success in such a manner that the bastards can take it away from you?

⫻ TWO

To look at it from the other side, why define failure in such a manner that it can be pinned on you from behind, that other people can nail you with the label, and the label is irredeemably damning?

As conventionally regarded, failure is a verdict imposed from without, and carries with it a double emptiness. The first emptiness consists in the fact that failure is not generally accorded the respect of being approached as a thing unto itself, but is thought of only as the absence of success, the hole that's left when the treasure has been dug for but not found.

The second emptiness, even grimmer, was neatly described by William Gaddis in 1981. In "a society where failure can reside in simply not being a 'success' ... [the] most ignominious defeats [of all are held] in store for those ... who fail at something that was not worth doing in the first place."

But failure doesn't *have* to be regarded that way. It doesn't have to be thought of merely as the absence of success, or the absence of anything. To put it simply, "lack of success" and "failure" are two different things. Lack of success is something that happens to you—or rather, doesn't happen—while seeking success. Failure is something you do instead. It is an active stance, an approach that draws from a far wider spectrum of options and leads on to a far wider spectrum of results than do the stances that go with making it.

It is not a coincidence that the imagery of success is relentlessly linear—one takes the road to riches, or cleaves to the straight and narrow path to respectability and advancement. Mere lack of success stalks that same rutted highway, only it doesn't get very far. True failure, on the other hand, takes the scenic route. Consider the quintessential flop, Don Quixote. Quixote doesn't stall on the thin pathway to succeeding; he bushwhacks through uncharted ground—frontier, if you will—on a globe-trotting mission through the dales and back alleys of failure. To describe *Don Quixote* as a book about a guy who doesn't succeed is absolutely, stunningly, to miss the point. The story, rather, is about the implacable dignity that accrues to someone who sets out to fail big, and with a pure heart.

Measured by the conventional American view of what striving is about, this is, of course, romantic nonsense. Saying *anything* even provisionally good about failure smacks equally of the incomprehensible, the subversive, and the morbid. But that's because the conventional view defines failure, *a priori,* as everything frustrating, substandard, bad. This is a view fostered by an extreme, deadening, and *willful* want of imagination. The want of imagination comes from a resolute inattention, and the inattention comes, in turn, from fear.

No one thinks about the textures, the nuances, of failure because no one wants to think about failure at all. It can't be talked about. In a society where infidelity, net worth, ovarian dysfunctions, and whether size matters are routinely discussed over dinner, failure remains taboo, an object of superstitious dread, the only F-word not in common parlance.

Some people can barely bring themselves to pronounce the syllables. In 1986, *The Wall Street Journal* reported on a business professor from Yale who forced his students, all of whom had previous work experience, to talk about their failures; "someone always ask[ed] if 'error' or 'mistake' [could] be used instead." This is roughly analogous to being in medical school and referring to human excrement as doody, but so general is the horror of failure that the baby words are not only accepted but encouraged in grown-up company.

The national dread of failure is nothing new, of course, though its prominence ebbs and flows; when business is in fashion, and success is all the rage, fear of failure takes on a proportionate virulence. The basic terror, though, has existed "from the outset" and derives, in a perverse way, from the exact circumstance that gave rise to the habit of more: from "the fabulous opportunities open to a new people on a new continent." In America, a "man's destiny [was] largely up to him." The land was unimaginably rich, and according to democratic orthodoxy, social classes did not exist. Facing neither barriers nor boundaries, one could rise according to one's diligence and abilities, or flop according to the lacks thereof. In America as in no other society before or since, character was fate.

There were only two problems with this ideal of America as pure meritocracy. First, merit did not begin and end with the sorts of skills and proclivities rewarded by the marketplace—unless, that is, you drained "merit" of its meaning so that it suggested nothing but the ability to make money. If you did that, merit did indeed equal success, both terms being equally vacuous.

Second, the model of America-as-meritocracy was never more than approximately accurate, and it became less so the more established and diverse America became, the more time and cultural experience separated the old arrivals from the new. Immigrants couldn't help it that they talked funny. Blacks, Jews, Catholics, and women couldn't help it that they weren't wanted in certain places. Nor were all the factors that tipped the scales of opportunity as gross or obvious as gender or race. When the Founding Fathers talked about separation of powers, they neglected to separate the power of certain schools from the power of certain industries, the influence of certain clubhouses from the influence of certain boardrooms.

None of this is news, of course, and that's precisely the point: It *should* have been abundantly clear all along that the American playing field was not exactly level, and the awareness that this was so *should* have injected some reality into the mythology of making it on merit alone. More pertinent to the present discussion, it should also have made less crushingly personal the possibility of failure.

Yet succeeding on pure merit was such a glorious, affirming, intoxicating ideal that in America people clung to it in spite of ample evidence that that wasn't precisely how things worked, and in spite of the fact that the mythology made life emotionally tougher for almost everybody. "To the lure of accomplishment was added the new shame of failure that could not be blamed on 'the system.'" Living *as if* deserts were generally just, the unsuccessful American "often suffer[ed] agonies at the sight of an old schoolmate driving a Cadillac." He was deprived even of the comfort of resignation by the half-truth that he, too, might have had the fancy car, the golf shoes with fringes, the wife with the polka-dot dress made not of rayon but of silk.

Too ready to let success be defined by the tokens of success, too willing to take sole credit when he did succeed, the traditional American could not shrug off a devastating self-blame when he failed. Either way, he tended to regard his strivings in a Promethean vacuum, overlooking the role of luck, of favors, of biases pro or con, ignoring virtually every aspect of context. When times were good, people tended to make money, and they thought they were damn clever and virtuous for doing so; when times were bad, they missed mortgage payments and boarded up the windows of small businesses, generally preferring a stoic despair to the making of excuses.

Neither despair nor excuses, however, were satisfactory substitutes for the simple and humbling acknowledgment that "success" and "failure" were not wholly in one's control. A new technology could make you or break you. Interest rates could make you look smart or stupid. Your biggest competitor could marry rich and quadruple his resources or he could slip in the bathtub and die. A guy from Bonn could get mad at a guy from Tokyo, a banker from Hong Kong could cable a dealer in Geneva, and everything could change. Five years' worth of "success" could vanish in an afternoon, quick and slippery as a shadow sliding over snow. There was just no knowing.

There should have been a species of relief in the realization that success and failure, as measured in money, partook in varying degrees of the accidental. But it was not in the traditional American psyche to embrace that relief, any more than it was part of the American psyche to factor in class biases when framing one's ambitions. In America, goals did not necessarily moderate in accordance with realistic prospects. The hunger for more prevailed, even when its cost was anguish, even when its cost was rage. In America, the unlikely was not the impossible. One should be able to transcend. Not to transcend was to fail.

But isn't the idea of failure itself—the harrowing, narrowing, paralyzing fear of it—something that ought to be transcended? Among people whose avowed goal is mastering their own fate, there is something abject—and, if you step back, something bleakly comic—in the knee-knocking dread that the label of failure could be pinned on them by circumstance, by consensus, by someone pointing a finger.

How meek we are! How we blanch with mute terror at the possibility of screwing up or of being passed by. How easily deflected we are from just getting on with what we ought to do. What, after all, is the worst that could happen?

/// THREE

Success and failure. Work and leisure. Life and life-style.

The eighties were a time when these linked and warring pairs, the push and pull between them, went a long way toward defining how we lived. These were the categories that signified, the ones through which our actual, active values could be inferred.

Not that one simply and conclusively chose success or failure, or signed on forever with the program of work or of leisure, or gave allegiance once and for all either to the demands of life or the niceties of lifestyle. No, the choices were always provisional, never absolute, and seldom wholly one's own to make. As to the results the choices led to—whether measured in money or job status or accomplishment or contentment—they were as varied and as full of nuance as life itself.

Yet there was something in the air in the 1980s that tended to deny those nuances, to reduce the infinite graduations to dry and flavorless instances of either/or. Rich or poor. Ambitious or lazy. Materialistic or inward. A winner or a loser.

Where did that reductive tendency come from? It derived from the unexamined and perhaps unconscious habit of thinking in terms of the marketplace model—as the business rah-rahs said we should, as the pragmatic fashion of the day demanded. In the marketplace, a number went up or it went down; a day was good or bad in direct proportion to the amount of money made or lost; people were worth more than you, or less. Why shouldn't all of life be so breezily unambiguous, so free of fuzz and rough edges? It wasn't that marketplace logic *explained* things, exactly; rather, it described them within a framework that suggested they didn't need to *be* explained: results mattered, judgments didn't. This, at a time when life seemed unprecedentedly uncertain and complex (as it had seemed, of course, in every decade before) was comforting.

Comforting, but dangerous. There was a certain brittle finality to marketplace verdicts; the dynamic of either/or was powerful but not nimble. If circumstances no longer seemed to warrant wild optimism, you had no choice but to be a pessimist; there was nothing in between. If conditions no longer seemed peachy to make you a success, then the same stark logic that had impelled you toward that version of making it now whispered failure in your ear.

The terror of that word, in turn, brought about a whining faintheartedness, a superstitious dread that clouded thinking, even among those for whom thinking clearly was purportedly Job One. At Harvard Business School, on the virtual eve of the October '87 crash, MBA candidates were complaining about being given case histories that turned out badly, as if the cases—which were *true,* after all— carried evil spells that would poison their careers. "We want to be successful," groused one student, "and they're telling us horror stories."

Well, chum, welcome to a universe where horror stories happen, and life goes on. Welcome to a world where things don't turn out exactly as you were so cocksure they would, where the right moves don't necessarily stay right long enough to make a brilliant career of, where half a decade's paper gains can vanish in a few hours—and where, if you *really* believe in the marketplace versions of success and failure, you have painted yourself into one hell of a tight corner. Success, by that reckoning, is predicated on the numbers going up, up, up, on the continuing manufacture of *more*. If the numbers come down, even if they stay nested where they are, you're left murmuring the F-word.

Words, however, change. So do the things the words refer to. Success doesn't need to be described according to the dry mechanics of making more money next year than this year. It can equally well be spoken of in terms of knowing more, understanding more, being more serene. For that matter, success doesn't need to imply progression at all. What about the ideal of *consistency*? To find a way of living, and to stick to it in the face of changing fashions and outside pressures—call it dignity, and if the maintenance of one's dignity doesn't count as a high form of success, then our ways of reckoning are hardly worth a nod. Similarly, optimism doesn't have to be defined in terms of a perennially rising economic graph, and the marketplace model doesn't have to be accepted as a particularly useful or desirable way of looking at anything except the marketplace. These definitions, these metaphors, are merely customary. They are devices meant to serve our convenience. When, in the course of shifting circumstance, they no longer do— when they make more people feel bad than good, when they motivate toward goals that no longer serve the commonweal—it is time to change them.

Fortunately, we are hypocrites in this regard: When the marketplace was cooking, when the go-go atmosphere flattered our ambitions and confirmed our drives, it seemed natural to install the marketplace as the central shrine and symbol of our hopes. Now that the gloss is gone and the rah-rahs have been chastened, it seems just as natural to nudge marketplace values back toward the periphery. Not that those values suddenly became inadequate in late

October 1987. No, they were paltry, purblind, and hazard-ously one-dimensional all along, and it only took the oddly relieving catharsis of the Crash to make that clear.

It took the Crash, as well, to point up the paradox in the eighties' insistence on *not settling*. Oh, those were brave words in the 1980s, the battle cry of all those bright and energetic men and women who were determined not to be left behind and not to be railroaded into a fate that was merely ordinary. If they had their hearts set on Stanford, they wouldn't be content with UCLA; if they wanted the cashmere, the lambswool would give them a rash. Less, perhaps, with joy than with defiance, these people had decided that nothing but the best was good enough for them. Anything else reeked of defeat, and "success" was what you went for so you wouldn't have to settle for anything else, so your world would know no boundaries.

But success eighties-style was itself a closely bounded precinct, with a mapped and hard-edged grid of options. You got an MBA. You went to law school. You did computers. You worked hard, and long, and you watched your butt. Yet for all its ferocious demands on time, energy, and some-times dignity, success eighties-style, if you were privileged enough to get onto its track, was really sort of easy—and sort of ordinary. Once you'd selected "success" as your aim—once you'd decided that success was the kind of noun that could be used that way—no further decisions were necessary. You pulled on your work clothes and followed the map.

But what about all the options that weren't *on* the map?

What about the back alleys and the winding roads, the sort of fringe places that were not in social fashion and might still be called frontier? If the destination was success, you didn't go there. That's where failure resided—as did other things that, once upon a time, were respected for the courage they demanded and the imagination they embodied: the independent and proudly disinterested thought, the cutting-edge work in the arts and in the sciences, the notion of social duty not as a fund one gave money to, but as something one acted upon.

In the brief and frenetic heyday of the eighties, it didn't seem that much of consequence was being given up by forswearing those back roads. The action was elsewhere. But in the long suspended moment since the day the eighties ended, it has begun to look rather different. It has begun to seem that maybe "success" itself had been a kind of settling, a limiting of oneself to those few worn paths that other people had defined, that led to rewards that other people had determined, and that other people, or blind circumstance, could take away again.

Did this add up to a destiny that was other than ordinary, a life that was self-chosen and self-achieved? With the fever of the eighties broken; it didn't seem so. It seemed more truthful to suggest that success eighties-style was a kind of victory that people settled for when they couldn't decide on a quest that was truly their own, in the absence of a calling that would be worth the risk of failing at.

Epilogue: Toward a More Temperate Time

ONE

Benno Collier had four phone lines and half a secretary.

Her name was Teresa. She had red hair, and she sat on the other side of a low partition. The partition didn't reach all the way to the floor, and sometimes Benno would watch Teresa kick off her shoes and scratch the instep of one foot with the toes of the other. When a call came in, Teresa would pick up after three rings if Benno hadn't. She'd announce the caller through the intercom, and Benno would respond by way of hand signals, raising his arm above the level of the frosted-glass screen between them. A single upraised finger meant she should ask the caller to hold. A finger making quick circles meant Benno would call right back. A hand waving good-bye meant Benno didn't want to talk to the person, and Teresa, in her most sympathetic voice, would say he was in an all-day round of research meetings.

At 2:07 in the afternoon of Monday, the fourth of April 1988, Benno was talking with a client in Denver when Teresa's voice came through the intercom. "Your wife is on four-three," she said.

Benno made quick circles with a finger.

A moment passed, then Teresa's face appeared at the top of the partition. "She says she's going into labor."

//// TWO

By the spring of 1988, America had settled into a slightly uneasy, noncommittal calm. Half a year after the Wall Street debacle, the country overall did not look much different from the way it had looked before. The mainstream economy was more than surviving; some claimed it was flourishing. Unemployment rates were more or less stable, and while prices at the grocery would soon be inching upward in response to the Midwest drought, consumers did not seem overly concerned. As the memory of October faded somewhat, people began to feel that the projected effects of the trillion-dollar loss in abstract wealth had been greatly exaggerated all along, blown up by a blend of blind fear and media hype. The markets themselves had returned to a relative sanity; they plodded along—as, before the eighties, they almost always had—gaining a little, losing a little, not doing anything worthy of headlines.

There had, of course, been casualties. Pensioners in Florida had seen their nest eggs crack, and developers in Arizona now had a harder sell on their hands. Certain New York restaurants had gotten palpably quieter; J. Bildner's, the pricey, so-called yuppie grocer in Benno and Sally Collier's neighborhood, had closed its doors and soaped its windows. Small cities like Portland, Maine, and Eugene, Oregon, found themselves littered here and there with the skeletons of uncompleted buildings from the boomlets of the hothouse years. The business press, bloated from the days when money news was the grabbiest news, found itself with a shortage of pizzazzy stories to tell and perhaps the beginnings of a shortage of people who were so intent on reading them. *Fortune* got skinnier. Dow Jones killed plans for a new magazine.

Yet there was a far more important casualty of the graceless and panicked ending of the 1980s: the hunger for more.

The Crash demonstrated the perils of the eighties version of that hunger the way a fall down stairs reminds someone he's been drinking too much. The tumble surprises almost more than it hurts, and in the wake of the surprise there is room for insight, reassessment. In the aftermath of the undignified rout that wrapped up the decade, a new sort of realism began taking hold—a realism more mature and much more real than the gung-ho mythology that had lately passed for pragmatism. Numbers *could* go down. Easy gains *did* tend to be neutralized by helpless losses. Against the impulse of growth was a slingshot effect that worked to bring things back to roughly where they'd started. Brash and unexamined confidence would take you just so far; when something really big happened, your own blustering success suddenly seemed as frail as a baby bird.

To be humbled without being destroyed is a piece of great good luck, and this is what happened to economic America at the end of the 1980s. It could begin to be acknowledged—without shame, and better late than never—that America was a nation among other nations, a player in a political and financial system larger than itself. The morning news now carried reports of what was going on in London and in Tokyo. Currency fluctuations were seen now not as adjustments other countries made *around* the dollar, but as ebbs and flows that included the dollar, and that were designed to keep a vast—and delicate— machine from going irreparably out of whack.

With the acknowledgment of interdependence came a more enlightened understanding of what competition meant—and didn't mean. Remember Richard Gephardt? He ran for President on the single issue of getting tough with perfidious foreigners—and was repudiated at the polls. In New Hampshire, in the South, even in Detroit, there was a postmodern understanding that blaming it on the other guy may have felt good but didn't help. Jesse Jackson got much farther on the message that task one was making the system work better and more fairly *here*—and that there existed a natural solidarity among all those for whom the system hadn't been working, all those who had been left pressing their noses against the window of the narrowly held prosperity of the years before.

If the talk of solidarity and new alliances was an inevitable feature of an election year, it was the breaking of the eighties fever that suggested that perhaps the sense of shared purpose, of mission, might now become more widespread than it had been for the past fifteen years or so. There was something conciliating about Black Monday— conciliating beyond the simple grim reminder that we could all go down the tubes together.

As the political events of the seventies had chipped away at the myth of national omnipotence, so the panic of '87 and the blahs that followed let the air out of business rhetoric and brought the bigshots back to actual size; and there was relief in this for all concerned. The financial milieu was humanized by its failure—as big industry had been by its setbacks in years past. Now that the ringmasters of the money circus had been publicly embarrassed, now that the grievous limitations of their magic had been exposed, there was less reason to resent them. They too labored under the fearsome knowledge that they were not in control of the game; they too could be baffled, helpless, beaten down. Yuppie-bashing, which for a brief time had constituted a new genre of snide humor, became passé as soon as yuppies started losing jobs, putting their apartments up for sale, admitting they'd been blind-sided. Now that they weren't moving so fast as to blur, the young professionals who had done so much to define the 1980s could be seen for what they were: a group of people dropped by historical chance into a given set of circumstances at a given time, doing their honest if conventional best to measure up to a standard then in vogue.

To measure up—that, after all, was what the quintessential eighties types had been trying to do; and the impulse, fundamentally, was no different from that which in decades past molded young adults into organization men or perfect housewives or hippie carpenters or activists. Social fashion was powerful; it had to be factored into what passed for free choice. The sense of what was fitting changed, the broad desire to do what was fitting did not.

By the spring of 1988, it had begun to seem that the sense of what was fitting was due for a revision.

⫻ THREE

Wear a suit that is ten years out of style, and you will probably get away with it. Time will have invested it with a sort of quaintness, of venerability, even of irony. Wear a suit that is one year out of style, and its datedness will seem glaring, tawdry, insuperable.

By the spring of 1988, eighties social fashions had begun

to look as bad as last year's suit. The rabid chase after the fast and famous dollar had already come to seem a trifle retro, a little out of sync. This happened fast—one night you went to sleep exemplary and in the morning woke up crass. Greed was no longer bragged about as though it were evidence of sexual vigor. The world of business became a less persuasive synecdoche for the world entire, and the expensive frills of lifestyle no longer sufficed for covering over the foursquare basics of life.

The pendulum was moving away from the excesses of an age of money, toward a more temperate part of its arc, a place where different values would pertain. Tentatively at first, almost bashfully, those values were beginning to assert themselves.

It began to be acknowledged that a meaningful measure of a nation's well-being could not be reached by oohing and aahing over its richest people, but only by taking an un-flinching look at all the tens of millions who weren't rich. If you cared enough to seek an honest picture of how America was doing, you didn't ogle the mansion where Donald Trump lived; you asked what kind of medical care was available to his gardener, where his housekeepers' children went to school. In the answers to those sorts of questions resided the germ of national pride or national shame, the evidence of whether America was living up to its promises.

As to the nature of one's own stake in that promise, that, too, was undergoing a revision. The eighties had steered people toward an insistently private stake—you carved your slice off America's wealth as though it were a wheel of cheese, and hoarded your little treasure like a mouse. By the values of the 1980s, it didn't seem to matter that the central cheese was being whittled away, and that after all those individual helpings had been consumed there would be . . . what?

The newer values carried with them a different sense of stake-holding. There was less emphasis on one's own little stash, and more emphasis on the role one played—as worker and consumer—in stewardship over America's wealth-in-common. Certain old ideas seemed new again: respectable wealth derived from adding value, not from skimming the top of the pot; financial whizzes who pulled dollars from a hat were no longer admired. Fortunes that subtracted from the commonweal were not fortunes to be celebrated in the media, but fortunes to be ashamed of, spent in secret like the proceeds of crime. As eighties social fashion had hissed forth the message that we were all free agents, so the newer values whispered that, in addition, we were all trustees.

With privilege came obligation. Indeed, an integral aspect of privilege was the ability to make a difference—to better one's community, to make one's company more responsible. And making a difference, in turn, was coming to be seen as the more durable criterion for measuring success.

Through the 1980s, as we have argued, success was progressively drained of its content, sucked dry of its meaning, until it denoted nothing more than having lots of money. This dry husk of success, being devoid both of weight and of roots, blew away on the first ill wind. In its place was left the recognition that a notion of personal achievement without a context of shared values was as cold and useless as a burnt-out star. What does an individual's success mean to the *rest* of us? What does it *create*? What sort of mark does it leave on the landscape—whether that landscape is construed as economic, or social, or moral, or as the literal earth, blanketed in fragile air, washed with tenuous water, dotted with mansions and shacks where people live? These are the questions the newer version of success must address in order to earn its stature and its dignity. Making money is a private affair, but success, so to speak, is by general consent; we, all of us, define it every day. We have a right to demand a real accomplishment, a making of something better, before we give someone our regard and our applause.

In dreams begins responsibility. The people currently alive in America—especially, perhaps, those tens of millions of young adults who were the offspring of America's peak hegemony and who are just now on the threshold of their ripest strength and fullest discretion—are the inheritors of great dreams and have been great undaunted dreamers on their own account. The tradition of frontier was bequeathed to them; the blind expectation of more was fed to them with their milk and cookies, handed to them, bubble-packed, with their battery-powered toys. Other dreams came their way as well: the convenient dream that with growing prosperity would necessarily come growing justice; the circular dream that American growth would prove American virtue, and that American virtue, thus confirmed, would make American growth eternal.

For a few brief decades, those dreams seemed almost easy; they seemed to dream themselves. They no longer do. They now cry out for careful and responsible shepherding. The challenge is largely one of translation and transition.

The dream of frontier needs to be translated into something that is not a lie and not a mere exercise in old-soldierish nostalgia. *Something* must seem new, and beckoning, and grand, and able to call forth the best in those who seek it; and we are past the point in our history when that something is likely to appear in the form of quantity. There will not be more land. There will not be more geopolitical power. There will not, in significant ways, be more money. Frontier, if it is not to become a brittle and self-mocking notion, has to be translated into the sphere of quality. A nation filled from border to border can always become a better nation—more equitable, more beautiful, more healthy, more serene. A people who are as wealthy as they are likely to become can always become wiser, more humane, more highly evolved in the uses of their wealth. Frontiers based on extent are not the only frontiers; they are, in fact, the only frontiers that vanish.

The translation of frontier from quantity to quality is one aspect of a more general transition from what might be thought of as the first phase of America's richness to the second—from the phase of stockpiling vast amounts of wealth, to the phase of finally addressing the often-asked, always-shrugged-off question, *What is all that money for?*

There is a tendency to imagine that the first part of this process is the hard part, and the second phase is easy. Just the opposite is true. To be sure, the amassing of wealth, either national or personal, is arduous and gritty work. Yet stockpiling wealth is easy in the sense of what it relieves one from. Making money simplifies the emotional landscape, focuses and also limits the attention. As long as the bucks flow in and the ante continues to be upped, there is a constant and explicit way of measuring progress. That measure is called *more*. You can count it and so you don't have to think about it.

Beyond the habit of more, however, wealth raises questions that do need thinking about. When it can no longer be assumed that we will all be richer next year, the happy crassness of the boom days does not suffice. What is called for is the guts to acknowledge that time-tried strategies are no longer working quite so well, and the imagination to see past them.

Without the comforting lie that eternal growth will eventually iron out our inequalities, we have to take responsibility for the way rewards are divvied up. If the current split offends our consciences, *we* have to change it. We cannot abdicate our own moral judgment in favor of some market-place mechanism that purportedly allocates rewards in a "rational" way. Unless, that is, we accept homelessness, terrible education, and substandard health care as rational.

Without the guarantee that work alone will lead to payoffs grand and burgeoning enough to keep us gratified and distracted, we have to consider more carefully the high and difficult ideal of a balanced life—a life that integrates labor and leisure, one that reconciles self-interest with an ethic of service, one that recognizes peace of mind not only as a desirable thing but as a moral achievement in itself.

And without the dangerous promise that more money can always be found somewhere, somehow, we have to develop the civilized knack of living well while living within our means.

Make no mistake—the prospect of these transitions scares the daylights out of people. The 1980s, in fact, will be remembered as a fundamentally dishonest and willfully blind holding out against the recognition *not* that things were changing, but that they had already changed. The American standard of living—what an arrogant phrase; as though it held within itself everything that could possibly matter—didn't level off in 1987, but in 1973. America's wealth-in-process—its promise of education and advance-ment, of opportunity for those on the fringes—has been getting squeezed for twenty years. The eighties, with their sudden fortunes and unabashed excess, posed as a reprise of the good old days, but were in actuality a noisy wake for a time already passed and painted over with the stuff of myth.

The irony is that the transition people have been so desperately fending off is a transition to a better time, a time when life will seem like less of a scrap. *What is all that money for?* One of the things it's for is to make money relatively less important. Among the poor, after all, a preoccupation with funds is understandable; among the well-to-do, it is unseemly, petty, unevolved.

As it is with individuals, so it is with societies. With the national fortune established, we don't *have* to make a fetish of the economically fastest track; it is, in fact, beneath our dignity to do so. It more befits our situation to promote the kinds of accomplishment that cover a far broader swath of human possibility than does the cramped category of things that people get overpaid for. We can afford to admire the flamboyant thinker, the eccentric, the noble failure. We have room, even, for people who are not selfish.

What is all that money for? It is, in part, to assert the power of those who buy against the power of those who sell. For all our brashness and swagger, we in America have been oddly meek in our acceptance of what the marketplace—both domestic and foreign—throws our way. We buy as if it were our duty to buy, as if it were the function of life to further the well-being of the marketplace rather than vice versa. What a missed opportunity there has been in this. We as a nation are the world's carriage trade; a prerogative of our wealth is not to do business with those we disapprove of. We can withhold our custom from those who pollute or exploit or poison. Faced with products tainted by bad faith, we can keep our hands in our pockets. We can, to some extent, buy decency by insisting that those who sell to us earn their niche, not just in the circle of getting and spending, but in the community of people who get and spend.

What is all that money for? It is, finally, for the providing of choices—and it is on this count, more than any other, that 1980s values went so sourly awry. At a time when personal options should have seemed unprecedentedly broad, the obsessions of an age of greed made them seem chokingly narrow. Was it fear that so constricted the passages? Was it an unspoken epidemic dread that the music was about to end and *you* would be the one without a chair?

Well, the music is not about to end, and it is perhaps not amiss to say that the 1980s were largely an emotional crisis posing as an economic one. The hard part was adjusting to the *idea* that the days of automatic more were over, that the new dynamic would be the subtler one of high-level holding steady. As a people, we fought that adjustment every inch of the way; yet it seems that the adjustment has been made. The eighties were our tantrum; Meltdown Monday was our spanking; now we are resigned, ready for a more temperate and a kinder time. Under the values that will guide this more temperate time, the hunger for more will certainly not vanish, but it can be redirected. More money, more tokens of success—there will always be people for whom those are adequate goals, but those people are no longer setting the tone for all of us. There is a new sort of *more* at hand: more appreciation of good things beyond the marketplace, more insistence on fairness, more attention to purpose, more determination truly to choose a life, and not a lifestyle, for oneself.

Dare we suggest that these new forms of *more* comprise a species of frontier?

//// FOUR

Just after 1:00 A.M. on April 5, Lucas Rex Collier was born. He weighed seven pounds, six ounces, had slate-blue eyes whose irises seemed to fill the entire space between the tiny lids, and a barely visible whorl of silver hair. Sally Collier had watched as the cord was cut and the child attached to her became somebody else.

Benno sat at the bedside, his damp shirt sticking to his back. He held Sally's hand as she nursed. They called the baby Locust, Reckie, the Wreck, and the Wrecker; he was twenty minutes old and already had four nicknames.

A nurse came to take the child away, and Sally Collier fell instantly asleep. Benno settled back in the green vinyl chair and laughed. It was a deep and silent laugh that came from the bottom of his chest and closed his throat on the way up. They were parents now. They had a kid who would grow up in their house, whom they would feed and teach to throw a ball. This kid was the person the future would happen to. Everyone had hopes, Benno thought, everyone had fears. Until you were a parent, they floated free, they applied to everything and nothing. Suddenly they all landed on your kid. It was damn merciful that the kid didn't know it, because the hopes and fears were an awkward bundle to carry around. Even if you were pretty sure, as Benno was, that everything would turn out O.K. He was more sure of it every moment. Sitting there damp and exhausted in what was getting to be the middle of the night, he decided that his son's world would still have its adventures and its second chances, its upward spirals called by whatever name, that the days of seeing life get better were not used up. Parents were by nature optimists. They had to be.

NOTES

INTRODUCTION

4 "Benno and Sally Collier" are real people, not composites. To protect their privacy, however, certain details, in addition to their names, have been changed. "Benno" does not work for Morgan Stanley; he is an equity salesman for a comparable company. He did not work for Dewey, Ballantine, though he was a practicing attorney for eight years with another leading Wall Street firm. "Sally Collier" did indeed work for NBC— that being the only network on strike in October 1987— though not in the precise capacity described. The "Colliers" do live on the Upper West Side of Manhattan, though perhaps not on West End Avenue. All other information concerning them is literal, and was obtained in a series of interviews conducted in late 1987 and early 1988.

4 "leaving the law": Tamar Lewin, "The Faster Track," *The New York Times Magazine,* 10 August 1986, 14.

6 "the end of business as usual": This was the headline of the lead article in the business section of the *Times* on Sunday, 25 October 1987.

8 "the underlying economy": From a presidential statement

issued on October 19, quoted in *The New York Times,* 20 October 1987.

8 "caught as much by surprise": "Fall Stuns Corporate Leaders," *The New York Times,* 20 October 1987.

8 "I don't understand it": Robert E. Allen, quoted in the above.

8 "We don't know": John A. Rolls, ibid.

10 "on some other": Studs Terkel, "On Some Other Planet," *The New York Times,* 25 October 1987, sec. 3.

11 "towns in Utah": The national and seemingly oblique consequences of Black Monday were considered in "Cold Winter on Wall Street," *The New York Times,* 13 December 1987, sec. 3.

1: THE MORE FACTOR

20 a man named Sanborn: For a fuller account of railroad-related land speculation in Texas, see F. Stanley, *Story of the Texas Panhandle Railroads* (Borger, Tex.: Hess Publishing Co., 1976).

20 College Mounds or Belchervilles: T. Lindsay Baker, *Ghost Towns of Texas* (Norman, Okla.: University of Oklahoma Press, 1986).

21 "who, in their own Countries": Benjamin Franklin, "Information to Those Who Would Remove to America," in *The Autobiography and Other Writings* (New York: Penguin Books, 1986), 242.

21 "not the constitution": Frederick Jackson Turner, *The Frontier in American History* (Melbourne, Fla.: Krieger, 1976 [reprint of 1920 edition]), 293.

22 "the freedom of the individual": Ibid., 266.

22 "no natural boundary": Tocqueville, *Democracy in America.*

23 Productivity in the private sector: These figures are taken from the Council of Economic Advisers, *Economic Report of the President,* February 1984, 267.

24 carrying costs on the national debt: For a lucid and readable account of the meaning and implications of our reservoir of red ink, see Lawrence Malkin, *The National Debt* (New York: Henry Holt and Co., 1987). Through no fault of Malkin's, many of his numbers are already obsolete, but his explanation of who owes what to whom, and what it means, remains sound and even entertaining in a bleak sort of way.

24 consequences for the individual wallet: The figures in this paragraph and the next are from "The Average Guy Takes It on the Chin," *The New York Times*, 13 July 1986, sec. 3.

24 For all the blather: See, for example, "The Year of the Yuppie," *Newsweek*, 31 December 1984, 16.

24 "for millions of breadwinners": "The Average Guy," see above.

26 the crabgrass frontier: With the suburbs again taking on a sort of fascination, this phrase was resurrected as the title of a 1985 book—*Crabgrass Frontier: The Suburbanization of America*, by Kenneth T. Jackson (Oxford University Press).

27 "the luckiest generation": Thomas Hine, *Populuxe* (New York: Alfred A. Knopf, 1986), 15.

2: NORMAL IS WHAT YOU'RE USED TO

29 The median age: *Statistical Abstract of the United States*, 1987 edition, table 20.

29 8 percent economic growth: "U.S. Expansion—Is the Nation Growing Fast Enough?" *Time*, 16 February 1960, 90.

29 year of greatest fecundity: *Statistical Abstract*, table 80.

29 "the decisive generation": Landon Jones, *Great Expectations* (New York: Coward-McCann, 1980), 1. This book, which to the best of my knowledge was the first demographics-based best-seller in America, remains one of the touchstone volumes on the baby-boom generation. While demographics, as Jones freely concedes, does not explain everything, it *helps* to explain

a great deal, and this book remains valuable for anyone who ever wondered why she had to share a schoolbook or why he had to wait three weeks to take his driver's test.

30 population increase between 1946 and 1964: *Statistical Abstract,* table 2.

30 as the United States did in 1953: "Business in 1953—A Keystone of the Free World," *Time,* 4 January 1954, 54ff.

30 39–23–33: Lewis H. Lapham, et al., *The Harper's Index Book* (New York: Henry Holt and Company, 1987), 42.

30 Americans spent more on entertainment: "A $40 Billion Bill Just for Fun," *Life,* 28 December 1959, 69.

30 more televisions than bathtubs: "Two in Every Home," *Time,* 28 February 1964, 93.

31 "there was no competition": From a personal interview conducted December 19, 1987, at MIT.

33 "Himalayan peak[s]": "Business in 1948—The New Frontiers" [There's that word again!], *Time,* 10 January 1949, 73.

33 "did not have to worry": Thomas Hine, *Populuxe* (New York: Alfred A. Knopf, 1986), 60.

33 "generational tyranny"; "setting the national temper": Jones, *Great Expectations,* 1, 7.

34 growing so fast: Analogously, in the sixties, it was not difficult to imagine that the nation itself, rather than 60 million individual adolescents, was enduring paroxysms of defiance and rage, yet somehow managing to have a damn good time while going through an absolute developmental hell. The seventies, similarly, could be dubbed the "me decade" not because human nature had suddenly become (more) narcissistic and hedonistic, but because those same obtrusive tens of millions were now trying to strike a bargain with fate: *O.K., so what do we get in exchange for our fading youth?* The

eighties, at moments, appeared to contain faltering steps toward national maturity, though, as we will argue, mere receding hairlines and spreading hips didn't constitute proof that we'd learned that much.

35 less than half their ... income: "The Great Shopping Spree," *Time,* 8 January 1965, 59.

36 Barbie's greatest year: "More Trouble in Toyland," *The New York Times,* 20 December 1987, sec. 3.

37 the newer exurbs: For an account of sub- and exurban development, eighties-style, see John Herbers, *The New Heartland* (New York: Times Books, 1986).

37 the values of belonging: To those who, like myself, grew up in a 1960s suburb where neighbors didn't visit each other's houses and often didn't even say hello, this notion of belongingness may sound strange. However, as William H. Whyte makes clear in *The Organization Man* (New York: Simon and Schuster, 1956), earlier suburbs had some of the feel of the prewar small town, and were in fact designed specifically to preserve that feeling in a time of job transfers, the breakup of neighborhood ethnic enclaves, and the very beginnings of the shopping-center age.

37 Housing costs were outstripping: In 1986, the National Association of Homebuilders reported that, in order to afford a median-priced home, a family needed an annual income of around $37,000. Actual median income, however, which had been virtually stagnant for nearly a decade, stood at $27,735. An even bigger problem for many young families was the lump sum required for a down payment. As of 1970, a typical 20 percent down payment came to $5,320; by 1985, that figure had nearly quadrupled, to $20,160.

39 a highly individual matter: As I hope is clear, I am not advocating a return to the sixties and seventies version of adolescence, or a return to anything. One of the things I *would* like to do, however, is to counter a creeping revisionism that

became fashionable in the 1980s, and which has sought to portray the liberal arts/introspective style of previous decades as a self-indulgent waste of time. For some, no doubt, it was precisely that. For others—who are now lawyers, businesspeople, artists, politicians—it was an opportunity to grow civilized.

42 "the true business of liberal education is greatness": Cited in "Unconquered Frontier" (that word again!), *Time,* 1 March 1954, 64.

42 any but those who studied phys ed: D. Norton-Taylor, "The Business Schools: Pass or Flunk?" *Fortune,* June 1954, 112.

43 more than twice as many ... business degrees: "Liberal Arts, Long in Decline, Are Reviving Around Nation," *The New York Times,* 9 November 1986.

43 the American Council on Education poll: These figures derive, to be precise, from questionnaires completed by 209,627 freshmen at 390 two- and four-year colleges. The survey is jointly sponsored by the ACE and the Higher Education Research Institute at UCLA. Unfortunately, direct comparisons with student attitudes in the fifties cannot be done through this survey, which was initiated in 1966.

In considering student attitudes, it is pertinent, though not surprising, to note that the relative on-campus social standing of various majors seems to go right along with the popularity of the subjects themselves. In 1971, according to Peter Cohen in *The Gospel According to Harvard Business School* (New York: Doubleday, 1973), MBA laureates were regarded as dim nerds and were the subjects of such mockery that, at commencement, students of other Harvard divisions hooted, hissed, stomped the bleachers, and made farting sounds when the B-school grads were announced; by 1985, MBAs had reached such a height of social fashion that someone was marketing a pin-up calendar of "Eligible Bachelors from the Harvard Business School."

44 "shopgirls from Bloomingdale's": Barbara Howar, "Gossiping About Gossip," *Harper's,* January 1986, 37.

44 glorification of the hot career: The media's lavish and generally sycophantic treatment of business in the 1980s is discussed at greater length in Chapter 6.

45 The William Whyte quote is from "The Organization Man: A Rejoinder," in "Organization Man Revisited," by Paul Leinberger, *The New York Times Magazine,* part 2, *The Business World,* 7 December 1986, 68.

3: WHY THE MIDDLE CLASS ISN'T FUNNY ANYMORE

47 The Franklin quotes are from "Information to Those Who Would Remove to America," *The Autobiography and Other Writings* (New York: Penguin Books, 1986).

48 "never establish any equality": This and the Tocqueville citations that follow are from *Democracy in America,* Part 1.

50 "took comfort for granted": Henry Steele Commager, *The American Mind* (New Haven: Yale University Press, 1950), 6–9.

51 "Must you wait": Louis Sullivan, *Kindergarten Chats,* cited in Frederick Lewis Allen, *The Big Change* (New York: Harper Perennial Library, 1986), 29.

52 92 percent of the inhabitants: "A Once Tightly Knit Middle Class Finds Itself Divided and Uncertain," *The Wall Street Journal,* 9 March 1987.

55 The figures and quotations pertaining to American income and spending in the early 1950s are taken from a remarkable and historic series of articles done by *Fortune* in 1953–54 on "The Changing American Market." Housing, furniture, food, luxuries, leisure—virtually every major segment of the consumer economy was examined in these pieces, which hold up extremely well not just in their analysis and projections, but as a brilliant contemporary portrait of an America just waking up to the realization of how shockingly wealthy it had become.

58 "we design a car": Quoted in "Cellini of Chrome," *Time,* 4 November 1957, 99.

58 "the new Early American Look": "The New Early American Look in Home Living," *Look,* 17 April 1956, 72.

58 Thomas Hine, *Populuxe* (New York: Alfred A Knopf, 1986), 6.

58 "an expression of outright . . . joy": Ibid., 4.

58 first blipped past 4 percent: *Statistical Abstract of the United States,* 1987 edition, table 764.

58 when real wages started to fall: For a discussion of real wage rates and their consequences, see, for example, Robert Kuttner, "The Declining Middle," *The Atlantic Monthly,* July 1983, 71.

59 1974: For a somewhat fuller account of the economic situation in 1974—possibly the most bedeviling year in U.S. economic history—see my earlier book, *The Big Time* (New York: Harper & Row, 1986), 141–43.

59 unemployment at 10 percent: *Statistical Abstract,* table 637.

59 losing manufacturing jobs: Ibid., table 670.

59 trend toward equality reversed: Barbara Ehrenreich, "Is the Middle Class Doomed?," *The New York Times Magazine,* 7 September 1986, 44.

59 middle class getting screwed: Because such a high proportion of Americans think of themselves as middle class, the question of whether the middle class is doing well or badly under a particular administration obviously is a huge political issue— one that generates a great deal of casuistry and statistical razzmatazz. It is beyond our scope here to trace in detail the arguments and counterarguments about how the middle class is faring; the reader should be aware, however, that certain conservative economists and pundits did maintain through the 1980s that the middle class was *not* shrinking and *not* in trouble, but that ways of reckoning middle-class status simply

needed to be redefined. I confess I do not give equal time to this viewpoint in the body of the text, for the simple reason that I believe it is off the wall. You can "devalue" the middle class and still call it the middle class, just as you can devalue the dollar and still call it the dollar; in either case, however, buying power and prestige have diminished.

59 families described as middle class: The 1985 figures are from the *Statistical Abstract,* table 731; the comparison figures from 1973 are from "The Mass Market Is Splitting Apart," by Bruce Steinberg, *Fortune,* 29 November 1983, 77.

60 women's earnings 65 percent of men's: *Statistical Abstract,* table 681.

60 real weekly earnings in construction, etc.: Ibid., table 676.

61 average earnings among "smart" middle class: "America's Middle Class—Angry, Frustrated and Losing Ground," *U.S. News & World Report,* 30 March 1981, 44.

61 one in every five college grads: Kuttner, "The Declining Middle," 70.

61 college degrees nearly quadrupled: *Statistical Abstract,* table 252.

61 employing more people: Ibid., table 661.

62 over 11 million lost jobs ... half ... went back ... for lower pay: "Middle-Class Squeeze," *U.S. News & World Report,* 18 August 1986, 41.

62 more employed/unemployed: Landon Jones, *Great Expectations* (New York: Coward-McCann, 1980), 151.

62 pay ratios in manufacturing vs. service: Steinberg, "The Mass Market," 78.

62 carrying costs on a typical house: Ehrenreich, "Is the Middle Class Doomed?" 74.

62 percentage of first homes: "America's Middle Class," 41.

63 price of new house increased 30 percent: *Statistical Abstract,* table 1275.

63 "the lower-middle class doesn't exist . . .": Paul Fussell, *Class* (New York: Summit Books, 1983), 44.

65 that quarter would grow to a third: Steinberg, "The Mass Market," 82.

4: QUIZ SHOWS AND THE NATIONAL PURPOSE

68 a rigged television quiz show: The quiz show scandals were one of the biggest stories of the late 1950s, and were widely covered—mostly from October through December of 1959— in all the major news magazines and papers. In the following, very condensed, account, I will cite sources only for direct quotations.

69 "the finest product": "The Big Fix," *Time,* 19 October 1959, 67.

70 "a raving lunatic": Ibid.

71 "a shocking state of rottenness": "The Tarnished Image," *Time,* 16 November 1959, 72.

72 the values that underlay the rules: I stress this distinction because, as I will argue later, especially in Chapter 11, I believe it to be at the heart of the ethical malaise of the 1980s. A sort of Catch-22 pertains: the weaker the influence of shared societal values, the greater the need for more explicit and more complicated laws and regulations. The more complex the laws and regulations, however, the more loopholes they inevitably contain, and, more to the point, the greater the temptation to "get around" them. Morality thus ceases to be an organic whole and becomes a sort of game in which anything not explicitly prohibited is allowed.

73 "like cucumber growers": Said by Fairfax M. Cone, executive committee chairman of Foote, Cone & Belding. Quoted in "Needed: A Cleanup," *Time,* 4 January 1960, 68.

73 "however thin we slice it": Alan Harrington, "The Self-Deceivers," *Esquire,* September 1959, 59.

74 "typical of business morality": "A Deejay's Exposé—And Views of the Trade," *Life,* 23 November 1959, 47.

75 "forced to think": "A Melancholy Business," *Time,* 26 October 1959, 54.

76 Asked California governor: The remarks that follow—from Brown, Kennedy, Rockefeller, Percy, and the Gainesville *Times*—were made during November 1959, and were cited in "The Issue of Purpose," *Time,* 16 November 1959, 27–28.

78 for America's own reassurance: It doesn't take a Freudian analyst to surmise that at least part of America's susceptibility to the ugly excesses of McCarthyism derived from an unacknowledged fear that maybe Communism *did* have something appealing about it; maybe the Marxist-Leninist message *did* address certain human longings not necessarily assuaged by capitalism triumphant.

78 "implied threat": Norman S. B. Gras, "The American Way of Socializing Business—Under the New Business Statesmanship," *Harvard Business School Alumni Bulletin,* Spring 1949, 50.

78 "who had proved how well": *Time,* 4 January 1954, 54ff.

80 "we have mastered production": Said by Richard Courts, ibid., 58.

5: "TO KNOW NO BOUNDARIES"

90 "If we close it": quoted in "Terrible Tuesday—How the Stock Market Almost Disintegrated a Day After the Crash," *The Wall Street Journal,* 20 November 1987.

90 "in the absence of any true calamity": Ibid.

91 a theme song for a James Bond movie: The movie, and the song, was "For Your Eyes Only."

91 "the generation doomed": This remark, by Landon Jones, was cited in "Middle-Class Squeeze," *U.S. News & World Report,* 18 August 1986, 37ff.

92 An average-priced new car: The figures in this paragraph are from "Middle-Class Squeeze," ibid.

93 "superconsumer whose mighty wallet": "Superconsumer Slows Down," *Newsweek,* 9 September 1985, 68.

93 only 27 percent had a microwave: The figures that follow are from "A Sense of Limits Grips Consumers," *The New York Times,* 15 March 1987, sec. 3.

97 "the unromantic generation": Bruce Weber, "Alone Together," *The New York Times Magazine,* 5 April 1987, 22.

97 "those faculty that were students": Said by William Kristol, chief of staff to Secretary of Education William J. Bennett. Quoted in "Education Chief Deplores Campus Radicalism," *The New York Times,* 15 May 1986, sec. B.

6: ATTACK OF THE BUSINESS RAH-RAHS

99 "It isn't creative": This was the motto of the firm Benton & Bowles, now part of D'Arcy Masius Benton & Bowles.

100 "trading passions": Tocqueville, *Democracy in America.*

100 "the almighty dollar": *Wolfert's Roost,* "The Creole Village."

100 pragmatic in his religion: For Commager's analysis of these tendencies, see *The American Mind* (New Haven: Yale University Press, 1950), especially pages 26–30 and 96–99.

100 "The *persona* of the American civilization": *America as a Civilization* (New York: Simon and Schuster, 1957), 274.

102 "The New Entrepreneur": This article, by Gurney Brecken-feld, appeared in the issue of 22 July 1978, page 12.

103 leading us down the tubes: By 1988, it should be noted, entrepreneurship, too, was being looked at in a jaundiced light. According to *The New York Times,* business experts were now suggesting that "rather than propelling the econ-omy to new heights, the constant spawning of companies may actually be sapping America's economic might." ("A Look at Entrepreneurs: Doubt on an American Ideal," 14 June 1988.)

105 "In more straightforward times": From an essay in *All Things Considered,* a collection of Chesterton's London *Daily News* essays and occasional pieces (Chester Springs, Penn.: Dufour, 1969, reprint).

106 Trump's views on peace: Ron Rosenbaum, "Trump: The Ultimate Deal," November 1985, 109. The magazine's cover, by the way, pictured the developer holding a white dove.

106 Avon CEO Hicks Waldron: N. R. Kleinfield, "What It Takes," *The New York Times Magazine,* 1 December 1985.

107 "Executive Fun and Games": N. R. Kleinfield, in *The Business World* (supplement to *The New York Times*), 8 June 1986, 52.

107 "has long appealed to many": Nick Lyons, "Gone Off Fly-Fishing," *The Business World,* 3 May 1987, 65.

107 the origins of the new business photography: Daniel Shaw, "Risky Business," *American Photographer,* November 1985, 74.

111 "high-tech baroque": "E. L. Doctorow: Pumping Out Success," *The New York Times,* 25 October 1987, sec. 3.

112 *The Corporate Warriors:* Douglas K. Ramsey (Boston: Hough-ton Mifflin, 1987).

112 "Soldiers of Misfortune": Jonathan Z. Larsen, *Manhattan, inc.*, May 1987, 106.

113 "many top executives": Kleinfield, "Executive Fun and Games," 52.

113 "chess on grass," "balls are much bigger": Ibid., 62.

115 *Conquistadores del Cielo:* Ibid., 59.

115 "modern business enterprise": *The Affluent Society* (New York: Signet Mentor, 1978), 81.

116 "era of me-first management": "The Age of 'Me-First' Management," *The New York Times,* 19 August 1984, sec. 3.

116 *Penthouse* commissioned a survey: Joe Mancuso, "After Hours: Private Lives of CEOs," December 1987, 135.

117 a former Harvard Business School professor: Edward Wrapp, "Don't Blame the System, Blame the Managers," *Dun's Review,* September 1980, 82.

7: A SICKNESS CALLED SUCCESS

121 "go where Americans"; "the attempt of some ... image makers": "Threats and Whimpers: The New Business Heroes," *The New York Times Book Review,* 26 October 1986, 1.

124 Sales of BMW, Jaguar, Mercedes: Alex Taylor III, "Detroit vs. New Upscale Imports," *Fortune,* 27 April 1987, 69.

124 "a sign of high vulgarity": Joseph Epstein, (writing as Aristides), "What Is Vulgar?" *The American Scholar,* Winter 1981–82, 15.

126 "the impostor phenomenon": There seems to be some disagreement as to who coined this phrase and when; as far as I can determine, it was first used by the psychologist Pauline Rose Clance, and discussed in her book *The Impostor Phenomenon: Overcoming the Fear That Haunts Your Success* (Atlanta: Peachtree Publishers, Ltd., 1985).

126 psychologist Joan Harvey: The typology that follows was discussed in Harvey's book, *If I'm So Successful, Why Do I Feel Like a Fake: The Impostor Phenomenon* (New York: St. Martin's Press, 1985).

129 "leisure, health, relationships": Ellen Hopkins, "The Young and the Sleepless," *New York,* 9 June 1986, 70.

130 "The Pursuit of Unhappiness": David Gelman, *Newsweek,* 21 May 1984, 79.

132 Douglas LaBier: The citations that follow are from *Modern Madness: The Emotional Fallout of Success* (New York: Addison-Wesley, 1986).

133 "power as a magical solution": Douglas LaBier, "Madness Stalks the Ladder Climbers," *Fortune,* 1 September 1986, 79.

134 *Nation's Business* and *Fortune: Fortune* citation ibid.; "When Your Work Life Drives You Crazy," *Nation's Business,* November 1986, 61.

134 "hit bottom when they reach the top": "The Strange Agony of Success," *The New York Times,* 24 August 1986.

134 "a false fantasy": Ibid.

134 "high and hooked on money": This quote and the others in this paragraph are from "Wall Street's Money Junkies," by Jay B. Rohrlich, *The New York Times,* 7 May 1987.

135 the suicide rate: *Statistical Abstract of the United States,* 1987 edition, table 121.

135 woman's chances of having an ulcer: Jon I. Isenberg, "The Ulcer Updated," *Town and Country,* November 1986, 178.

136 "made success in America": "Greed and Envy," *The New Republic,* 27 February 1984, 6.

136 "the new ideal of success": Christopher Lasch, *The Culture of Narcissism* (New York: Warner Books, 1979), 96.

8: A TYRANNY MISCALLED TASTE

138 In 1958, a Frenchman . . . ; In 1967, 480 million sold: Roger Beardwood, "Bich the Ballpoint King," *Fortune,* 15 August 1969, 122.

139 The sales of Mont Blanc pens: Per Koh-I-Noor Rapidograph Inc., U.S. representative of Mont Blanc.

140 "status pen . . . status handbag . . . status loafer": Holly Brubach, "Flaunting It," *Vogue,* January 1987, 204.

141 "age of designer water": "Water to Go Anywhere Under the Sun," *The New York Times,* 5 July 1987, sec. 1.

142 "conspicuous consumption of valuable goods" . . . "a means of reputability": Thorstein Veblen, *Theory of the Leisure Class,* Chapter 4.

143 "the propensity for emulation": Ibid., Chapter 5.

143 "the pecuniary life": Ibid., used throughout as a shorthand for America's money-centered social structure.

143 a life of gross inequality: The examples that follow are from Frederick Lewis Allen, *The Big Change* (New York: Harper Perennial Library, 1986), 28–29.

144 "the banquets of the rich": Here, for example, is the menu of a dinner for forty, given by Randolph Guggenheimer at the Waldorf-Astoria in 1899:

Buffet Russe
Cocktails
Small Blue Point Oysters
Lemardelais à la Princesse
Amontillado Pasado
Green Turtle Soup
Bolivar
Basket of Lobster
Columbine of Chicken, California Style
Roast Mountain Sheep, with Puree of Chestnuts
Jelly

Brussels Sprouts Sauté
New Asparagus, Cream Sauce and Vinaigrette
Mumm's Extra Dry and Moët & Chandon Brut
Diamond Back Terrapin
Ruddy Duck
Orange and Grapefruit Salad
Fresh Strawberries
Blue Raspberries
Vanilla Mousse
Bonbons, Coffee, Fruit

145 "What is, is wrong"; "The tendency of the pecuniary life": Veblen, *Leisure Class*, Chapter 9.

146 "shopping was the unifying principle": Ellen Hopkins, "Born to Shop," *New York*, 16 June 1986, 42.

147 "patron saint of shoppers": Ibid.

147 93 percent of teenage girls: Myron Magnet, "The Money Society," *Fortune*, 6 July 1987, 26.

147 "gradually became obsessed": Hopkins, "Born to Shop," 47.

147 "You can almost hear": Ibid., 46.

148 "impoverishment by substitution": Charles Reich, *The Greening of America* (New York: Random House, 1970), 162.

148 There was the young woman: The examples that follow are from "The Shopping Addicts," *Newsweek*, 18 March 1985, 81.

149 economists were bewailing: See, for instance, Lester Thurow, *The Zero-Sum Solution* (New York: Simon and Schuster, 1985), esp. 208–10.

149 five dollars owed for each dollar saved: See Lawrence Malkin, *The National Debt* (New York: Henry Holt and Co., 1987), 3–16.

149 interest payments as much as health care: "Middle-Class Squeeze," *U.S. News & World Report*, 18 August 1986, 37ff.

151 "there was no recession": "There's No Recession in the Luxury Market," *U.S. News & World Report,* 23 November 1981, 53. The prices quoted in this paragraph are from this article.

151 What "you're seeing": Sandra Shaber, senior economist for Chase Econometrics, quoted in "There's No Recession," above.

151 sales of stretch limousines doubled: Eileen Keerdoja, "Stretching Out the Drive," *Newsweek,* 8 April 1985, 84.

151 the average age of a first-time fur owner: Magnet, "The Money Society."

151 American consumption of French champagne: Bernice Kanner, "Brut Force," *New York,* 19 January 1987, 9.

152 "luxury items and services": Mary-Margaret Wantuck, "Marketing to the Big Spenders," *Nation's Business,* August 1985, 42.

152 "the art of selling": N. R. Kleinfield, "The Art of Selling to the Very Rich," *The New York Times,* 15 June 1986, sec. 3. The citations in the next four paragraphs are from this article.

155 the *arriviste* "a patriot": Brubach, "Flaunting It," 204.

155 "demonstrating what we all wanted"; nouveau riche "a compliment": Ibid.

155 "buy social status immediately": quoted in Magnet, "The Money Society."

156 "that the haves are ... beholden": Brubach, "Flaunting It," 205–6.

157 "in the metaphysics of the market: George Dennis O'Brien, "The Christian Assault on Capitalism," *Fortune,* 8 December 1986, 181.

158 real-life rich studied television rich: See, for example, Stephen Drucker, "Psyching Out," *Vogue,* January 1987, 208.

9: THE WAR BETWEEN LIFE AND LIFE-STYLE

161 It was coined in 1929: Daniel Czitrom and David Marc, "The Elements of Lifestyle," *The Atlantic,* May 1985, 16.

162 " 'others' who seemed so alien": Ibid., 20.

163 "the property of mass-marketing": Ibid., 16.

164 *The Nine American Lifestyles:* Arnold Mitchell (New York: Macmillan, 1983).

164 more than 150 concerns were paying: James Atlas, "Beyond Demographics," *The Atlantic,* October 1984, 50.

164 the substance of the SRI study: Very briefly, this study began with a Riesman-inspired division of people into "inner-directed" and "outer-directed" groups. The outer-directed group was further broken down into Belongers, Emulators, and Achievers; the inner-directed group was divided into the categories I-Am-Me, Experiential, and Societally Conscious. Outside these essentially middle-class groups were the "need-driven" Survivors and Sustainers. The ideal posited by VALS was the "integrated" personality, described as psychologically mature, tolerant, understanding—i.e., very much like a life-style expert.

164 "once an expression of tolerance": Czitrom and Marc, "The Elements of Lifestyle," 20.

166 a 1987 *New Yorker* cartoon: Edward Koren, in *The New Yorker,* 1 June 1987, 30.

167 "feeling poor on $600,000 a year": Title of an article by Brooke Kroeger in *The New York Times,* 26 April 1987, sec. 3.

167 "sort of reduced [them]selves": Said by an unnamed twenty-six-year-old investment banker, quoted by Kroeger in "Feeling Poor."

168 "save lives or produce spark plugs": Ibid.

169 "chasing the same things" ..."[apartments] in Aspen": Ibid.

171 "the woman with $1,200": "The Year of the Yuppie," *Newsweek,* 31 December 1984, 14.

171 "new pastime of 'competitive eating' ": Ibid., 20.

172 "we're willing to ... sacrifice ... free time, relaxation": Ibid.

172 "the biggest wave"; "the same flamboyance": Said by Joanne Martin of the Stanford Business School, ibid., 24.

10: THE JARGON OF ACTIVE CHOICE

193 the financial writer Andrew Tobias: The following anecdote is from Tobias's *Playboy* column, "Quarterly Reports." This installment was titled "Compensation." *Playboy,* December 1986, 146.

193 "no longer [had] any relation": "The 1929 Parallel," *The Atlantic,* January 1987, 63.

193 "hint of unreality": Tobias, "Compensation."

194 "if Freud were alive today": N. R. Kleinfield, "Men and Their Money: The Passion of the Eighties," *Esquire,* February 1984, 39.

194 "render unto Caesar": Matthew, 22:21.

11: GHETTOS OF THE CONSCIENCE

195 "sleaze wave": "What's Wrong," *Time* (cover story), 25 May 1987, 23.

195 "Club Fed": George Rush, "Club Fed," *Manhattan, inc.,* June 1985, 82.

197 "Throw them out, fellas": "The Wrong Dream," *Manhattan, inc.,* April 1987, 59.

197 "transaction mentality": Quoted in "What's Wrong," 15.

197 "an age of Hessians": Quoted in Myron Magnet, "The Money Society," *Fortune,* 6 July 1987, 29.

197 One pundit exhumed . . . Polybius: Bernice Kanner, "What Price Ethics?" *New York,* 14 July 1986, 34.

197 "as if trapped": "The Decline & Fall of Business Ethics," *Fortune,* 8 December 1986, 65.

198 "ethics pays"; "marketplace does reward . . . integrity": quoted in "Harvard to Get $30 Million Ethics Gift," *The New York Times,* 31 March 1987.

198 "a case of throwing money": "Harvard's $30 Million Windfall for Ethics 101," *Business Week,* 13 April 1987, 40.

198 "merely paying lip service": "Ethics 101: Can the Good Guys Win?" *U.S. News & World Report,* 13 April 1987, 54.

198 "business ethics . . . a growth industry": David Vogel, "Could an Ethics Course Have Kept Ivan Boesky from Going Bad?" *The Wall Street Journal,* 27 April 1987, 24.

198 "a few sullen questions": "Shad the Lawgiver," *Fortune,* 11 May 1987, 154.

199 "be fascinated to see": Quoted in "Harvard to Get $30 Million," as above.

199 "A university which hasn't decided": Quoted in "Harvard's $30 Million Windfall," as above.

199 "They still have to sell": Ibid.

202 the broadest discrepancy in income: For discussions of the implications of this situation, see, for example, Robert B. Reich, *Tales of a New America* (New York: Times Books, 1987), chapter 14; and Lester Thurow, *The Zero-Sum Society* (New York: Basic Books, 1980), esp. those sections dealing with the interplay between income distribution and productivity.

204 "what soft porn is to ... love": Peter Drucker, "Ethical Chic," *Forbes,* 14 September 1981, 173.

204 blame on educational system: Allan Bloom, *The Closing of the American Mind* (New York: Simon and Schuster, 1987).

12: THE NEW LEISURE MEETS THE WORK ETHIC

209 "The Good Life": Special issue of *Life* dated 28 December 1959. In the discussion that follows, information pertaining to 1959 is from this source unless otherwise identified.

210 "How Do YOU Rate": Russell Lynes, ibid., 85.

214 "the human use of human beings": Norbert Wiener, *The Human Use of Human Beings: Cybernetics and Society* (Jersey City: Da Capo, 1988; originally published in 1950).

219 "a lot of people [were becoming] ... expendable" ... "canned entertainment and spectatoritis": Paul Goodman, "The Mass Leisure Class," *Esquire,* July 1960, 70.

219 "a kind of madness" ... "a feckless, aimless meandering": "Happy Idle Hours Become a Rat Race," *Life,* 28 December 1959, 117.

220 "The opportunity is so unprecedented": "Leisure Could Mean a Better Civilization," ibid., 62.

222 "symbolize[d] an entire generation's disenchantment": Lewis M. Andrews, "Communes and the Work Crisis," *The Nation,* 9 November 1970, 460.

222 "work crisis" . . . "renegades from Yale": Ibid.

222 "This book, being about work": *Working* (New York: Pantheon, 1974).

223 worker absenteeism at auto plants; common for 15 percent not to show up: "Is the Work Ethic Going Out of Style?" *Time,* 30 October 1972, 96.

223 the proportion of people reporting themselves dissatisfied: Ibid.

223 Insurance companies had to refigure their worker compensation scales: "The Great Male Cop-Out from the Work Ethic," *Business Week,* 14 November 1977, 156.

223 "run[ning] out of dumb people": "Is the Work Ethic," as above.

223 "they considered menial or unpleasant": Ibid.

223 "maybe we ought to stop talking": Ibid.

224 number of women in the labor force: *Statistical Abstract of the United States,* 1987 edition, table 653.

224 41.5 percent held jobs in 1967; 52.4 percent in 1976: "The Great Male Cop-Out," as above.

224 the number of men neither holding nor seeking jobs: Ibid.

227 "A New Take on Type A": Article by Marilyn M. Machlowitz in *The New York Times Magazine,* part 2, *The Business World,* 3 May 1987, 40.

227 "a terrible class aspect": "The Work Ethic: It Works Best for Those Who Work Least," *The Progressive,* June 1981, 66.

228 In a 1968 survey: The figures and quote that follows are from Daniel Yankelovich and John Immerwahr, "Putting the Work Ethic to Work," *Society,* January/February 1984, 58ff.

228 the "good" years 1984, 1985, 1986: "Middle-Class Squeeze," *U.S. News & World Report,* 18 August 1986, 37ff.

229 fully 40 percent of employed Americans earning less than $11,000 dollars; 10–20 million staying out of work force: "America's Army of Non-Workers," *The New York Times,* 27 September 1987, sec. 3.

13: THE F-WORD

237 "a society where failure can reside": "The Rush for Second Place," *Harper's,* April 1981, 31.

239 "someone always asked": "Business Schools—and Students—Want to Talk Only About Success," *The Wall Street Journal,* 15 December 1986, 29.

239 "from the outset"; "the fabulous opportunities"; "a man's destiny": Sloan Wilson, "Happy Idle Hours Become a Rat Race," *Life,* 28 December 1959, 118ff.

240 "To the lure of accomplishment"; "often suffered agonies": Ibid.

243 "We want to be successful": Quoted, without attribution, in *The Wall Street Journal,* as above.

INDEX

About the Author

Laurence Shames is the former ethics columnist for *Esquire* magazine. He is also author of *The Big Time: The Harvard Business School's Most Successful Class and How It Shaped America*, which was named one of the ten best business books of 1986 by *Business Week*. Currently he is a freelance journalist whose articles have appeared in such publications as *Playboy, Manhattan, inc.,* and *The New York Times*.